THE
GOLDEN
CORD

The Prophetic Alchemy of
the Lord's Prayer

THE GOLDEN CORD

The Prophetic Alchemy of the Lord's Prayer

Adonijah O. Ogbonnaya, Ph.D.

CrossPower Publications
Lansing, Illinois

The Golden Cord: The Alchemy of the Lord's Prayer
CrossPower Publications Copyright 2009 literature arm of AACTEV8 Int'l
(Apostolic Activation Network
Aactev8 International
P.O. Box 5053
Lansing, Illinois 60438
+13127525490
Web www.aactev8.com

First edition
First printing
ISBN 978-0-9727913-0-4

Library of Congress data
Alchemy, Prayer, Provisions Personal Growth, Spirituality. The Lord's Prayer, Will, will of man, Will of God, Kingdom, Heaven, forgiveness, Temptation, spiritual power, transformation, Bible study,

TABLE OF CONTENTS

ACKNOWLEDGMENTS

Since Christmas 1970 when I returned to Nigeria a few weeks after that encounter on the road to the farm, God has placed many people in my life who have helped me on the way. Mr. Josiah Ikedi trained and mentored me in business as is the custom of our people and encouraged me to go school. Bishop Edward Ezenwafor for fiery street preaching on the streets of Onitsha in 1971. A. A. Nwodika who baptized me at Nkisi River helped me to stop going for altar call for salvation every time the door was open. Rev. N. C. Thompson who truly in the ministry is my Father for he turned me on to study that still bears fruit today. He sent me to Jalingo in Northern Nigeria as a young pastor of fifteen. There by the help of Rev. Alfred and Marianne Bohr who were missionaries to Nigeria. It was through them and their children that I came to Canada before coming to the USA.

There are many people to thank. I must thank my wife and great friend Benedicta Chinyere for her love encouragement and support. She has continued to support the work of the Kingdom to which we have been called even when it has not been easy. Her joy even in the face of hardship continues to be an inspiration. I thank God for all my children and what they have done to educate me as much as I have educated them. To my church family Life Church of Chicago lands that have supported the work we have been doing around the world. Thanks to my dear brother and friend and his lovely family Bishop Freddie Steele "twin." Only Heaven knows how much you have done to encourage me. To a man with a Father's heart and woman with a mother's heart, Bishop Ruddel and Audrey Bloomfield, thank you. Again to the Bohrs Mom and Dad, words cannot express how much I love you. I am grateful to Apostle H. Daniel Wilson, my apostle, for your encouragement. I also want to express my gratitude to Dr. Arvid J. Lindley, the former president of Hillcrest Christian College who took a chance on a sixth grade African pastor and opened the door of education to me. Wherever you are, may the Lord bless you and your seed. Of course all the errors and misunderstandings in this work are mine solely.

THE GOLDEN CORD
INTRODUCTION

This is a book on prayer. One cannot be theoretical about prayer. It would be high display of a lack of authenticity. Therefore, I will introduce this book by giving you a sneak peek into one of the major experiences of my life. In so doing the introduction will be partially autobiographical. As those who know me may attest, I am often reticent about autobiographical excursions in public preaching and lectures. But being impressed to write on prayer, I find no other way of broaching the subject and maintaining authenticity without being testimonial.

My Prayer life is greatly influenced by the Hebrew system found among the old Igbos of my home and later on by the Siddur. I also learned much attending Christian schools run by missionaries. In reading the New Testament and attending missionary schools, what especially caught my imagination was the Prayer taught by Jesus and the prayers he prayed. When the disciples said "teach us to pray," he prayed what we call today the Lord's Prayer. The Lord's Prayer was recited everyday at my grade school and took on deeper meaning for me. Several times while praying the Psalms and reciting the Lord's Prayer I had a vision of the Lord. In one of those occasions, I received the call to preach but prayed no attention to it.

From 1968 to 1970, I secretly attended a small full gospel Church led by an Elder called Mr. Oko. My Father was not very keen on that as he believed it would remove me completely from our tradition. In 1969, Mr. Oko took us to a convention. I was filled with the Holy Spirit and began to speak in tongues in that convention. There I had visions of another world. I must have spent over three hours at the altar though I was not yet baptized in water. When I came back home, my Father was not happy. He stopped me from going to this crazy people church, but the die was already cast. I prayed continuously in my new found language as I walked and meditated on the experience of being caught up. My spirit was filled with sweet ecstasy. In fact I was having so many visions that my Father and some of his friends began to come to me for answers to certain troubling issues. During my stay in the small church, the leader gave me opportunities to preach and to teach although I was the youngest there.

In September of 1970 on the way to the farm. I began to say the Lord's Prayer "Our Father who art in Heaven, hallowed be thy name. Thy Kingdom come, thy will be done on earth as it is in Heaven." As these lines flowed from my lips, I knew something was happening to me. It was as though someone else was speaking through me. I could not resist. I kept speaking. I could hear myself saying "give us this day our daily bread" and the rest that follows but the whole landscape melted away—the trees, the field and the hills in that moment began to move as if it was liquid oil reflecting light. Powerful lights shone through. I could still hear myself as if in a distance, faintly still whispering the Lord's Prayer as my whole being was passing through dimensions that until this day I can hardly find words to describe. I stood before a vast stream of indescribable light, rivers of golden fire, and waves of blue flame as we find towards the end of a burning candle but infinitely larger in dimensions. The streams of light and fire gave forth sounds of great harmony. I saw men and women clothed with garments reflecting various colors of light that mimicked the rainbow. I beheld creatures, the like of which I have never seen. I heard my inner man speaking the name of The LORD in Hebrew. I spoke the name of "Jesus the Messiah." The sound from my voice was like a song from myriad voices. Sound poured out from every pore of my body; my whole being was a harmony of praise. My body was not my body; it become transparent light. I could see through my body. I remember hearing the question: Do you believe? Without hesitation I responded, "Yes, I believe." In that one moment I experienced the God of Abraham, Isaac and Jacob in His great love, beauty and terror all at once.

That moment with the Lord's Prayer opened up for me the vistas of the heavenly dimensions. The pattern and process of this prayer was the magma in which the stone of my prayer life was formed. Of the numerous spiritual experiences I have had through the years, this has been so indelibly imprinted into the depth of my

12

soul that I find myself returning to the Lord's Prayer in times of confusion and meditating. The meditation has never failed to yield fruit. One thing that that experience with the Lord's Prayer did for me is that it affirmed my faith in Jesus Christ as the Way, the door into that eternal realm. I came to the conclusion that He did not just teach the prayer as something for us to recite by rote or to turn into mere traditional shibboleth. It came to represent for me *a glory cipher, a Kingdom code, a power formula.* The Lord's Prayer holds for me within its sentences, gates, channels of deep spiritual terrain that our souls can traverse in God our Father. It holds keys that can unlock the spiritual possibilities in our body, soul and spirit and launch us into deeper spiritual experiences. This prayer is for me the Golden Cord which threads from this temporal dimension into eternity.

I know by experience that when we pray we open up Gates and channels for traveling spiritual dimensions. Since then the Lord's Prayer has held a supernatural fascination for me. I have spent hours meditating on it and experiencing numerous spiritual journeys, visions and dreams and entering into the world it was meant to open up to the disciple of Jesus Christ. This is just the beginning of the lessons I have learned from this prayer in the past forty years. This first volume will be more philosophical, but the next two volumes will be application of things mystical and practical, which the believer mystic can use to enhance their spiritual walk with the Lord. The Lord's Prayer, I consider to be the golden cord of prayer that can be used to pierce through dimensions and upon which we can hang our prayer life in our pilgrimage upon this earth and seek to enter the mansions of our home in the heavens.

Those experiences notwithstanding, I write as an apprentice who is still learning from the Master. In matters of spirituality, it is the personal inner experiences that are often paramount to me—of course, not without reference to objective reality. In a sense I am an empiricist, giving more credence to my inner experiences of God than to mere dogmatic assertions and formulae.

This book is written to help you with your spiritual life, especially in the area of prayer. Seeing that there is so much that is propagated today as spirituality that is not biblically–based and some even go against Judeo-Christian perspectives, many honest men and women have given up on spiritual processes or in the least become suspicious of anything that speaks of mystery. Some have developed the fear that being spiritual may make them susceptible to all sorts of malicious and pernicious entities. It does not help that much of what we hear from so many is focused on dealing with demons or the devil and marginalizes the completed work of Jesus Christ. All these notwithstanding, there is no question that prayer plays a strong role in the development of authentic Christian spirituality.

Prayer can work in all sorts of practical ways in your life. In this book, I will provide you with a guide on ways to enter into prayer and tap the supernatural realm. In it, I describe straightforward ways to understand and practice your spirituality. You will encounter certain interpretation and principles that have been proven in my life and in the lives of many throughout the world. The teachings and ideas contained in this book will help you transcend some of the spiritual constructs that have limited your ability to overcome certain obstacles. You will discover that through prayer you can actually access a life of miracles and joy. Keep in mind that prayer has been given to you as a key that can help you make quantum leaps into new territories and spheres of wellbeing and wholeness. There is a great inner current of power that was placed in you when you became God's child through Jesus Christ. It is not necessary to die with it still stuck inside of you. You do not have to keep wandering in the wilderness of powerlessness. In this book, you will tap into language and process that will help unleash that inner power of Christ in you for whole life transformation. The language of prayer especially as we find in the Lord 's Prayer, is language for releasing miracles directly into your life-world.

The book proceeds like this: The first part—from chapters one to six—deals with the meaning of prayer, prayer and the human emotion, the Holy Spirit and the human emotions, varieties of prayers, methods of prayers and atmosphere for effective prayer. Second part is an excursion on the Lord's Prayer.

PREFACE

Jesus said, "When you pray, say:

> *Our Father*
>
> *Who art in Heaven,*
>
> *Hallowed be thine name*
>
> *Thy Kingdom come,*
>
> *Thy will be done on earth*
>
> *As it is in Heaven,*
>
> *Give us this day our daily bread,*
>
> *And forgive us our trespasses*
>
> *As we forgive those who trespass against us;*
>
> *And lead us not into temptation*
>
> *But deliver us from evil,*
>
> *For thine is the Kingdom,*
>
> *The Power*
>
> *And the Glory,*
>
> > *Forever. Amen."*

Adonijah O. Ogbonnaya
Chicago, Illinois, 2009

PART 1

THE MEANING OF PRAYER

CHAPTER ONE

THE MEANING OF PRAYER

P rayer is meditational harmonizing of our being with the nature and purpose of God. It is the concerted effort of our whole being to become attuned to the creative Spirit of the Creator. It can be done collectively or individually. It can be done by thought, emoting and even attitude, in quite serenity or boisterous sound and movements. Prayer is very powerful. This power of prayers is often affected by the attitudes we hold; both about the one to whom with pray—God and for whom we pray—others and ourselves. As relating to God, we must have an attitude of the faith, "for he that cometh to God must believe that He is and that he a rewarder of those who diligently seek Him." (Hebrews 11:6) As relating to others, we must express love and forgiveness because God measures back to us the measure we meet out to others, as relating to ourselves acceptance and grace because self-hatred is the root of unbelief and lack of forgiveness. These are catalysts for the power of prayer. How deep we can go into God and this power depends on how much we are willing to let go of the wounds and inner pain we harbor either against God, others or ourselves. One prayer, which the Lord Jesus taught us to pray, commonly called "The Lord's Prayer" calls us to live as we pray, and to pray as we will live. In other words, our daily thoughts, actions and beliefs must strive for the same level of attunement with God that we seek in prayer.

Thoughts and ideas have powerful impact on prayers. It can be argued that our every thought has the same impact as a prayer. The longer a thought is held in mind, the more power it possesses. The New Testament focus on the mind sees it as a builder that actually contributes to help or harm, bless or curse every individual that we hold in our thoughts or in our spoken prayers. This is so important that it was included in one of the beatitudes: "Blessed are the pure in heart (thought) for they shall see God." In tuning our being to what I term "the God wave," it also helps to foster our relationship with the Divine in all its forms. Whether we are praying for ourselves or for others, our thoughts are important. If people have asked for prayer, it is important that we surround them about with intentional thoughtful concern. As people of faith it is important that we saturate the world with thoughts of Divine compassion and love. The pulse of our thought reaches out and affects even those who have not asked specifically for our prayer help. This is our likeness to God. This is why Paul insisted in Phil. 4:8:

> "Finally, brethren whatsoever things are true, whatsoever things are honest, whatsoever things are just whatsoever things are pure, whatsoever things are lovely, whatsoever things are of good report; if there be any virtue, and if there be any praise, ***think on these things.***"

I believe that the POWER of prayer travels through **thought** and mood. When done effectively, prayer is the light of Christ's nature traveling through our thought and words to the dimension, location, situations or persons for which we are praying. It is not that prayer is "telling God what to do," rather prayer is the creation of a tabernacle of thoughts, ideas, words in which the glory of the Lord may travel and dwell. If we can align thoughts ideas and words with the Word of God, our prayer can be the means for manifesting the perfect Will of God in any earthly situation as it is already in Heaven. When prayer is effective, God releases glory and energy which radiates its content to whatever dimension our thought is willing to carry it. Thus we read Eph. 3:20: "Now unto him that is able to do exceeding abundantly above all that we a**sk or think,** according to the power that worketh in us." The power that "worketh" in us is the Holy Spirit of Christ impregnating our thought and will in such a way that God works in us and through us to transform the world. If the power that works in us is God Himself, then our very prayer is the interweaving movement of the Divine energy moving from within us to

God and returning back to God so that God is all in all in our prayers. The basis of this movement of God's power or Divine energy in a human being is the commitment of thought, imagination and speech to God. When committed to God, they, as the expressions of the deepest desire of man, can carry not only the positive power of God, but even the negative influence of the demonic. When not aligned with God, it can carry negative pathology. Nevertheless, it takes whatever we ask or think and multiplies it by God or the demonic. Given this power then there is need for purification of our desire for prayer to be effective and righteous. True prayer moves beyond the principle of asking and even supersedes the human conscious thought process. This is the mystery of prayer in that God can answer unformulated thought and that which is beyond words. In fact we read in Isa. 65:24: "And it shall come to pass, that before they call, I will answer; and while they are yet speaking, I will hear."

Prayer is feet by which we walk the way of divinity and enter the door of eternity. It is the vehicle whose engine is Christ leading us from the judgment seat to the Mercy Seat wherein shines the sacred flame burning over the hidden manna, the ever living rod of Aaron, and the words engraved upon clay of tablets by the finger of YHWH (Jehovah) ELHM. In prayer, we turn our full attention to the mercy seat; we gaze intently at the sacred flame of faith and envision hope even in the wilderness. Prayer is a Divine love language whose wondrous lyrics are joyfully tuned by notes of worship, adoration, thanksgiving, praise and jubilant dance before the One who sits within the flame, even the Son of God. It is the sacred flame of eternity breathed upon our temporality.

When we pray, we activate the instrument for crossing over with Lord Jesus Christ through the storm tossed sea of life. As one prays, they instigate purification of emotions, thoughts and feelings, body, spirit and soul that permits them to pass over to the supernatural sphere and to enter into these mysteries hidden behind the flame into the Ark of the Covenant. For this to happen we must, as Paul tells us, "pray with all prayer and supplication." Prayer that releases the supernatural and suspends natural boundaries must itself be from the Spirit of God. It is when prayer flows from the very heart of the Holy Spirit that it can transform all carnal operation of the flesh and mind so that we can be transported directly into the presence and throne of God. In prayer, we enter into the sacred mystery, of which Paul speaks when he says, "For one who speaks (prays) in tongues does not speak to men but to God; for no one understands, but in his spirit he speaks mysteries." (1 Cor. 14:2)

As children of God, our prayers must flow from a heart fully surrendered to the Spirit of Christ directed by the inner longing of the spirit within. It is the Holy Spirit that empowers and nudges us to become more intimate with God our Father. As we develop a life of effective prayer, we can go through this mystical gate of fellowship not only by a one time in-filling of the Holy Spirit but a constant in-flow of the Spirit of Christ. When we pray, we crash the false walls of our rationalism and are carried on the wings of grace. The Holy Spirit answers the inner longing of our will and reaches into our subconscious; we groan with sighs of anticipation for the re-freshing which comes from the Lord Jesus Christ. Like the bridegroom longing for the bride, God in man reaches through the darkness and looks face to face upon himself with the frailty of our human eyes and speaks mouth to mouth with our stammering tongue of clay. Fire, Holy fire burning in the soul toward God—that is what prayer is. The glowing fervency for God and love for Him sounds a har-monious cord because prayer has been used to tune our soul as a musical instrument to the God-sphere. Through prayer then let us enter into the Holy of Holies. Let us die to the natural that we might live supernaturally; let's burn the flame that we might overcome the darkness that surrounds us and be raised by the crucified Christ, who is that Light, to new life.

The relevance then of prayer for human life cannot be over–stated. There are numerous accounts of its many structure and forms in various contexts. Even the skeptics of the secular world are now buying into the potency of prayer. Prayer is among the acts known to ground human persons while thrusting them into transcendence. Prayer is a creative principle within man far exceeding what the mind has even dared to grasp in its fallen nature and frailty. When eternity completely swallows time and the influence of prayer upon the universe and human affairs are unveiled, the least that can be said is that prayer has kept the world from the grasp of the abyss and held it often from plunging headlong into the precipice of a personal and social demonic black-hole. The excellence of prayer is also seen in its power to resist the oppressive power of the demonic which strives to take over our personal and communal world. In prayer human beings soar upward into unfathomable mystery. In prayer we fall upward into the heart of God and God comes "downward" into our humanity[1].

Prayer is the spiritual praxis that the Holy Spirit uses to release us from carnality into true spiritual friendship with God. By its sweet communion we gain deeper knowledge into God. Thus it is the key given to us by our God to unlock mysteries of the inner sanctuary of the heavens. The Bible calls us to pray without ceasing. It is an act for all seasons. This command is based on the assumption that prayer done in season and out of season releases us into that Divine righteousness and pleasure which is the life of Christ. Here in prayer is the secret of the believers' subjective intimacy with the objective God who is the object of his/her supreme devotion. Through this Divine introspective focus on the God who has come to live in the intimate center of his/her being, the believer transcends the bondage of the mundane and is drawn into divinity which in circuitous ways reconnects to the mundane as sanctified reality. Every now and then the believer must consciously enter that inner sanctum and travel the Path called Jesus to the truth and the life which He IS.

By constant prayer and tuning of the heart to the rhythm of Divinity, the daily life of the child of God is filled with new courage and strengthened to face the ungodly forces of the universe that array themselves against him/her and God. Here in the intimacy of Father and Child, the long process of glorification initiated by God in the garden, confirmed by the call of Israel, reinforced by the covenant of blood and set ablaze upon the altar of fire, is now confirmed at the altar of the blood and body of the Lamb whose horns the believer takes a hold of in prayerful delight. Here in prayer we return to the primal purpose of Divine creative image and likeness in which we are made a little lower than Elohim. (Ps. 8) What is the chariot of wind by which we fly into that realm of the angels and become a radiating image of our Father? Prayer, I say. It is where we pass beyond the veil through the luminous darkness (Howard Thurman)[2] into the supernatural light, bypass the flaming sword having being clothed by the love of God in His Christ and then proceed to eat of the fruit of the tree of life.

As one of the most significant spiritual principles, prayer provides a solid ground for growth and intimacy with God. When we pray, we are able to make choices based on the influence of the Holy Spirit who knows the innermost thought of God and not based on our desire or thought deriving from worldly patterns or processes. By prayer our will becomes congruent with that of our heavenly Father and our spirit is tuned to the highest harmony with truth and righteousness with Christ who, being its strings, makes our lives music for the Divine dance.

Our actions and plans in life if not seasoned with prayer become ineffective and out of sync with divinity. For a lack of prayer results is a lack of spiritual concentration and robs us of a focusing vision—God—which is capable of setting our affections in order of righteous priorities. Prayer is a most significant undertaking which demands the commitment of all our being and provides perspective from the eternal on the spectrum of our entire life. Thus, lack of prayer is not merely regrettable; it is a destructive inflow of negativity into our being which cuts us off from true life.

Lack of prayer is the worst drainer of spiritual energy and causes most of the disintegrative chaos within the believer and the communion of which he/she is part. It is at the heart of much disunity and failure of nerve into which great men and women of faith sometimes fall. Somewhere at the root is slack or even worse the complete neglect of genuine prayer. Again I must reiterate that prayer in this sense is not me working to be accepted by God, rather is my falling unrestrained into communion with my Lord and my God so that I in communion feed on God's eternal presence. Where the circle of prayer is broken, power begins to wane and the elegantly weaved thread of genuine fellowship begins to pull apart. Lack of prayer often leads to self-justification and prideful resistance of the Holy Spirit. I saw so much of this when I was a pastor, where people who refuse intimacy with

God want to make decisions affecting the flow of God's Kingdom. May God help us. When prayer is lacking, because one is no longer looking steadily into the heart of God, one becomes self-focused.

Prayer is a mighty weapon for effectiveness; conversely, its lack is a mighty weapon in the hand of our carnality and whatever enemy that seeks our downfall. This is especially true in ministers. Its lack in them can be devastating to the people they tend because this lack or slack keeps them out of touch with the inner realities of their own lives. This lack may often lead to rationalization of the seeming spiritual inadequacy or legalistic conformism in which God is absent. Both of these often parade themselves as holiness. It may keep us from discovering the truth about ourselves; thus, we end up ministering from a false center.

Prayerlessness may be terrible, but a false kind of prayer or ungodly prayer is destructive in and of itself. This false kind of prayer which one finds among some circles in Nigeria which ignores the word of the Lord Jesus but focuses on the emotional despair of the people and works on their desire for revenge is a false prayer. Its focus is often the devil not Christ. It is answered but never by God. It can often create a negative atmosphere that can bring into manifestation the inner pain of the one who is praying. Nonetheless ,what has been shown in Nigeria is that an effective spirituality requires a prayerful life. A prayerful life helps you identify Divine priorities for your life. A prayerful life leads you to transformative actions. A prayer-focused life activates and encourages an atmosphere of mutuality between believers. A prayer-focused life opens us up to the flow of Divine life. A prayerful life produces true humility because it is a God-focused life. Close contemplation of prayer will cause awe at God's grace which brings us sinners with all our inadequacies and lack of worth close to such a Holy God, without immediate annihilation of our essence. The person who prays truly often becomes overcome with the depth of God's mercy and grace. This prayer consciousness will silence the pride of life as one is filled with the glory of the Lord, hush the lust of the flesh as one is filled with godly love, and wash the eyes from the lust of the eyes as one gazes intently on the beauty of Jesus Christ.

Relationship by its very nature demands communication. Our relationship with God demands that the inner spring of prayerful communion with God flows continually. This spring (prayer) waters the garden of our communion with Christ. Jesus the Messiah often went apart to drink from this spring. Out of this fountain of prayer flowed miracles, signs and wonders, wisdom, knowledge and revelation. (Matt. 14:23ff; Mark 6:46-47) The Spirit of the Lord which came upon Jesus was the Spirit of prayer and intercession. If we follow Jesus in this regard, prayer will be the hallmark of our lives. Every spiritual person is truly a person of prayer. As water is to fish, so prayer is to the spiritual person. Entrance into the inner sanctum, the Holy of Holies, the Ark, the Mercy Seat, the piercing blue flame between the cherubs are accessed only through prayerful communion with our heavenly Father. As children of God our Nephesh, our normal soul; Neschemah, our higher soul; ruach our spirit; yea, even our physical body often longs for the heavenly Father's embrace. In prayer (as deep communion with God) this longing is filled. Our love is set ablaze, our hunger satisfied, our thirst quenched, as we enter into the chamber of Divine love through prayer. Often we will find ourselves drawn away from the hustle and bustle of life into the sanctum sanctorum (holy holies) where the Father and the Lover of our souls waits to overflow our being with love and mercy. If the Lord God is the highest love of our being, we will seek to join our being to His Being, our spirit to His Spirit, our heart to His heart, our mind to His Mind and our will to His Will, and yes, our body to His Body. In prayer we share in fullness of God-life. When we have thus shared in this fullness, we move into our world with Him as we embrace her hurting, dying and hungry who truly need the life we have touched in prayer.

Our earthly life with all its attendant needs and demands prayerful communion with the Creator. We are created by God (says Rufus Jones, the Quaker Mystic) to exhaust ourselves. Our energy dissipates, our strength fails, our resources run dry, and we must go to God, the Source of our life, in prayer. Our wisely crafted solutions to our intractable problems shatter like worn out crystal against adamantine; to find our way we must plunge into the heart of God. All of these are God's way of assuring our

flight to the refuge of prayer.[3] Yes, even our finitude, as Jacque Ellul says, is the cru-
cible in which our Heaven piercing prayers are forged. God gave prayer as a way of
replenishing our spiritual, psychological and physical supplies. By prayer we acknowledge our total dependence upon the Lord. We can do nothing by ourselves,
absolutely nothing. If we go on our own we lose our way, if we speak on our own
we lose our words, if we fly alone we fall; ***therefore, we pray***. I flee to the chamber
of prayer within my heart that my God may truly be the One that speaks and does,
moves and has being within me and through me.

Prayer is one way, probably the most vital way, of replenishing the earth. By
it we subdue. Through it we receive the capacity for continuous dominion. In
practicing it we become more like our Lord through whom and with whom we
communicate. Through prayer the trees of our lives become more fruitful and our
seeds are watered toward multiplication. Because the source of all these is not ourselves but God (for the Excellency of the power is of God and not of us), prayer
becomes absolutely necessary. If we would ameliorate the poisonous effect of the
carnal self so poisoned by the old serpent, ***we must pray***. Jesus said pray that you enter
not into temptation. Prayer therefore serves as our covering from the tempter's snare.
It does not mean that we are not tempted but because we are focused on God and
radiated by Him, we can withstand. If we fall we will not stay fallen.

Whoever we communicate with, we bear their fruit in our thought and actions.
Lack of communication with God is communication with self, world and Satan
which leads to falling away from God and into temptation. If we do not pray and
communicate with God, it means that we are sharing our love with someone else
and our expectation has moved from God to self, world or the devil. It is imperative
that human beings share their need with Heaven's heart. Prayer moves the need
of the world heavenward. By it we traverse the store house of Heaven, releasing
its supplies into the atmosphere of earth's open fields. Prayer is work more important and greater in power than preaching and teaching because their unction flows
from it and touches the heart about whom we preach. It is, therefore, not only important that we commence, continue and consummate all our acts as children of

God in prayer but that we become prayer. As delight in His glorious presence and live consciously in it every day, we will begin to see the great day in response to our prayer of presence. Manifestation of the glory and its continuous abiding will we come to the place of this type of prayer.

How is prayer to be effective? What makes prayer avail much? For Christian prayer to be effective and avail much four things must happen: prayer must be God focused, Christ informed and centered, and Holy Spirit enlivened and directed, and other concerned. The Father of light must stand at the center of the circle of our prayers. Unless God is at the center, we lose the life of prayer and our prayer life fails. God-focused, not man-focused, nor need-focused. All the prayers of Jesus were God-focused. The God of Israel was the singular focus of all the prayers of Jesus. John 17 and other recorded prayers of Jesus were God-focused and informed by his relationship with the Father. He also was other concerned in his prayer. But that other concern flowed from what he heard from the Father's heartbeat. Effective prayer appends more time listening to the heart of the Father than telling Him what to do.

Effective prayer is grounded in righteousness. Righteousness, if I may say to the dismay of some, is not always right action but rather the state of the heart and its intentional motion. This intentional motion must be Love. There is no law against love. There is no sin where foundationally love is and springs forth into its own streams. Though some dirt may fall upon it, it remains pure and clean, for God is love and love is of God. The righteousness from which prayer must flow in order to be true and effective is God himself as expressed lovingly toward God, neighbor and self. Effective and availing prayer flows in vertical and horizontal love.

When prayer is true, one is able to pan the silver of true doctrine and find where the gold of knowledge is refined. By it one enters into the secret chambers of the earth and releases the treasures of darkness. Only in prayer as entrance into the Divinity, does one put an end to darkness. With that LIGHT he searches the deep recesses of the Kingdom store house and finds treasure. With prayer we take a hold of the God who is Light and so are able to find our way in the thickest darkness. A man of prayer cuts a cell into the place forgotten by men of lesser consciousness who have been enchanted with fleeting values of the age. He often removes himself from noise of the world and his head and ties himself to the crimson thread dangling and swaying until Heaven finds him and pulls him into its bosom. He transforms the ordinary means of the earth into the extraordinary highways of holiness. By the fire of his hunger, even his breath become flight into divinity, his word become the seed of God planted into the heart of the world. By prayer the rocks that are often men's heart become burning sapphire and the dust is transformed to gold nuggets. By prayer the man or woman of God assaults the rock-hardened heart of the sons and daughters of Adam and lays them bare without lifting up a finger or voice of vengeance. The praying man or woman tunnels through the walls and facades built up by fear and doubt because they see; by the eyes of the Spirit, Divine treasures hidden in the soul of people. The prayer warrior though praying, in the dark closet radiates the light of God to the furthest reaches of God's creation. One day as I was praying I got caught up into another realm and suddenly realized that:

This place of prayer where I go, no bird of prey knows the hidden path to it. The enemy's eyes does not peer through; no evil demon abides or sets its camp there. The false lion does not prowl there. That is why he seeks so much to pull me down and away from Divine intimacy and to uncover me from this secret place. For in that secret place I know the intimate embrace of my Shepherd and lay there by the still gentle waters of my Shepherd's gentle stream listening to the whispering melody of His voice to the depth of my depth. I am brought into the inner chambers of my Lord. I see the keepers of His rainbow, revelations of beings, creatures fearful and awesome, radiant and beautiful. O my Lord. What a wonderful beauty I see in this place! I do not want to leave. I want to stay, but He gently nudges me back and on the wings of grace I glide back gently here. From there I emerge only to feel chills of fear and tears for the sons and daughters of my Father, my brethren among whom the enemy has set camp. I look up, I breathe deeply, and I smile, and take courage because I have been with the Lion of my Tribe. My heart is submerged in praise and beatific adoration, radiating all over me. Glory be to my Beloved for His love. It is well, I say.

The prayer of the believer flows from pure emotional delight combined with the force of the Divine intellect out of which emanates sanctified imagination which works itself into transformative reality. This is what I believe is committed by 2 Chron. 7:14:

v^{a}yikaan^{a}uw `amiy '$^a$sher niqraa'- sh$^a$miy `^{a}leeyhem v^{a}yitpalluw viybaqshuw paanay v^{a}yaashubuw midarkeeyhem haaraa`iym va'$^a$niy 'eshma` min- hashaamayim v^a'eclach l^{a}chaTaa'taam v^a'erpaa' 'et-'artsaam^5

14 if My people who are called by My name will humble themselves, and pray and seek My face, and turn from their wicked ways, then I will hear from Heaven, and will forgive their sin and heal their land

What is communicated from the passage is that when authentic prayer flows from the Divine Spring of life it is:

1. Transformative—in that wherever its river flows it brings healing and life. Its transformative balm comes from the fact that it is embedded in the consciousness of God's absolute rule over God's people. God has the capacity to make and remake because God is the zero point from all proceeds and to which all must go. At "God-Point" any change is possible. Since they are "my people," they are in fact at the "God Point". "While" is not conditioned because they are the ones who need transformation; thus, the phrase "if my people."

2. Devotional—in that it flows from deep devotion to the Master. The concept kav-nah' in the Hebrew evokes the archetypal idea of a man on bended knee, vanquished not by the enemy but by forceful devotion to that which he sees as being infinitely greater than his mind can grasp. This awe-sense brings him down to touch the root symbolized by the kissing of the feet and coming into subjection. He/she lets himself or herself be subdued by its radiating and loving presence. This humility is the essential process of Divine human combination creating an atmosphere for an expanding life. It opens the frontiers of human consciousness. By prayer the unmapped areas of our innermost being opens to the exploration of prayer.

3. Kenotic—self emptying embodiment of humility. In the Chronicles passage God requires humility as part of the process of prayer. Humility is kenotic. Kenosis, as we see in the Phil. 2, is a requirement for the meeting of eternity and time as we see in the Lord Jesus Christ.

4. "Pressing in"—this is what I understand the word translated seek in the KJV to mean. The Hebrew word *baqash* (baw-kash'); speaks to primal rooted search of the soul for its bridegroom. In fact it is a mode of worship or prayer whereby one presses with one's whole being after someone or something—in this case God. We press into the glory. We press into the presence to experience its fullness. We press till we break through or until the Divine breaks upon us with its floods of grace and mercy. It is not just that we beg or beseech God for something but that our desire is for Him not merely to procure a thing but God as God is the focus of our pressing in.

5. Turning-whirring—this is the sense of the word *shuwb* (shoob) used in this passage. It is the idea of repentance. It is not merely a single act of turning but root disposition and willingness to turn back away from a particular act or way of life. It is sort of turning of the wheel which turns so as to move the object connected to it away from one point to another. But conversely it is also the turning or a transition from one state of being and doing to another. As used here it does not mean to return to where one started but to where one veered off the right track and to rebuild the broken breach. By it we reopen the wells that have been covered by dirt. In praying it is to bring back home again the heart. This can be done in the mind or in the recess of the soul. Prayer also allows us to cease from certain acts or behavior that may have overtaken us. We continually convert and experience deliverance over and over again. Thus, when I pray, I fetch my thought, emotion, imagination, intellectual processes and bring them back home again. It is the also the idea of recovery, refreshing, relief and rescue. Through prayer restoration occurs and often there is reversal of adverse conditions. In prayer I can retrace my steps and take corrective measure that erases certain bad choices.

CHAPTER TWO:
PRAYER AND HUMAN E-MOTION

Defining the human emotion is rather difficult given the fact that every field of learning from Anthropology to Zoology claims to have insight into it. So I am just going to focus on the common notion of the emotion as the human capacity to translate experiences through feelings. Emotions maybe deeper than feelings; but they are so intertwined that no one has been able o separate them. "Emotion" according to Keith Oatley of the University of Toronto, *"are those processes that both engage us in the world in a way that promotes well-being, and that signal to us and to others how these interactions are going, that is to say whether we are or are not flourishing."*[6] The Bible ties emotions to both the works of the flesh and fruit of the Holy Spirit. This means that they are connected in the core to the ingredients that form our spirituality. When we see the connection of emotions to the Holy Spirit; they help us relate to each other in a meaningful way; but when they are tied to the flesh, they lead us to produce what the book of Galatians calls "the works of the Flesh." If we emote anger, it births rage, wrath, strive and violence. When our emotion is of hatred it does the same thing and results in, violence war and strife. If greed is the motion of being, it leads to emulations, covetousness and bitterness. When prayer grows out of the Emotions of fear, anger and envy, it leads to witchcraft, idolatry and superstitions. Revenge is not emotion; it is an act resulting from an emotion filed through the feelings of anger or hate. Lust is an emotion which as we see in the book of James can inform prayer, and thus make it less effective or keeps even good prayer from being answered. 1. Fear, 2. Hatred, 3. Anger, 4. Greed, 5. Lust, 6. Envy—These are foundational to the works of the flesh. Prayer can indeed grow from these emotional centers, but they are hedge breakers and serpent releasers.

The other groups of emotions which we find together in the New Testament are: 1)Love, 2) Joy, 3) Peace. To me these three emotions have the greatest impact on prayer, as they are the primary offspring of the Holy Spirit from which gentleness, longsuffering, goodness, temperance and faith flow. I cannot accept the psychological idea that faith is feeling or an emotion. That is not to say it does not affect the emotion but rather that faith is usually contrary to the immediate emotion or mindset of the believer. The Holy Spirit travels on the wings of love, joy and peace to make our prayers more effective. These emotions, when they are present, evoke faith and allow the Holy Spirit to work toward the transformation of the six negative at least for a moment. We need then to learn how to harness the positive emotions for prayers, especially if they will build up our spirit and prepare us to act like God our Father. This is why we must be filled with the Spirit.

How do we deal with the emotion and use it effectively in prayer? First, we learn how to breathe by using the Word of God. This may done by intentional breathing done in between a short whisper of a passage of Scripture that speaks to the inward man. For example: breathe in deeply for four counts; then say, "the Lord is my shepherd" as you gently breathe out. You may do the same with short phrases that describe who the lord is to you. Breathe in 1, 2, 3, 4; breathe out while saying "the Lord is my light." Breathe in 1, 2, 3, 4; breathe out, "the Lord is my Salvation" and so on. You can do the same with verses that affirm your identity in Christ. Another way of aligning your emotions with positive prayer process is to cite Scriptures that speak directly to the feelings you need to emote.

What word fitly defines the emotion within the Scripture? The Hebrew word Leb often translated "heart" is more than just the organ of blood flow; it sometimes denotes the emotion, but I believe that soul is more connected to the emotional aspect of the human being. In the Scriptures the soul is shown to carry all the dimensions of the feeling which define emotion. The soul is said to be in anguish

Gen. 42:21 and to be in bitterness in, I Samuel 1:10; Job 3:20; 7:11; 10:1. Appetite is attributed to the soul. (Ps. 31) The soul rejoices, thirsts, is downcast, yearns and clings. (Psalm 35:9; 42:2, 5 ff. Furthermore, it can be at rest, or agitated, consumed with longing or feelings of guilt, pleasure, sorrow or pain. It can be spoken to and commanded to listen, to hope or despair. All these are things we often attribute to emotions. It is all these things that give the emotions their potency in prayer. "The emotion," Thomas Aquinas states, "is the impulse by which the soul is drawn to a thing." It follows then that it is also an instrument by which we are drawn to the highest object of the human spirit which is God. But the emotion is not just a drawing to but also the instrument of repulsion that causes one to flee from an object of terror. The person being drawn to God involves their emotion. One religious scholar Rudolph Otto had said that God is "mysterium tremendum et fascinans." God is both an object of fear and fascination. In prayer not only is the emotion key to our passionate seeking and holding to God, it is the key to our physical equilibrium. The emotions are never silenced as long as there is a desire to take a hold of God. No matter what prayer it is, it must tap into the emotion and channel it to the object or subject of its desire. To say that prayer should not be emotional is to say that the body should not be involved in prayer.

We have been taught to fight passions since the days of the Stoics—the goal was to attain *aptheia.* The church even came to teach that the absence of passion was the qualification for receiving from God. In prayer we were told that we were to use the emotion without being emotional; we were to have joy without enjoying it; we were to be angry without feeling it emotionally. In all these was the assumption that it is possible to separate the emotional from the rational. We were in fact to have feeling without feeling it. We are to be enthused without becoming enthusiastic. We were to be excited without being excitable. People were inculcated with so much fear of the emotion. I must say that prayer lost much of its fervor when passion was sent packing. Whether you accept that emotions are cognitive, perceptual or affective, the human person will be incomplete or at least poorer for not being in touch with it and prayer will lose much of its zest without it.

Our emotions are connected to our beliefs, desires, values and thought process. Our emotions are more than a complex of beliefs and desires, neither are they entities separable from us as persons. The emotion has instinct, intuition, intention and interactive force. Instinctively, it ties to our basic need for survival. Thus, it deals with our embodiment and participation in the concrete world. Being thus embodied, it is attuned to your need for relationship and care. It can measure to a large extent the authenticity and inauthenticity of an act, speech or gesture directed to our person. They are part of us that attach to our beliefs about our world, self and others. Even the negative emotions which are not act sserve to attune us to our environment. For example anxiety may lead a Christian to prayer. A feeling of anger may tune us to the vibration of things we do not like. Fear may cause us to veer away from danger.

Many Christian mystics and teachers seem to have developed a litany of choruses calling for the abolishment of the emotion from the sphere of prayer. But I find no such support in Scripture. There is no call to forgo the emotion in prayer rather there seems to be a call for the purification of prayer and an encouragement to pursue prayer with holy intensiveness and fervor. This intensiveness cannot exist if the emotion is left out. Emotion is a key aspect of the human person. Some glibly say things like "joy is not an emotion" or happiness is not emotion. That is a li, for all the fruits of the Holy Spirit call on the emotions and are intricately connected with the human emotion purified of course by the Holy Spirit.

Mark 11:24-26:

24 Therefore I say unto you, what things so ever *ye **desire***, when ye pray, believe that ye receive them, and ye shall have them. 25 And when ye stand praying, forgive, if ye ought against any: that your Father also which is in Heaven may forgive you your trespasses. 26 But if ye do not forgive, neither will your Father which is in Heaven forgive your trespasses.

This passage of Scripture in which Jesus deals with prayer is directed to the human emotion. Desire, believe-feeling of joy at the reception of good news—

like everything that has to do with the human body, it is so easy to dismiss it and denigrate its importance for the spiritual life. But the emotion with all its problems is necessary for our spiritual well being. Pure and positive emotion adds to the power of prayer and improves the outcome of prayer. When praying, our thought process regarding the events of our life has been can positively or negatively affect the meaningfulness and effectiveness of prayer. This process of heart purity is something that causes breakthrough in prayer or brings hindrance to our efforts. What your thought processes, feeling process, images are about before, during and after prayer can improve the power your human spirit in its mutual interaction with God. Prayer, arising out of purified emotions is means to draw the power of the Divine into the circumstance of our lives for which we pray. The emotion amplifies the force of whatever it does and in prayer it gives more power than one can ever imagine. Emotions have a great deal of reservoir of force available to them for the lifting up the human person who can harness them. Purifying and focusing the emotion in prayer taps into that reservoir and quickens you as a person with the confidence and increases their chance receptivity from the heavens. By this I am not talking about emotionalism and vain repetition, rather I am referring to the speaking of the language embedded by God in human beings for effective navigation of the universe in which God has placed them.

Rabbi Kook in his notes points out that the Hebrew verb **lelaptihel** or *lehitpalel*— "to pray" - is in the reflexive tense. This emphasizes the aspect of prayer's spirituality as intricately connected to the emotion and its impact on the whole man. The state of contemplation brings out an outpouring of directed emotion, beyond the soul's normal range. Prayer bathed in passionate emotion has the power to fulfill desires because there is a power in the world which is greater than the sum total of the problems. That power comes to reside in any human being through Jesus Christ. For we read "as many as received him to them he gave the power to becomes the sons of God." (Jn. 1:12) The diminished effectiveness of so many prayers through this century has to do with the denigration of the place of human emotion. But the emotion is the chariot wing of prayer, which passionately ignites of the fuel of the soul, sets it ablaze by the power of God and its vibratory pitch chases the night of despair and the evil beast away. When directed by the positive vibration of the Holy Spirit's presence, prayers that flow from a pure emotion release power and force for the saturation of the supernatural into the atmosphere. The power of a prayer charged with emotional intensity informed by purity supersedes routine prayer in its ability to release miracles. Emotional purity is especially helpful when praying for others. This may explain why the Lord Jesus Christ insisted that that we forgive our enemies and love them so that the force of prayer flows in emotional purity which not only benefits those for whom we pray but benefits us. For we read "blessed are the pure in heart for they shall see God." Because of the possibility of the emotion to be hindrance to our prayer, we must bring it the fiery center of the Shekinah. Most people do not know this and tend to pray only for themselves and those that they know and like and avoid praying for those who may have hurt them. Christian prayer is the training of the emotion to vibrate the emotion at the level of Divinity. Praying for others, especially those that you do not know, even those who may be at odds with you releases a powerful force from the unconscious that benefits you as well as the recipients of the prayer, and helps to purify your emotion for intercessory effectiveness.

Prayer in its emotional aspect deals at the most primitive level of our being. This is underscored by the fact that when we are "caught up in the spirit" we return to the primordial language of hidden and pent up emotionality, whose only sounds are groaning that cannot be articulated in conventional parlance.

Different types of prayer call forth different emotional states. The emotion that attains prophetic prayer is not the same that attains intercessory prayer. That which attends confessional contrition is not that which attends prayers of exuberant praise, thanksgiving or glorification. Some prayers are labor intensive others are not. The emotion in prayer produces changes based on the experience and the need. There is no way that we can come to a place of emotionless prayer even when we see Christ face to face. The very longing of our heart to be united with our Father causes our soul to cry out. Most of Christian prayers, unlike other religions grow our deep compassion for the world; when we see the world in its current state and far removed from the intended ideal of the heavenly Father, our heart moans in prayer. When we see the sick, when we see the oppressed, when we see the abused, when see the lost, our hearts cry out with passionate plea for their salvation. When they are saved, we release our emotions also in joyful praise. We could never logically reach the threshold of the heart of Christ and the Father if our emotions are shut off in prayer. To understand this we see how many times Jesus shed tears or grieved in the spirit for His people.

There is a phrase used in the Scripture which shows that God intents to elicit our emotion in our relationship with Him. Empathic words: "For we do not have a High Priest who cannot sympathize with our weaknesses, but one has been tempted in all things as we are yet without sin. Let us therefore draw near with confidence to the throne of grace, that we may receive mercy and may find grace to help in time of need." (Heb. 4:15-16) Feelings do not sum up emotions, rather they form a small part of it. So then prayer is not about how one feels though feelings do play some role in it. All kinds of feelings are often manifested in prayer depending on what the praying one is going through and how they seek to enter into the heart of God or deal with their problem. Depending on what the prayer is, joy is an appropriate expression as much as sorrow, sadness, exuberance, guilt, etc. etc. So do not confuse a particular feeling as a sign of effective prayer, rather it is the momentary signature of the situation in which you are going through upon your body. The thing about feeling is that one feeling can be used to silence the other in quick flash of thought and focus. Emotion in prayer helps one to discern the mind of the spirit in issues of justice and equity. It can also tune the heart to compassion and mercy as it flows from the Lord. Emotion cues to the intuitive subconscious location of the Divine voice. In the Deut. 6:5:

> "And thou salt love the LORD thy God with all thine heart, and with all thy soul, and with all thy might." (KJV) This is repeated in Mark 12:30: "Love the Lord your God with all your heart and with all your soul and with your entire mind and with all your strength.'" Mark 12:30 (NIV)

Prayer is not just talking to God but the assessing, valuing and empathic consideration of decisions and choices in light of Divine nature. In prayerful emotion our being learns to align itself with beauty of the Lord and you may sense His displeasure in cases of our lack of discipline. It is our emotion that cautions us as to approach God with reverence and not with arrogance and rudeness which oft tends to be confused with faith. Yet, if we can bring the force of our emotions to bear positively on prayer, we can change the vibratory resonance of any atmosphere and make it conducive for prayer and for reception of what is birthed as the result of our prayer.

Because of the capacity of the emotions to confuse our motivation and led us into spiritual quicksand, we need the Holy Spirit. When we get to the edge of our emotions, we tend to lose focus and to become confused and sometimes we do not know what to do. This capacity of the emotion to mislead means that we need the Holy Spirit to make sure that our emotions do not set up idols which may end up displacing the purpose of God in our lives. This means that while emotions are vital to prayer, if they are not hoed by the Spirit of God and channeled through the will as sanctified by the Holy Spirit, they may force us to set up idols or spirits whose major function is to flatter our wishes to our own destruction. So God gives the Holy Spirit to protect us from ourselves mostly, especially as it relates to our prayer lives. Why this Divine protection as it relates to prayer? Because in prayer we are more likely to meet various entities who seek to distort our goal and offer us false images which are not in submission to the image of the God or ourselves.

CHAPTER THREE

PRAYING IN THE SPIRIT

Because of that possibility of emotional distortion we must pray in the Spirit. If only to create an objective sense of communicating with divinity without the noise and static of our prejudices, then praying in the Spirit is worth it. And Paul makes this clear when he says in Rom. 8:26-27:

> 26 Likewise the Spirit also **helpeth our infirmities**: for we know not what we should pray for as we ought: but the Spirit itself maketh intercession for us with **groanings which cannot be uttered**. 27 And he that searcheth the hearts knoweth what is the mind of the Spirit, because he maketh intercession for the saints according to the Will of God.

Our infirmity consists in our ignorance of the Divine method by which we should approach the throne and the limitation of the language this side of Babel. We do not know how to form the words in our barbaric sinful language that can penetrate the fiery veil of the heavens. When we approach the gate, there the cherubs with the flaming sword await our stammering tongue and stand in the way of our passage. There we cannot speak the password. The only password of the initiate here is the name of the one who said "I am the door."

> John 10:7-9: "Then said Jesus unto them again, Verily, verily, I say unto you, I am the door of the sheep. 8 All that ever came before me are thieves and robbers: but the sheep did not hear them."

We know that whatever we ask the Father in the Name of Jesus, that He does it. We also know that if we ask Jesus for something because we are "in His name" he will do it for us. But there is an infirmity deep within our souls—something deeper than just saying the name of Jesus. Our intellect gets in the way of our ability to speak to Heaven in way that conforms to the Will of God. We are often in trouble because we confuse our present desire with the Will of God and our prayer language becomes the language of self. Note that the passage does not say "we know not how to pray" but "we know not what to pray." It is the "what" to pray not the "who" to pray to or the "how" to pray that is our problem. "What" refers to things or outcome that we desire in our pursuit. The breaking out of the Spirit upon our apathy and materialistic enclosure is what helps us in the quest for the "what" that is pleasing to God. This passage implies that there is a way we ought to pray for "what." In order words everything that we desire has the specific language which it will listen to and hear. There is a language for everything which is the object of our desire, but we do not know the language for it. If it is true that whatsoever we ask the Father in the name of Jesus He gives it to us, it means that the problem is not the that our prayers have not been answered but we have not yet spoken the language of that which has been given to us. How can we speak to the "what" we do not know? The Spirit is the one with the linguistic capacity to speak to the things which have been released from the mind of the Creator by their own language in order to cause them to come into manifestation. This infirmity is the result of Babel. For at Babel it is not just man's language that was confused, but our ability to speak the language of things that have been freely given to us by God has been closed up. At Babel there was also a confusion of our ability to hear God and the universe in which we live. If the Holy Spirit does not check the emotions, we can become victims of the nine confusions of Babel. Confusion of hearing, confusion of speech, confusion of communion with physical structure, confusion of love with lust, confusion of spirituality with materiality, confusion of noise with voice, confusion of man of with God, confusion of grace with human works, confusion of murder with sacrifice. All these are healed with the coming of the Holy Spirit which is the miracle of hearing, the miracle of speech, the of true miracle communion, the miracle of love, the miracle of voice, the miracle spiritualization, the miracle of grace and the miracle of sacrificial activation of divinity.

The Spirit helps our infirming by speaking the language of the manifestation of what we have been given, cutting short the interruption in the heavenliest and causing that for which we have prayed and which according to the promise of the Master has been given to us to flow joyfully into our lives. Our infirmity in this case is not the removal of apathy but the use of irrelevant language. But through the Spirit, prayer becomes the decisive instrument to uplift us and cause us to plunder and make manifest what the enemy is holding captive in the ethereal sphere. It is here that the Spirit must move beyond the modern or even post-modern rational technocracy. In fact by the definition of prayer as that which the Spirit does with us and sometimes for us because we lack the language of manifestation, we can say that modern man does not know how to pray. This infirmity even cuts deeper. It is the undue enthronement of rationalistic processes over the intuitive orientation of man in religion. The superficial supremacy of the emotionality over spirituality incapacitates even the prayer of the so-called religious.

The Spirit helps our infirmity. This is not a mechanical process that gives occasion for rote structuring of prayer, but the Holy Spirit touches the most imperceptible aspects of our human spirit tracing its many motions and seeking to direct that impression by transmitting the right sequence and energy to that which is sensitive in relation to the Will of God. Through the Holy Spirit's influence on our soul, we commit to the Christological Kingdom Process. This Spirit's in prayer transitions us from inefficiency to efficacy. For in prayer the Holy Spirit is the agent of Divine efficacy that can raise our primary occasions to eternal actualities. So why is the helping necessary? Why is praying in the Spirit necessary? This is why. We often know how to pray, we know who to pray to but the articulation of the alignment of our circumstance and true need with the Will of God escapes us; here the Spirit being God speaks to God who knows and is able to align our will with the Divine Will and to give the linguistic vehicle for what we need must travel to manifestation in our context.

42

The Spirit helps our infirmity by taking upon itself to make intercession for us—intercession—the Holy Spirit functions as the go between the believer, *"us,"* and the Father to plead on our behalf things which are hidden in our unconscious that we cannot put into words. Here, the Holy Spirit bears the burdens of our lives and pours them directly into the heart of the Lord God. This is not we interceding for others but the Holy Spirit operating in our life's situation and picking up and cleaning hidden things that may lead to self-deception. If we consider the struggle in which the believer is engaged with the enemy, the fact that God chooses to use His Holy Spirit to impact us directly and create an atmosphere favorable to the union of our will to God's Will and Thought should not surprise us. We do not know why we sometimes get the sense of urgency to pray, but the truth is that the Holy Spirit strikes the cord of our spirit propelling our soul to act in such a way that produces sound in the supernatural sphere. This sound or voice (*kol in* the Heb) allows an entrance of light that swallows darkness and opens the channel for us to tap into eternity. We enter the place where time as we know it in the world is no more. Through this helping of our infirmities, we hear the tone of the Heaven as our soul passes through various dimensions and is impressed upon by the Will and Thought of God making my being a wing for the flight of the harmony of world wholeness.

The helping of our infirmity by the Holy Spirit changes how we conceive Divine process and how we calculate and understand time. Guided by the Holy Spirit in prayer, our being enters into the mind of God and hence beyond time. Since we are there by the very Spirit of God, we can become agents of change of time by seeing it from eternity. When time is seen from eternity, it ceases to be. Literally, we become the seat of Divine light piercing the dark background of night. Through this helping of the Holy Spirit we develop spiritual lucidity which transforms all subsequent and I dare say even past actions by the nature of God with whom we commune.

In helping our infirmity, the focus is not to fit God into our ego or to force God to conform to our proscribed patterns, rather the Spirit's intent is genuine communion of God with God. It is an inner Divine conversation to which we are privileged to eavesdrop. Only that which God does truly communicates with God at a God level and can truly affect a Divine outcome. When God ceases to act with God and leaves us to ourselves or to another, it becomes demonic and subject to Divine judgment. For prayer not be demonic it must be directed by the Spirit of God who is God and be summarized in the love of Christ.

In helping our infirmities, the Spirit helps us to remember Divine thoughts, ideas and images erased by the trauma of incessant attack of demonic powers against us. We certainly cannot find fault with the memory of the Holy Spirit. For as God is all seeing and all knowing, so is the Holy Spirit. One specific thing that the Holy Spirit does in helping infirmities is to bring up Scriptures in our mind and then give us the unction to speak the Word in order to accomplish a particular purpose. The Lord Jesus said, "He shall bring to remembrance whatsoever I have said to you." "That which I have taught you" in my estimation is not merely that which proceeded from the three years of His earthly life but the inclusive communication of all the eternal Logos and Rhema proceeding from God to humanity. Thus, that which "I have taught you" will include all that God has spoken from the creation of man to the end of time. The Logos is eternal speech from eternity and has the very nature of God. The Holy Spirit brings into our mind that which has been eternally in the mind of God. In intercession this is essential because here what is at stake and held up by the weakness of man are the eternal purposes of God seeking to work itself out in the life of humanity. This intercession flowing from the unutterable groaning refers to kind of a Divine code decipherable only by God. How do I know it is code? In verse 27 we read, "He that searcheth the heart knoweth what is in the mind of the Spirit." This is similar to the code book of revelation which no one in Heaven or on earth or beneath the earth could open except the Lamb of God who is God in incarnated. Paul in speaking of praying in the Spirit affirms the idea of the spirit code. In 1 Cor. 14:2 we read, "he who speaks in a tongue does not speak to men but to God, for no one understands him; however, in the spirit he speaks mysteries."

Praying in the Spirit puts our thought far away from any creature and communicates it directly into God. One of our infirmities is the tendency toward repetition that Jesus warns against in Matthew. But the Spirit bypasses this by providing us with language and capacity far exceeding the vocabulary of our ordinary learning. Another mode then of our infirmity is the fact that our natural communication is understandable even to the enemy of our faith. The devil can read our strategies and fears in our prayers. Our language of prayer carries with it our inner fears that the enemy cannot know otherwise because the heart of man is a closed book to everyone, even man himself, except God who is able to search it. The Holy Spirit on the other hand is God and communicates with the Godhead in language that God has reserved as intimate conservation between Him and His children. Thus Paul, says it is a mystery, yes, even to the one in and through whom the Holy Spirit operates. How do I know that it is a code decipherable by God alone through His Holy Spirit? Paul says, "no one understands him for he speaks mysteries."

Furthermore, our infirmities consist in not always being certain of the Will of God and therefore having a tendency to pray in cross-purpose to the Will of God in contexts where we have very heavily vested our emotions. The comparative constancy under which various themes, ideas, needs and images strive to influence our lives may cause us to choose lines of actions merely to maintain our comfort and as result become detrimental to our well being. The Spirit is not affected the same way by these phenomena that combine to assault our loyalty to the Divine Will. The Spirit is not prevented either by emotion, rational limitation or lapse of memory from absorbing completely into the Will of God since it is God. Superfluous conditions remain not so much outside of its purview as to the fact that they are unable to sway it away from Divine Will and purpose. The Holy Spirit does not fall prey to forces that separate from God for He is God.

The Holy Spirit in helping our prayer experiences is perpetually conversing to the Godhead the pressure under which we labor. Through its agency the Godhead comes to move upon the waters in the dark places of our soul bringing the God nature to bear upon it and transforming our habits and motions. The Holy

45

Spirit as intercessor holds the solution to the elaborate fragmentation which leads to linguistic, rational, temporal disorientation and subjects us to hubris and limits our communicative possibility with God and with one another. Let also say that I believe that praying in the Holy Spirit can also help us communicate effectively with another human being whose reason or other factors prohibit from grasping what our heart is trying to communicate, but by praying in the Holy Spirit our spirit can communicate in Divine clarity to them.

The purpose of the Holy Spirit in prayer is to make actual the possibility of resolving the communicative dissonance, our emotional disharmonies, biophysical enclosure and mental limitation as it relates to God and our fellow human beings. This disharmony and all such are many times caused by an inner misunderstanding of who we are as it relates God's good will towards us. This kind prayer that we speaking of here are not analytical but intuitive harmony creating movement which means which causes prayer to be:

> Less a linear communication with God, and more an effort to better
> understand one's self, using God as a prism. And, as Kook extrapolates,
> to better understand ourselves through God, we must direct our hearts
> and minds, "to contemplate God via prayer."

The Holy Spirit by praying through us and for us creates for us as it were an organismic compensation by applying supernatural systems—Divine energy flows from the eternal realm into the structure of our spiritual communication system. But it must be remembered that this work of the Spirit, this ability of the Spirit to indwell humanity and to flow communicatively between Man and God is only made possible by the **hypostatic** union of Human and God in Jesus Christ. The Holy Spirit talks to God from inside humans because God first became human in Jesus Christ. Now God does not only see our infirmity but through Jesus Christ the Godhead can be touched deeply by our infirmity and seeks to help us. From this great experiment the Spirit can now actually use human nature to reveal hidden mysteries lying deep in the recesses of man back to Heaven. In helping our infirmity the Holy Spirit performs the task in us now here on earth, which the ascended Christ performs in the presence of the Father and the angels—Intercession. Some of the tasks of the Holy Spirit include: 1) To open the door so that we can continually tap into the vast powers made available to us by God by praying directly into the heart of God. 2) To enlarge our accretion of revelational knowledge that comes through times of intimacy with God. 3) To bring about the expansion of feelings of absolute dependence upon God that causes us to cry to God for our total salvation. The Holy Spirit has the Divine Technology that can cause our emotional outputs to conform to the nature of Christ. This is called the Mind of Christ—the interweaving of our emotions with the Holy Spirit allows us to pray effectively and in harmony with the Will of God.

CHAPTER FOUR

VARIETIES OF PRAYER

"Praying always with all (types) prayer and supplication in the Spirit, and watching thereunto with all perseverance and supplication for all saints." Ephesians 6:18

Prayer flows in various ways and is carried by various currents. In fact prayer flows maybe even affected by the ministerial gifts or spiritual gifts of the individual. As such anyone may pray in particular flow, but one who is powerful or passionate in a stream of gifting may cause higher vibratory resonance by the greater deposit of the Charismata in them in that area. In this case it may be well for believers to find out how effective their prayers are when they pray within particular stream. No matter what kind of prayer one is involved with, it calls for spiritual vigilance and perseverance. It should also have as its main purpose to edify and build up the body—as Paul says "for all saints."

PROPHETIC PRAYER:

Prophetic prayer signifies both a re-appropriation and a transformation of the insights of Divine man. Now this kind of prayer is based not only on need but also on love. It is neither mere incantation nor a meditation but a spontaneous outburst of intuitive insight. Indeed, heartfelt supplication is the essence of true prayer. Prophetic prayer does not involve begging and even complaining. Prophetic prayer is not the same as what scholars call prophetic religion. It is a verbalization of Divine intuitive grasp which literally prophesizes to the circumstance based on what it has seen in the supernatural realm. One of the reasons for the giving of the Holy Spirit is the desire on the part of the Lord to move prayer from mere petition to prophetic output. When we fall down at his feet to worship and adore his Lordship as his servants, we open for the saturation of the Spirit of Christ and the release of Prophetic prayer. For we read in Rev. 19:10 the **testimony of Jesus is the spirit of prophecy**. As followers of the Son of man our prayer is prophetic annunciation of the Kingdom of God and prophetic denunciation against the Kingdom of darkness. In prophetic prayer we call on the universe to obey our God as proclaim His majestic name. So our prayer when it flows from the testimony of Jesus which is the spirit of prophesy, says to the world: "Hear ye the word of the LORD." By this prayerful prophetic of "Thus saith the Lord GOD," we call the world to cease from its foolishness and from following its own spirit and begin to see God's purpose. This is the essence of the in-filling of the Holy Spirit which we read in the book of Acts 2:17-21

17 And it shall come to pass in the last days, saith God, I will pour out of my Spirit upon all flesh: and **your sons and your daughters shall prophesy**, and your young men shall see visions, and your old men shall dream dreams: 18 And on my servants and on my handmaidens I will pour out in those days of my Spirit; and **they shall prophesy**: 19 And I will shew wonders in Heaven above, and signs in the earth beneath; blood, and fire, and vapour of smoke: 20 The sun shall be turned into darkness, and the moon into blood, before that great and notable day of the Lord come: **21 And it shall come to pass, that whosoever shall call on the name of the Lord shall be saved.**

The reasons for the outpour of the Spirit is the empowerment for prophesy, vision, dreams and prayer, and the capacity to call upon the name of the Lord for signs and wonders. All these are geared to the salvation of the person and the world. The blood, fire and smoke are reminiscent of sacrifices offered under the

Mosaic covenant. The final goal of all the sacrifices is the salvation of they who call upon the name of the Lord. Prayer has become, for many, nagging at God that the very sense of prophetic prayer has been put to the back burner. Those who look for the great and terrific day of the Lord must turn to Prophetic prayer.

Prophetic prayer removes the shroud of darkness which grows from negative confessions. It illuminates our stammering language by the outreach of the Spirit bringing it into pure articulation of Kingdom outcomes. The Holy Spirit moves prophetically to help us to release creative life process into the body of Christ, the Son of God. It is by this inflowing of prophetic prayer that there is steady uplift and empowerment to construct the channel through which Divine energies of life flow until the knowledge of the glory of the Lord covers the world as the waters cover the sea. That this prophetic mode of prayer that is essential for the spiritual health and growth of the people of God is seen in the early church where prophetic announcement was seen in prayer.

There is no solution for the present loss of spiritual force and the poverty of soul and body, the feebleness of visionary input, except the people of God awaken to the fact that merely having gatherings is not going to cut it, but that there must be applied prophetic mode of prayer at various levels of the universe which reinserts Divine value into the realities of the world. Prophetic prayer flows from a deep embrace of the fellowship, drinking from the deep well of God's throne. We must become inebriated from this spring of Divine mystery, imbibing from the pure love of its creative force, and let it flow as a pure living spring from our innermost being. Prophetic "prayer is born out of the intense earnestness and out of the consciousness that only God, through us as feeble organ of His Will, can accomplish what we seek and what we need" for the true transformation of the world. By prophetic prayer there arises clarity of vision for the people that results in profound changes. When we enter the realm of prophetic prayer, light breaks through as pray and we are often inundated with the river of God's energy from the throne. Such unbounded power comes when our prayer moves from mere utilitarian petition to prophetic outflow release from the Holy Spirit which has been freely given to us by the Lord.

Prophetic prayer is warfare prayer conquering obstacles, refreshing the soul and settling the vast storm of restlessness. Prophetic prayer is coming and will work in a mighty way throughout the world and upon the lives of God's people. It is an operation of grace given to those who search for God with the same fervency as the early church. When prophetic prayer comes, as it will, the people of God will influence the course of the cosmos causing the secret channels of the universe to give up their treasures for the benefit of the Kingdom of God. In the word of Rufus Jones Prophetic, "Prayer will lift us to new levels of experiences, put us in touch with an intensely transforming fire that brings transfigurative energy and make our impossible possible." Prophetic prayer flows throughout the Book of Psalms. Often we see David move from petition to prophetic affirmations. Sometimes prophetic prayers may come as the result of specific revelation from the Father: Matt. 16:16-19:

16 And Simon Peter answered and said, Thou art the Christ, the Son of the living God. 17 And Jesus answered and said unto him, Blessed art thou, Simon Barjona: *for flesh and blood hath not revealed it unto thee, but my Father which is in Heaven. 18 And I say also unto thee*, That thou art Peter, and upon this rock I will build my church; and the gates of hell shall not prevail against it. *19 And I will give unto thee the keys of the Kingdom of Heaven: and whatsoever thou shalt bind on earth shall be bound in Heaven: and whatsoever thou shalt loose on earth shall be loosed in Heaven.*

Matt 18:18-20:

18 Verily I say unto you, Whatsoever ye shall bind on earth shall be bound in Heaven: and whatsoever ye shall loose on earth shall be loosed in Heaven.19 Again I say unto you, That if two of you shall agree on earth as touching anything that they shall ask, it shall be done for them of my Father which is in Heaven. 20 For where two or three are gathered together in my name, there am I in the midst of them.

What these two passages show, though they do not deal directly with prayer, is that there are revelational, edificative, authoritative, and communal aspects to prophetic prayer. This does not mean that other flows of prayer do not have revelational insights but that there is unique and greater flow of revelation in prophetic prayer.

The Hebrew word *halipet* **Tefilah** is the act in which the Divine in man corresponds with the ultimate is at the heart of the prophetic. The very act of entering into intimate conversation with God unleashes the prophetic because it calls forth the source of plenty in the time of need, mercy in times of judgment, peace in times of war, love to transcend hate, light to overcome darkness and God to abide with man in the frailty of humanity. Prophetic prayer can call forth joy in the time of sorrow. At the depth of prophetic prayer in its true authenticity is God breaking into human consciousness by a creative word. By this prophetic inherency, prayer speaks forth Heaven's blessing and wellbeing. Prophetic pronouncement in prayer can help the one for it is being offered hold the demonic storm surges at bay. By its revelational declaration prophetic prayer—what is called in the Hebrew **Kavanah**—aligns the word, mind, thought imagination with the Spirit and opens the pathway for the inflow of the Glory of the Lord—the *shekinah* into the earthly realm. Prophecy flows from the **Shekinah;** hence, when prayer taps into the **Shekinah,** it stops being mere petition to prophetic utterances. Prophetic prayer will often manifest when the praying one has touched that sphere of the glory with the Divine arrow causing its cloud to shower the soul and earth realm with manifestation. Prophetic prayer is not a thing that implies that only official prophets can pray prophetically. Prophetic prayer transcends whatever system the religious system, of the world and its false consciousness has concocted as the final expression of God apart from the Word of God. If this is the case then the expression of prayer now possessed by a majority of the churches must change in favor of the dynamic of the Holy Spirit, which Christ has given to the church.

Prophetic prayer is not the description of the circumstance we face to God but a speaking into the inner truth of our situation using the Word of God to transform it and dethroning whatever false power that has raised itself against God's Will and Kingdom. It is consistent with the Word of God and calls forth deliverance. By this prophetic prayer we identify with the Word of God and not with the statistic of human rules and principles. It announces what God wills and allows because its revelational insight puts it in touch with the current of Divine energy, which it then helps to flow through the people of God. Furthermore, it is not just one individual praying for the people while they listen in awe to their prophetic skill, but it is in itself a release of the Kingdom impulse within the people of God. This kind of prayer allows the people of God to corporately affect the manifestation of life upon the plane of human existence. Here the body vividly envisions the Kingdom and calls it into manifestation from its hidden realms. Prophetic prayer because of its revelatory insight touches the taps into heart of the Father for those in the shadow of death and His desire to move them into the dayspring of life. The poor and oppressed are released and the windows of Heaven are opened over the thirsty plains of human soul.

Because the body of Christ is a prophetic body, it is important that we should attempt to understand the place of prophetic prayer in the world in light of our definition of the Kingdom of God in which we now live. It illustrates the difference between transformative prayers flowing in power from the timid pleas without insight and reveals the true meaning of our new humanity in Christ. The understanding of any prophetic prayer depends upon the conviction that the praying believer has a unique place in God's heart and God's Kingdom and the salvation of the human race for which God has so graciously granted the Son.

Prophetic prayer is deeply rooted in the fact that human thought and action, life and suffering, are the subject of God's redemptive purpose. Of course prophetic prayer does not ignore the realities of the person's community but plumbs the inexhaustible depth of Divine and causes us to understand and depict the destinies of mankind with conviction flowing from an appreciative comprehension of the living sympathy of Christ. The Holy Spirit flows through our prophetic prayer posture, gives unction and draws the believer into cosmic order, binds the spirit of man to the spiritual sphere and fills the whole life with the pervading consciousness of the interconnection of worlds. It is here that the mighty phenomena which brings refreshing and receptivity into wasteland of human hopelessness and despair can move people to steadily receive the mighty wind propelling them to escape the fragmentation of life and bring them into wholeness—Shalom in Christ.

When the church engages in prophetic prayer in earnest, it organizes its spiritual energies to deal with the injurious effect forced upon peoples' lives in the form of thoughts, imaginations and concepts that raise themselves against the knowledge of Christ. (2 Corinthians 10:3-60) The power of people who engage in prophetic prayer is not their perfection but in finds its strength in the organization and practice of the Word God as written in Scripture and apprehended in the inner most sanctum of the Spirit as the throne of God. Thus, by prophetic prayer one seeks to reach in that moment into the Holy of Holies behind the veil calling forth the abundant life made possible by the death of Jesus Christ upon the cross. To such as pursue it there opens up to them new vistas of power from above releasing below an overflow so that the praying person becomes an embodiment of Heaven on earth possessing joy, truth and peace, providential immediacy and protective ability as it is in Heaven.

Prophetic prayer should be saturated by praise, adoration and worship. Prophetic prayer is prayer centered wholly upon God and His eternal characteristics and announcing such to the world for its transformation. In prophetic prayer God's majesty, glory, and power; His beauty His eternal love; His mercy and grace should be the ground. Prophetic prayer must always begin here.

CLEANSING PRAYER:

As we approach God in prayer we come through so many formative issues that have affected our clarity of motivation. In the inner levels of our souls we have learned some lessons many of them valuable but also many of them are hindrances to our honest and transparent approach to God. Some of our actions, attitudes and mentalities are nothing but rubbish and must be brought to the fire altar and the purging waters of God before we can proceed any further in prayer. In fact if we are honest many of them are tares, which have grown with the Divine wheat of God's love. We need to find them by prayer, detach them by the process that David sets forth in his psalm of confession, and burn them. They must come under him purifying fire of God's Holy Spirit. This facing of the worst aspects of our lives as we seek to become more intimate in prayer is demanded by the nature of God. This cleansing prayer *does not* bring us salvation, but it prepares us to intercede and to be an effective witness to others. David said, "so that I might teach transgressors your way."

We do not do this mainly because we are afraid of punishment from God but for the purification of our inner motives so that we are not living our lives or praying for others from a false center, thereby hindering our power and effectiveness. The pain that may result if we do not let go of the un-God aspect of our habit, mood and behavior not caused by God but by the exposure of uncleanness to the perfect Son of a Holy God. Our inner world with all the things we still carry does not stop God from loving us but it stops us from being completely available to God in particular ways. Unless these undesirable elements of our lives are dealt with, we may not make full proof of our gifts, power and ministry. So if we must be true effective in our prayer lives and become healers in the world, we need continually to come to the place of purification and cleansing—at the foot of the cross, the place of skull where sacrifice is made and the blood of the Lamb is poured out. We do not come out of fear because there is no more wrath, but we come out of love without condemnation to pour out our "reasonable service." We want to present our bodies as living sacrifices, holy and acceptable to God." This cleansing prayer needs to be at the foundation of all prayer to make us burn with affection and zeal for God and for others as opposed to burning with the fullness of our ego and lust for things.

Naturally then, one important step in personal prayer is asking for forgiveness of sins if one is to be effective in the walk with God. Psalm 51 is our best-known prayer of penitence in the Bible. (Psalm 51) Cleansing prayer places us on the altar of the God's fire so that the flame may pierce our innermost being. Effective relation with God means that our lives must be transparent (not perfect in activities but in love) before Him at all times. We are transparent before God. It is not the transparency that we have before God by virtue of His omniscience that is really the issue in our prayer but our own transparency towards Him that removes our spiritual blockades. God's ability to see all our sins does not remove them, but our ability to lay them bare, in a sense, permits God to remove them. Until God's transparency becomes my transparency, my sins remain because I am still attempting to hide my sins in the face of Divine transparency.

Cleansing prayer is more than confession. It is the deep penetration of the inner core of our being to see the root cause of our sentiments moods and behavior. This is what David does in Psalm 51. Sometimes confession can just be the flippant "I was wrong." It should not be so when dealing with God. However, when seen from a more deeper perspective, we can see that cleansing prayer is reaching to the core marrow of the act, sentiment, mood or behavior and laying them bare in all their ugliness and shame before the Lord, being assured of grace because we come through the doorway sprinkled by the blood of God's Son. When we come to cleansing prayer, we ought to move away from the confused attempt to generalize our sins and the tendency to explain them away. In cleansing prayer we move away from the partiality inherent in our understanding of our own act. Above all we must seek cure from the hopeless tendency to externalize our faults and project them to a source outside ourselves. In cleansing prayer we place before God every single occurrence every habit, every mood, every behavior every spiritual incompetence as a matter of spiritual urgency whose removal is indispensable to our spiritual survival.

The end or at least the lessening of every evil habit is the removal of self-justification and self-righteousness defense by the perpetrator. Unless deep cleansing prayer is undertaken, many of our prayers remain in the lower realm and do not pierce through the second Heaven into the third Heaven because often they are still founded on a dung heap of unresolved spiritual incompetence (sins). No progress is going to be made spiritually unless this aspect of prayer is restored to the church. Every movement which ignores cleansing prayer merely deals with the superficial externalities and does not have the power to transform its generation in their core being. Spiritual warfare is not a substitute for cleansing prayer. In fact many become casualties of the war because they engage in spiritual warfare without dealing with the hold which the other side has in their soul. Any attempt to replace this cleansing orientation of prayer with warfare may result in fact in the enemy being able to turn the weapon of the presumed warrior against him or her. Where cleansing prayer is not real, people may change how they dress how they dance, dress and speak but their inner core remains far away from God's heart and His Kingdom. All that happens in such cases is that the people become more and more self-focused, seeking new spiritual thrills and spectacular stories about the spiritual dimensions but having no real effect on the community. When we engage in cleansing prayer, we open up ourselves to the tide of the cleansing flood of God's Son who then unleashes in us the creative force of the Father for the changing of our world.

To show how deep cleansing prayer works in us, notice that in Psalm 51 David approaches the Lord Elohim not based on his own merit but based on the inner structure of the nature of God. God's multifaceted mercy is reached for "have mercy on me O God" says David, "according to thy loving-kindness unto the **multitude of your tender mercies. . . .**" Mercy is like a river's waterfall which in its variegated crashes washes upon the contrite. The first thing that cleansing prayer is conscious of is the inundating flow of the mercies of God. The heart of Heaven and the compassion that flows from it are the only reason for the opportunity to approach God. The second thing that cleansing prayer must be conscious of is the deep and intensive nature of filth that fills the one who approaches the Holy throne of the Lord. David uses several phrases to describe what must be done to the stain carried by the person who comes to cleansing prayer: 1) Blot out 2) Wash thoroughly, 3) Cleanse. 4) Purge. To grasp the issue here take a look at the words which David uses to describe the act, habit, behavior. He calls: 1) Transgression. 2) Iniquity. 3) Sin. 4) Evil. (It is four-dimensional. It has affronted every quarter of the Divine name.) It did not just affect Him, it affected every aspect of the Kingdom; yes, even to the sixth dimension. It affects the height, the depth, East, West, North and South. How is it to be dealt with? I must put "I" at the center as the perpetrator of the act. It is "I" who transgressed.

The cause, the originator is I. The ego cannot be absolved of its place in the activities that stains and separates me from the ideal image and likeness in and for whom I was created. Secondly, the act was generated by me, not as a surrogate for someone else but as my offspring and cannot be casually banished from my presence. Because it is mine, I cannot remove my gaze and focus from it without lying to myself and trying to lie to God. (I John 1:8-10) The cleansing prayer demands that "I" be placed as the center of the act and that "Me" as a possessive personality know that whatever sins "I" have committed belong to me. It is this that moves one in the cleansing prayer to justify God and not the self. David put it this way: "that thou mayest be justified when thou speakest and be clear when thou judgest." (v.4) The depth that calls forth cleansing prayer is the fact that while this is something I do and possess and while I am the originator of this act in the now, I am not the origin of its species. I believe this is what Paul meant when he said "… Now it is no more I that do it but sin dwelleth in me." (Rom. 7:20b) Its existence and power goes beyond my formation as "I." Its flow is in my being as the result of a spiritual-genetic inflow, which has been part of my race. I must then resort to someone greater than me, more ancient and more adept than myself to deal with this act. Knowing this David resorts to God and asks God to do seven things: 1. Hide his face from the act, 2. Create in me a clean heart, 3. Renew the right spirit within me, 4. Restore unto me the joy of the salvation, 5. Uphold me by God's right Spirit, 6. Deliverance from the guilt of misleading others to lose their soul is affected, 7. Open my lips and I shall praise thee.

The target of cleansing prayer is to let God into the innermost sanctum of the person, that is truth in the inward parts, and to know wisdom in the hidden parts. What happens to the praying person when the cleansing prayer has done its work and God has been released to do His work in the person? 1. Purity—I shall be whiter than snow 2. Knowledge of Divine wisdom is gained. 3. Knowledge of Divine joy. 4. Spiritual alignment—broken bones shall rejoice. 5. Continuous consciousness of God's presence is developed. 6. Instructive—I shall teach sinners transgressors thy way. 7. Doxological lifestyle—my tongue shall sing aloud of thine righteousness.

A cleansing prayer touches the core of our being and causes us to face our personal, communal and racial sins. This type of prayer brings us face to face with what God wants from us. God is not looking for material sacrifice but rather is looking for a living sacrifice which was given in His Son Jesus Christ. But when we sin as Christians we must go deep into our innermost being and allow God to deal not just with what we have done but also with who we are.

SUPPLICATIVE PRAYER:

Supplication can mean either to ask simply for something or to pray or to entreat someone's favor or even to call for something. In some rare instances it can mean to demand for something. But I am using it here in terms of a reverent asking for or calling for someone's help in time of need. (Luke11:9-13, James 5:17-18, 1 Kings 8:37-40, 54-55) The prayer of supplication involves a clear focus on the area of need in which we desire God to make an impact in our life. If we take up the prayer of supplication, we acknowledge our limitation as it relates in resolving the issue or need which have in the immediate or anticipate will confronts us. To supplicate means to petition or entreat someone, in this case God, for something. Supplicative prayer must be under girded by deep passion and fiery zeal for relationship otherwise it veers into idolatry. It is not unusual for supplication to be fueled by deep spiritual burden. In supplication we come to God as Father and King who has the fullness of all the resources that are more than enough to meet our need. God is rich enough, strong enough, powerful enough. Prayer of supplication flows from that point of need. All Children of God are aware of this kind of prayer. Our hunger to seek God's face often leads to this prayer. Jesus said, "ask and it shall be given to you…" This asking for something adds value to our life here on earth comes under the prayer of supplication. It is not the same as seeking or knocking, for Jesus Himself makes distinction among them. Petition means to ask for something. Because we are wholly dependent upon God for life, He loves to have us ask for things. Perhaps this is the most used and misused prayer of all time. We all want material prosperity and popularity—but whenever we ask for material things we should remember to add, "Your will be done." Although God cares about anything that concerns us and He wants us to ask Him for what we need, yet it pleases Him most when we ask for the Holy Spirit and the characteristics of Jesus.

This asking dimension of prayer is underscored in the teachings of Jesus in Matthew 7:7. He said, "Ask and it shall be given to you." This asking dimension of prayer is also seen Ps. 2:8 where just for the asking God is willing to turn the nations over to His asking children: "Ask of me, and I shall give thee the nations for your inheritance, and the uttermost parts of the earth for thy possession." In another place, Isa. 7:11-12, God says to one of the kings of Judah whose heart was filled with fear through his prophet, "Ask thee a sign of the LORD thy God; ask it either in the depth, or in the height above." The king Ahaz said, "I will not ask, neither will I tempt the LORD." But asking the Lord for anything is not a temptation, rather the purpose and use of the gift being request carries within it blessing or curse for the supplicant. To show how powerful this prayer of supplication can be in the believer's life, hear what Isaiah said in 45:11: "Thus saith the LORD, the Holy One of Israel, and his Maker, Ask me of things to come concerning my sons, and concerning the work of my hands command ye me." In Zech. 10:1 the supplication is directed to the weather and the atmosphere: "Ask ye of the LORD rain in the time of the latter rain; so the LORD shall make bright clouds, and give them showers of rain, to everyone grass in the field." The supplicant receives whether they ask alone or in agreement with others of like mind or like needs. Matt. 18:19: "Again I say unto you, That if two of you shall agree on earth as touching anything that they shall ask, it shall be done for them of my Father which is in Heaven." In the New Testament it is interesting to note that most places where Jesus tells us to ask there is in the vicinity of that context the idea of God as Father. This is a type of prayer that affirms our progeny and our place as children of God. There is nothing out of limits in the prayer of supplication. We read in Matt. 21:22, "And **all things**, whatsoever ye shall ask in prayer, believing, ye shall receive." But this cannot be taken in isolation of other texts. We also read in John 14:13-14, "And **whatsoever** ye shall ask in my name, that will I do, that the Father may be glorified in the Son. If ye shall ask any thing in my name, I will do it."

In most of the contexts where Jesus tells us to ask there are foundational assumptions. First, that God is our Father. Relationship with God is assumed. At one point Jesus says, *"Your Heavenly Father* knows what you need before you ask him." It is this relationship that puts us in the right to pray. Prayer of relational affirmation should under gird prayers of supplication. Second, out of this relationship grows the other foundational assumption or condition, "believe." Children believe that their parents can afford what they ask until they are told otherwise. That relationship births a confidence that can move the hardest of heart. This trust is indispensable to asking the Father for anything. Thirdly, there must be an abiding, an unwavering, and a continuous dwelling in the presence of the Master as opposed to the constant materialization of petitions. In John 15:7-8, Jesus says:

> "If ye abide in me, and my words abide in you, ye shall ask what ye will, and it shall be done unto you. Herein is my Father glorified, that ye bear much fruit; so shall ye be my disciples."

The asking must be done in the name of the one who has these three conditions summarized in Him. Jesus is the Son showing a relationship with the Father that is inseparable; secondly he has unshakable trust in His Father and only does what he sees the Father do; thirdly He always abides in the Father and the Father is always abiding in Him. In fact this abiding is so strong that He says, "I and the Father are one" and at another place he says "he that has seen me has seen the Father." Thus, use His Name to ask is a confirmation of our relationship, trust and rootedness in the Father.

> John 16:23-26: And in that day ye shall ask me nothing. Verily, verily, I say unto you, **Whatsoever** ye shall ask the Father in my name, he will give it you. Hitherto have ye asked nothing in my name: ask, and ye shall receive, that your joy may be full. These things have I spoken unto you in proverbs: but the time cometh, when I shall no more speak unto you in proverbs, but I shall shew you plainly of the Father. At that day ye shall ask in my name: and I say not unto you, that I will pray the Father for you:

There is another condition for asking that is revealed in life of our Lord and articulated for us in James. The purpose of our asking must be in tune with the glory and praise of the Father. We must not ask merely out of lust or for the purpose of hurting others. These are the only hindrances to obtaining our desire from the Father. Our asking must not be to war and strife. All these things are contrary to the nature of our Father and the one in whose name we pray. These are internal conditions of the heart that may hinder us from receiving what we ask. There is a strange connection between asking out of strife and internal restlessness, which is really unbelief. Faith is peaceable and restful because it is confident in its relationship with the one from whom it is asking. James also tells us another reason for our not receiving. **We simply do not ask. We just wish. We complain** therefore we do not have. **We must ask.** James says, "ye have not, because ye ask not."

There is yet another point that our asking must address, "for what purpose are we asking?" If the purpose for the asking is consistent with the nature and intention of God then we cannot be said to be asking amiss. Note the language of James "that you may consume it upon your lust...." This is an issue of intention and motivation.

4. Prayer of Thanksgiving

1 Thess. 5:18:

In everything give thanks: for this is the Will of God in Christ Jesus concerning you.
(Paul of Tarsus)

Gratitude unlocks the fullness of life. It turns what we have into enough, and more. It turns denial into acceptance, chaos to order, confusion to clarity. It can turn a meal into a feast, a house into a home, a stranger into a friend. Gratitude makes sense of our past, brings peace for today, and creates a vision for tomorrow." **Melody Beattie ~**

"The transmitter of Divine gifts to man is the heart, continually moved to gratitude, and the transmitter of temptations to the soul is discontented thought for ever moving in the heart. Again Lips forever giving thanks receive God's blessings, and a heart filled with gratitude unexpectedly receives grace" **(The Philakolia: Direction to the Hesychasts)**

The way we use the phrase "be thankful" suggests that gratitude is not merely an act but "who one is." So when we read over thirty-five times in the Authorized Version "give thanks" there is an implicit assumption that this verbal words of thanks form who we are and frame our attitudinal output in the world. If we look at the Hebrew and combine all the words that convey the idea of gratitude to God and even to human beings, we notice that it is used more than a thousand times. This tells us that if we would pray effectively we must cultivate a kind of **ontology of gratitude** which creates a **cosmology of praise**. Gratitude is in itself a spiritual practice that can transform our world. It is not a state of mind but of being. It is intrinsically a grammar of being and spirituality that communicates authenticity. For the believer, it is the ecological milieu within which their spiritual life has its ebb and flow. The way each one of us goes about showing gratitude may differ, but for the believer who has an effective prayer life this mode of being in the world is indispensable. The believer's relationship with God and the created world, which he/she believes is the gift of a gracious God to humankind, calls forth this flow of gratitude in believer. The practice of gratitude in prayer can increase our ability to deal with the circumstances that befall us.

Prayer of gratitude is a way of looking beyond the causality of life and instead of the ho-hum attitude to return to joy by being surprised by the wonder in the so-called mundane. Prayer of gratitude puts us in a place where, instead of feeling cheated by God and by life and looking incessantly for things to get better, we see ourselves as been intrinsically better than things, no matter what they are. Comparing, competing, and cross-referencing our achievement and inadequacies burdens us with care and can have devastating consequences for our spiritual lives. They grow out of ingratitude. When this happens we are led to live in perpetual dissatisfaction. Dissatisfaction creates artificiality and exaggerates our lack thereby causing us to set up idols other than God who we believe can meet our ever-gnawing need. But they never do meet them. The problem with absence of gratitude is that the things we want are never really for the glory of God or the benefit of others but for assuaging our greed—which remains ever present eating up soul's energy, until we develop this life of grateful song. Gratitude is a devotional because it grows out of our love and hunger to see the Will of God done. And when we are grateful and committed to the Will of God, our hearts receive good medication—that helps us realize our commitment though the process may be painful. Paul's injunction "in everything give thanks" challenges us to take a posture of expressive gratitude for everything and everyone based on how we see God rather than on how we see the situation or what may appear to be the immediate failure of persons we meet. There is an adage that describes people in terms of seeing half full or half empty glasses. I encourage you to use gratitude as your inner eye to look at the inherent goodness of life in all its ebb and flow. For gratitude is an affirmation of the goodness of God and the prodigious outpouring of mercy upon us.

Prayer of gratitude turns our eyes away from gaps or lack to providence and plenitude. Gratitude is not about how we see things, rather it is about how we know God. The problem with many prayers offered even among believers is that rather than exude ontological gratitude they tend to focus on utilitarian deficiency. They tend to focus on how difficult life has been. So many prayers are spent reminding God of how we can barely make it, how little good can be found in life itself that it is any wonder that God does not roar in thunder from the heavens. This is not a denial of the difficulty we often go through as we pass this way but rather a call to set ourselves above circumstance and to embrace the joy of the Lord as a way of healing our innermost disappointments. Prayer of gratitude is about God-focus, not about the often-tedious process by which we take hold of our daily purpose or destiny. Gratitude says, "I will focus on the goodness and plenitude of God."

When our lives are charged with gratitude, we will give thanks for anything or anyone who has benefited you and even for our enemies. Prayers of gratitude spring from a deep sea within the innermost sanctum and bubbles up to mouth of the righteous effortlessly. "Praise is comely for the righteous." (Ps. 33:1) For those of us who love God and whose life overflows with His love gratitude is like a free flowing tap pouring forth pure satisfying water both to the individual and to those who come into contact with them. Establish a habit of gratitude; sign it upon your heart and you will be made whole in more ways than one. A heart flowing with prayers of gratitude will chase away anger, pride, resentment, and selfishness. Prayers of gratitude open our heart to the universe. Practice the prayer of gratitude by making giving thanks and praise and blessing a major part of your everyday life and see how many miracle the universe releases to you. There is a Hebrew tradition that calls us to express gratitude at least a hundred (100) times a day thus, saturating the day and total environment with gratitude.

The word often translated in the KJV as "thanks" is the Hebrew *odoh* (*howduw*) for example in Psalm 136, "O Give thanks to the LORD for... Good, for His mercy endureth forever." Ps. 136:1 (***Howduw la-Yahweh kiy- Towb Kiy l^eowlaam chacdow.***) This word is more connected to the raising of the hand in acknowledgment of God not just as the source of good but as good itself. But nonetheless it carries with it the idea of gratitude as duty embeds in grace. The words *adot* (***toda***) thanks, *hkarb* (***bracha***) "blessing," and *lalah* (***halal***) to shine or to shine a steady light upon someone or something is usually translated "praise." It can also mean to raise high. These are all words of gratitude and power. These four words convey a sense of the universal obligation of gratitude which humankind especially believers owe God for His beneficence. Even a causal look at one's life demands gratitude for all the benefits of Divine Providence. There are general and personal gifts of Divine inflow that we in all our wildest dreams could not conjure up, so we bow in the prayer of gratitude. The gifts which God gives each day are indescribable so we join Paul and say, "Thanks be to God for His indescribable gift!" (2 Cor. 9:15)

Learning ***to be thankful*** is one of the best ways to combat a sense of victimization and self-pity, despair, hopelessness and perpetual fatigue. Thanksgiving should be a part of every conversation not just prayer. One of the major sins of 'the perverted generation' is that of ingratitude. According to Romans chapter 1, lack of gratitude is the seed of most evil acts that go against the will and purpose of God. The members of the perverted generation of Romans chapter 1 are not grateful to God for being God; they want Him to be something else so they make a substitute. They idolize. The women are not grateful for being women; they seek to act as men. The men are not thankful for the creation of women; they must substitute themselves and even animals for women. The men are not grateful for being men. Children are not grateful for the parents they have. Their parents can never do enough for them; they are not grateful for the little their parents are able to afford for them. Parents are not grateful for their children; they compare, complain castigate and complicate. And this lack of gratitude ends in the removal of the Spirit of God from their heart and they become darkness instead of light.

An understanding of gratitude is of great significance to the flow of God's power in our lives. Gratitude is one of the key ways to avoid much of the errors against which the Scripture cautions. Prayer of gratitude keeps us in the place of truth and checks the sinful impulse to believe that we are the source of our successes. The prayer of gratitude opens our eyes to see, so that we do not arrogantly presume that our developments and progress are based on our own resources. Prayer of gratitude can be an antidote to the type of thinking which marginalizes God and misjudge others. Our objective in the spiritual life should be to integrate gratitude into every aspect of our prayer life so that it is the oxygen that causes prayer to moves. When it becomes the environment in which prayer is exercised, we would receive more extraordinary answers to prayer. Often our immediate situations and the pain they cause move us to justify our accusations, complaints and even curse our lot in life. Gratitude is the cure.

This is why every prayer must be girded and saturated with praise adoration and worship of God. We come to God in praise and glory requesting that our prayers be answered, and then return glorifying and praising God for all. When our prayers have been answered, it is God incarnating Himself in the Name of His Son into our lives again. In praise, adoration and worship we are not being sentimental about our feelings for God, we focus on God's nature and this focus leads us into reverential awe out of which flows worship. We worship in Spirit and in truth as gratitude helps us to focus on God who is Spirit and Truth. A grateful heart knows there is a God, who based on the goodness of His nature answers prayers. Prayers of gratitude, as I have noted, embody praise and thanksgiving and are exemplified in Psalm 100, Acts 16:16-34, Psalm 149:4-9, and 1 Thessalonians 5:15-19. We find that as gratitude saturates an atmosphere, the glory of the Lord flows freely into the atmosphere as we see in the dedication of Solomon's temple in 2 Chron. 5:11-14:

11 And it came to pass, when the priests were come out of the holy place: (for all the priests that were present were sanctified, and did not then wait by course:12 Also the Levites which were the singers, all of them of Asaph, of Heman, of Jeduthun, with their sons and their brethren, being arrayed in white linen, having cymbals and psalteries and harps, stood at the east end of the altar, and with them an hundred and twenty priests sounding with trumpets:)13 It came even to pass, as the trumpeters and singers were as one, to make one sound to be heard in praising and thanking the LORD; and when they lifted up their voice with the trumpets and cymbals and instruments of musick, and praised the LORD, saying, For he is good; for his mercy endureth for ever: that then the house was filled with a cloud, even **the house of the LORD;14 So that the priests could not stand to minister by reason of the cloud: for the glory of the LORD had filled the house of God.**

Gratitude will bring down the cloud of glory even easier than fasting. A prayer of gratitude is a revelation of delight and reaches the throne quicker than most prayers, for it is written, Ps. 37:4: *"Delight thyself also in the LORD; and he shall give thee the desires of thine heart."* To delight is to move delicately and with finesses, to express joy with a kingly flare yet with softness and fluidity. At least that is my understanding of the Hebrew word *awnawg*. It is to be in constant motion as one who is dancing with a beloved partner and enjoy the movement. As we see here it is the harmonization of the atmosphere with God's nature and purpose. When that is done, it makes way for the release the glory of the Lord. One of the keys to this is gratitude.

The effect of the prayer of gratitude on negative conditions is well attested in Scripture. The best know, example of the power of prayer of gratitude in the midst of a negative situation making a big difference is the prayer of Jehoshaphat in 2 Chron. 20:21-23:

21 And when he had consulted with the people, he appointed singers unto the LORD, and that should praise the beauty of holiness, as they went out before the army, and to say, Praise the LORD; for his mercy endureth forever. 22 And when they began to sing and to praise, the LORD set ambushments against the children of Ammon, Moab, and mount Seir, which were come against Judah; and they were smitten. 23 For the children of Ammon and Moab stood up against the inhabitants of mount Seir, utterly to slay and destroy them: and when they had made an end of the inhabitants of Seir, every one helped to destroy another.

With the watering of gratitude prayer, we dispose ourselves to quickly answered prayers. Sometimes it is not that our prayers are flawed in and of themselves that keep them from being answered but the fact that they are bathed in the waters of ingratitude and discontent. What hinders us from praising God will hinder us from effective prayer if we let it. It can also hinder us from loving others. A heart of gratitude brings us into the inner chamber of the King—God. When we give thanks with all the facets of what that means even in seemingly negative situations, we are affirming our faith in God. This brings joy to God because it lets Heaven know that we are not confused about what is ultimate and who is truly in charge. Gratitude is one of the most powerful weapons available to would be intercessors. Gratitude removes one of Satan's greatest weapons against our lives out of his hands. Here is where we silence his roar and his movements. **Be thankful. Count your blessings. Delight yourself in the LORD.**

PRAYER OF INTERCESSION:

The word *Llpty* (**ythpalal** "to entreat") is what is translated to intercede in some versions of the Bible. This is really to entreat the favor of great person on behalf of one who has wronged them or one who needs their help. To intercede is to go or come between two parties, to plead before one of them on behalf of the other. In the New Testament it is the translation of the word *entygchanein*; the Latin uses the word *interpellare* in Hebrews 7:25. Some theologians suggest that we separate "Mediation," which means a standing in the midst between two contending parties for the purpose of bringing them together to represent. This is what Christ did for us. But they do not tell us what to call what someone who travails in prayer for another to God. I think that the word "intercede" may rightly be use for that kind of activity. When we take it upon ourselves to pray earnestly for other people, we enter into the realm of intercession. To enter into intercession, we must have a heart that really loves the Lord and cares about the things God cares about. In a sense it is to pray for someone that they may receive a special dispensation of grace from God. The great danger surrounding any people who have no intercessors is aptly stated by Ezekiel. Ezek. 22:30–23:1:

> And I sought for a man among them that **should make up the hedge**, and **stand in the gap before me for the land,** that I should not destroy it: but I found none. Therefore have I poured out mine indignation upon them; I have consumed them with the fire of my wrath: their own way have I recompensed upon their heads, saith the Lord GOD.

One who does not intercede is a breaker of the hedge and in fact is in danger of letting the serpent out. Often one who is not interceding is complaining, gossiping, passing judgment and condemning. Let not that one think that the serpent will spare him for he that breaks the hedge or even leaves it in disrepair will feel the bite of the serpent. Where intercession is not constant there is indignation, fire, wrath and over-powering Divine vengeance. So God actively seeks someone who can in fact make up the hedge by standing in the gap. Prayer of intercessions means that the believer is taken upon himself to stand between two people who have a quarrel and plead for peace. The following Scriptures bear this point out. Moses the man of God says:

Deuteronomy 9:20: And the LORD was angry enough with Aaron to destroy him, but at that time I *prayed for* Aaron too.

Righteous Hezekiah interceded for the people.

2 Chronicles 30:18: Although most of the many people who came from Ephraim, Manasseh, Issachar and Zebulon had not purified themselves, yet they ate the Passover, contrary to what was written. **But Hezekiah *prayed for them***, saying, "May the LORD, who is good, pardon everyone.

Job's healing and goods were restored when he interceded for his self-righteous friends

Job 42:10: After **Job had prayed for his friends**, the LORD made him prosperous again and gave him twice as much as he had before.

Jesus Christ our Lord interceded for Peter even though He knew that Peter would deny him.

Luke 22:32: But **I have prayed for you, Simon,** that your faith may not fail. And when you have turned back, strengthen your brothers."

Acts 8:15 When they arrived, **they prayed for them that they might receive the Holy Spirit.**

Jesus' major work for us in Heaven before the throne of the Father is entreating of God's favor on our behalf. Hebrews 7:25: "Therefore he is able to save completely those who come to God through him, because he always lives to intercede for them." When we intercede for others' we come closest to God's heart. We are more like Jesus. Jesus, in Heaven, is our High Priest and His ministry is to intercede with the Father for His disciples (us) and for all mankind. When we join Him in praying for others, we are most like Him. The natural outflow of being like Christ is to pray for others, especially as relates to the issue of Salvation and deliverance from the evil one. Jesus tells us as disciples to pray for others who are being called to the vineyard. In Matt. 9:37-38, we read, "Then He said to His disciples, 'The harvest is plentiful but the workers are few. Ask the Lord of the harvest therefore, to send out workers into His field.'" In praying for workers in the vineyard of the Master, we are interceding for the salvation of the world, by proxy if you may. For you see the key to the harvest of souls is that God sends effective harvesters into the field of human souls where love has given birth to true intercession. It is true that we are to pray for the unsaved but the direct intercession is for believers and for workers that God is calling from the body of His Son. The New Testament does explicitly teach intercession for the believer and the unbeliever in the command to pray for all men. We may go from the fact that Jesus died for the world, to the idea that He was given for the world to intercede for them. But the general orientation of the New Testament points the believer to intercede for one another. Our effective witness to the non-believer is powered by our willingness to intercede for them.

The first occurrence of intercession is the picture painted of our Father Abraham as he stood face to face with the Lord and pleaded for mercy over Sodom and Gomorrah. The word also occurs where others are pleading on behalf of Abraham as he seeks land to bury his late wife in Genesis 23:8. Abraham said to the elders of the city, "If you are willing to let me bury my dead, then listen to me and ***intercede with Ephron son of Zohar on my behalf.***" (NIV) It is also used in 1 Samuel 2:25 where Eli asks, "if a man sins against the LORD, who will intercede for him?" But Eli did not intercede for his sons, so they died from the judgment of the Lord. The man of God, Samuel exemplifies intercession. 1 Samuel 7:5: Then Samuel said, "Assemble all Israel at Mizpah and ***I will intercede with the LORD for you.***" In 1 Kings 13:6, we see how a stubborn king got himself in trouble with God and through intercession was restored to wholeness.

71

Then the king said to the man of God, "Intercede with the LORD your God and pray for me that my hand may be restored." So the man of God interceded with the LORD, and the king's hand was restored and became as it was before.

Another great example which in my mind is the greatest in the Old Testament is the intercession of Moses for the people of Israel when God wanted to wipe them our but Moses put his own welfare on the line to shield the people from the wrath of God. We read in Numbers 21:7: "The people came to Moses and said, "We sinned when we spoke against the LORD and against you. Pray that the LORD will take the snakes away from us." So Moses prayed for the people." Several things we must understand about intercession. First, it is directed to the Lord God, never to the devil or demons or human beings. We are not told to intercede for a demon oppressed, depressed, possessed person rather we are told to cast the spirit out. Secondly, a good intercessor may place himself/herself in the line of God's fire and must be willing to lay themselves down for the people for whom they intercede. There is always a sacrifice that the intercessor must make. It may mean that they need to spend hours in prayer and fasting for the person who is in need. We may intercede for someone to be saved from the legitimate consequence of their action. Thirdly, we may intercede for healing of sickness. Fourthly, we may intercede for direction in life's journey. Fifthly, we intercede for salvation of our unbelieving friends, family and fellow citizens. Sixthly, we can intercede for the weather to change in favor of the work of God. Seventh, we can intercede for the government of the land. We can intercede for people in any geographic location. Eight, we may also intercede for believers who are in trouble because of the Gospel. This is exemplified in Acts 12:5: "So Peter was kept in prison, but the Church was earnestly praying to God for him." This prayer of intercession was answered when God sent an Angel to set him free.

Intersession is not just for the super spiritual as has sometimes been conveyed. Any believer can get involved in the prayer of intercession. There is command in the book of James directed to the general body of Christ. Specializing intercession is problematic because it seems to excuse many from interceding, for it creates a self-styled elite class of Christians who disdain and disregard their brethren. James 5:15-18:

> 16 Confess your trespasses to one another, and *pray for one another,* that you may be healed. The effective, fervent prayer of a righteous man avails much. 17 Elijah was a man with a nature like ours, and he prayed earnestly that it would not rain; and it did not rain on the land for three years and six months. 18 And he prayed again, and the Heaven gave rain, and the earth produced its fruit.

The prayer of intercession which we see here is directed for the benefit of the body of Christ. Elijah is only used here as illustration of the power of prayer not an example of intercession. We must not confuse judgment prayer with intercession. It has become common for people to pray down judgment on people and call it intercession. Intercession is directed to healing and deliverance. Prayer of judgment runs a different stream from intercession and must be distinguished if the believer is not to veer off into witchcraft and self-seeking vengeance which may in fact poison his/her spiritual stream. It is not intercession when judgment is called but intercession when healing is prayed for and reconciliation is achieved.

CHAPTER FIVE
METHODS OF PRAYER

"Praying always with all prayer and supplications in the spirit" Ephesians 6:18

VOCAL METHODS:

In the vocal method, prayer is said out loud, alone or in groups. Vocal prayers are best known because man is a talking animal. We make statements such as, "say your prayers," speak a word to the Lord," cry to the Lord. Twenty-two times in the King James Version of the Bible the Psalmist uses the word, call, to refer to his prayer to the Lord. This shows how common the vocal type of prayer is. In fact this method of prayer is so common that many church people consider other types of prayer irrelevant or unchristian. In the simplest terms, prayer is talking to God—speaking to the Creator in conversational manner. But the problem is many of us speak to God but we do not wait to hear Him talk back to us. First, the power of vocal prayer is that: One, it articulates our hidden desires. Two, it makes our unconscious conscious so that we are clear about what we are saying to God.

Third, it creates a certain level of confidence in that we hear our voice as it resounds in the environment giving us the feeling of not being alone and not merely talking to ourselves. Everyone from Adam to Moses, from Moses to David, from David to Jesus and all the way to the present day talks to God in some form or another. But the real issue who does God speak back to? True vocal prayer is manifested when it moves from it merely being our talking to a conversation between us and God. One of the ways to make vocal prayers effective is simply put our thoughts into question form to the Father as a child would, and in this way rather than telling God what to do you elicit a conversation with Him. Vocal prayers should be interspersed with moments of quiet waiting for response from the Father. **Let God talk too**.

CONTEMPLATIVE METHOD OF PRAYER

Contemplative prayer has been given a bad name among evangelicals and many of my evangelical and Pentecostal brethren who view it as merely an eastern religious invasion into Christianity. But this is a misunderstanding of the impact and meaning of spiritual methods. There are phrases that convey the idea of contemplation in the Scripture. The dictionary defines it as thoughtful, meditative, deep in thought or to be lost in thought, pensive, reflective or introspective. Contemplative Prayer is "being lost" in the beauty and wonder of God and His creation, acknowledging His greatness in all things. It begins in silence. "Silence is the mastery of the future life," said an ancient Christian Father of the Hesychast movement. In contemplation we lay aside all thoughts that do not have direct bearing on the work of salvation. It is in this silence and stillness that we come to know God in a unique way. "Be still and know that I AM God." (Psalm 46:10) We can only practice this method successfully if we remove all distractions from our inner man or even our external man. The second way then to be effective is to find solitude. It can be done with Scriptures or the lives recognized men and women of God or even by revelative reflection on the creative genius of God our Father. At issue is the place not of the mind but the intuitive imagination in prayer. As King David says in Psalm 119:148, "within my imagination I picture, your precepts." The Scripture supports the harnessing of the intuition and imagination as instruments of prayer. The Hebrew words translated "meditation" can also be translated "contemplate" in Joshua 1:8. The word translated "meditate" is the word **"hagah"** (*wagiyhaalah*) **hlhygiw>** (thou shall mediate); the idea here used can mean to imagine, mourn or mutter and study a matter, can also imply to contemplate in isolation. Another word used is the word **suwach** **x l wuusu** (in Gen. 24:63 speaks of communing or complain in a mournful way or musing, talking and simply just praying, but in this case it is nurturing of a thing in the mind until it comes to fruition or manifestation. This method of praying focuses on the creative imagination and can be harnessed to focus prayer's power on its target. By the use of the mind, we can reproduce the patterns of the upper realm in the mundane realm. Here the believer uses his spiritual capacity and gifting to reproduce in the material realm the things, which the eyes of the Spirit have seen.

The imagination of the believer when focused absolutely on God or any aspect of God's being can bring success and fulfillment because the mind joined to Christ synthesizes the future and the present. When we use the mind method of prayer, we structure our spiritual experience for greater reception of Divine inflow. Focusing the mind in prayer is not necessarily the use of the natural mind, for the natural mind is enmity with God but the spiritual mind is what is called for here. If the natural mind is enmity with God, then there must be a release of the self from the carnality of the natural mind. This intentional release of the natural mind and moving into the spiritual mind or the mind of Christ facilitates our co-operation with the mind of God. In this method of prayer we are moved to clear the field of all mundane and worldly anxiety honing into and focusing on the beauty of the Lord or some aspect of His being that moves us at that moment. In contemplation we quiet our inner tumults and phase out all worldly sounds by centering our spiritual imagination on what is ultimate and lofty. In this we rest in God. This is our inner being enjoying God's Sabbath. Getting into this kind of prayer demands an antecedent positive posture that causes the soul of the praying person to come to grips with the fact that all it knows about God is nothing compared to that which can be known of Him. In that place the praying person then enters into willing release or a self-emptying of what is known in order to plunge headlong into the mystery called God. The power and effect of the mind when turned over into the mystery of God causes us to transcend our present tendency to list, describe and analyze our situation for God and move into a faithful resting because our mind is saturated by Him and not our needs. Actual intimacy with God culminates in points of knowledge, love, ecstasy or other empathic experience of the heart of God. Praying thus our soul gazes in loving awe on the glory of God.

MYSTICAL METHOD OF PRAYER:

"He that speaketh in tongues speaks mysteries unto God." The word "mystery" is used so many times in the Scripture by Paul that is seems to strange to me that there are some Christians movement who avoid it. But prayer is meant to penetrate the mystery of the universe. It is communing with Divine mystery in our inner man calling it to reveals itself. According to Heiler, the two highest types of prayer are the mystical and the prophetic. Mysticism in its Christian context represents not a synthesis of the sound, light and feelings but the silencing of all in the presence of the indescribable and incomprehensible nature of God. It silences human thought and language. In this speaking mystery the depth of our intellect, our will our hearts and soul communicate beyond the normal language and words which we know for the languages which we know are much too weak to convey the height and depth to which we have be brought. That is why only those who speak in tongues really approach this. But even they can come to the place where only groaning will do. It is also a universal religious phenomenon in which one allows his spirit to a plunge into the unknown by faith in order to access the celestial sphere. Here the aim is union with God, who is generally portrayed in supra-personal terms, unknowable by reason, beyond description, overpowering light or depth to which man can only answer with silence. In mystical prayer the idea of silence not just of sound but of the thought is very important. Sometimes, this prayer begins by picturing God in terms of the substances that are used to describe Him in Scripture but pushes the mind or the imagination to the point where it loses it denotative and descriptive ability and one is left only with silence. Ideas about God are not transformed into pictures on which the human soul or spirit soars beyond the terrestrial, but becomes silenced as one plunges into God.

Mystics see God that transcends personality, one that is best described as the Absolute, the infinite abyss, or the infinite ground and depth of all being. Mystics see prayer as the elevation of the soul and spirit to God. Though the mystic does not deny the intervention of God in history as we find in the Bible, he sees revelation as effective mainly in terms of an interior illumination rather than literal letter of

Scripture. He understands what Paul meant when he said, "the letter killeth, but the spirit gives life." To him/her, the Master's word, "the word that I speak to you, they spirit and they life" rings true. Mystics often speak of a ladder of prayer or stages of prayer, and petition is always considered the lowest stage. The highest goal in prayer is to culminate in Divine ecstasy. They may use singing, chanting, moaning and groaning, joy and music, hymns alone or in groups but these are seen mainly as means to reach that silence in which one plunges into the depth that cannot be described. They crave a Silence in which the material universe is "dead" and closed out; the world's distraction and noise silenced; the door of the heart opened to the Lord and the will disappears into the Will of the Godhead. The mystic may use Working Prayer which is dedicating the day's work joyfully and honestly to the Lord. She may also turn daily vernacular into prayer is bringing God's name back into everyday language—"Thank God" or "Thanks be to God"— during conversation. The mystic prays from the heavenly place. He is a supernatural traveler who can locate himself or herself spiritually in any place and pray across dimensions.

MEDITATIVE METHOD OF PRAYER

By meditation we are referring to the active use of the mind, which may include the feelings. Meditation is consciousness awareness of God, self and the world by taking into oneself the Word acts, or a precept of God, and allowing it to saturate one's being. Meditation can be done with anything, yet Christian meditation requires as its testing instrument the Word of God. There are proven methods of meditation in the Bible and in the experiences of Christian saints which have shown results to which the believer may resort depending on their maturity. Meditation is the road many Christians travel to becoming truly spiritual in their walk. Unlike some of the other kinds of prayer, meditation is not just an intuitive art veiled in mystery. Usually it applied to a passage of Scripture, or our own situation in life, or to any active way in which we try to understand God or ourselves. It is *thought* focused on God or God's world. Meditation has great richness and is easier to do than contemplation because the tools are ready for it, such as language and other symbolic expression. We may think about the meaning of joy or a wonder and sign performed by God. It is more akin to the thought grasping an idea. Moving the mind from hostility to genuine love and reverence takes work and co-operation with the Holy Spirit. This conformity of our mind with the mind of the Holy Spirit demands that we develop a way of concentrating deeply and considering the Word of God. The meditative capacity of the mind is affirmed by several New Testament passages: Rom. 8:6; Rom. 12:1; I Cor. 2:16. The Greek word used is usually the word *meletao* which means to revolve an idea in the mind and use the imagination. Most of the time in Scripture when the word occurs, it is in the context of the word of meditating on the Word of God. In Psalm 1:2 this is clear as it says, "But his delight is in the law of the LORD; and in his law doth he *meditate* day and night." Thus, in meditation we enter the go out to the field or the garden of the Word of God or nature creating a kind of evening to the outside world so that we can lift up our mind's eye and behold the beauty of the Lord out of the Word. In Joshua 1:8, we read:

> "This book of the law shall **not depart out of thy mouth**; but thou shalt **meditate therein day and night**, that thou mayest observe to do according to all that is written therein: for then thou shalt make thy way prosperous, and then thou shalt have good success."

Three key points about meditation are mentioned in this passage. First the mouth is important for meditation. Phrases taken from the Word of God, or sentences from the Scriptures, and repeated is a vital part of meditation. This is not vain repetition. For no repetition of the Word of God or the true name of God is ever vain. The second aspect is *thinking* on the words concepts and using the reason as way to grasp the concepts in the Word of God. Thirdly part of meditation is to active adherence to the ideas and concepts contained. Doing something for God can also be seen s meditation as way of getting into the meaning of what one is meditating upon. The idea espoused here is also supported by (Psalms 77:12) "I will meditate also of all thy work, and talk of thy doings."

The memory is also important in meditation. Hence the principle of remembrance David says in Psalms 63:6 "When I *remember* thee upon my bed, and *meditate* on thee in the night watches." We can meditate by deliberately recalling our experiences with God or other works of God. When Jesus said "remember me," it is call to mediation. When God says to Israel "remember the Sabbath to keep it holy," it calls us to mediate on the creative work of God and His power. The Sabbath is meant to be a day of meditation. It is a day of creative focus on the nature and work of God. Furthermore, in Psalm 119:15 David insists that meditation is a way of developing reverence for the ways of God. "I will meditate in thy precepts, and have respect unto thy ways." According to Psalm 119:23, it is one way to handle verbal attack by others. "Princes also did sit and speak against me: but thy servant did meditate in thy statutes." When we lift up our minds unto the celestial and express our love, our memory of the mighty acts of God are activated and recreated in our mind. Meditation on God and His might shames our base pride and deals with perversity within us. "I will meditate in God's precepts as answer to my sinful tendencies." Psalm 119:148: "Mine eyes prevent the night watches that I might meditate in thy word." Psalm 143:5: "I remember the days of old; I meditate on all thy works; I muse on the work of thy hands." Luke 21:14: Settle it therefore in your hearts, not to meditate before what ye shall answer. In 1 Timothy 4:15, Paul tells us to "Meditate upon these things; give thyself wholly to them; that thy profiting may appear to all."

Meditation on the person of Jesus Christ can produce in the believer a sense of the full joy which our Lord spoke of. It is a way of forming the image of the Master in our inner being. As we practice meditative prayer, we enter into God and God enters us and we are open to the source of tranquility available to us as human beings in our Father. By this kind of prayer Christ is formed in us and we are able to deal with some personal conflict and chaos that threatens to invade our lives. Deep meditation on the things of God and on the Word and work of God allows wholeness and Divine love, the beauty of God, to stream into our daily experiences. When we meditate on the things of God, we open up ourselves to the eternal nature of God which then takes form within us and flows into the world.

Meditation is a great tool for self-discovery, self-examination and honesty to God and the universe in which we live. As we meditate we can get to know ourselves and our purposes in life as the Holy Spirit lights our inner man and names our soul for the Kingdom. Meditation allows us to look deeper beyond the temporary and helps to rouse us up from our deep sleep bondage to the unconscious and prepares us for better visions of ourselves and the world. It is a great way to arouse the prophetic spirit and unleash dreams of great things within oneself.

Part of meditative prayer is also the principle of self-questioning. Ask yourself who you are in God; who you were yesterday? Who you are today in the now? Who will you be in light of what you know or think you know about God? Meditation is way to live life in wakefulness, moment by moment. Meditation increases awareness of yourself, world and the spiritual world in which you move that is actually going on behind your own eyes. Meditation has intrinsic value or else God would not have recommended it to Joshua nor would the psalmist have spoken so eloquently of the indescribable joy and comfort it brought to him.

ACTIONS OF GRACE AS METHOD OF PRAYER

This is a prayer not accompanied by word or deep contemplation but the simple thought of doing something for someone which carries the grace of God into their life. Offering an act to God as a prayer is one of the easiest prayers yet often neglected by us in our daily life. It is the intention and focus of the act that makes it a prayer. In giving alms or offering help, I offer it up to the Lord as prayer for the person to whom it is given. Doing a particular act in this way can help others experience the grace, power and glory of God.

ATMOSPHERES OF EFFECTIVE PRAYER

EFFECTIVE BODY PRAYER MUST BE PRAYED IN THE SPIRIT OF AGREEMENT.

T he principle of unity and agreement is seen even in the building of the tabernacle of worship in the wilderness. God says to Moses in Exodus 26:11, **"And thou shalt make fifty taches of brass, and put the taches into the loops, and couple the tent together, that it may be one."** Psalm 133 states unequivocally the benefits of the principle of unity for the flow of Divine blessings, Ps 133:1–134:1:

> *1 Behold, how good and how pleasant it is for brethren to dwell together in unity!* 2 It is like the precious ointment upon the head that ran down upon the beard even Aaron's beard: that went down to the skirts of his garments; 3 As the dew of Hermon, and as the dew that descended upon the mountains of Zion: *for there the LORD commanded the blessing, even life for evermore.*

The exclamation of David in this passage *(shebet 'achiym gam- yaachad),* "For brethren to dwell together as one," points to the unity of the people as a symbolic expression of God's nature. This God is also One, His Name is ONE. The word translated "dwell" *(shebeth)* is derived from the root word *yashab* which means to sit down in proper order as judges will sit on the bench with the intent toward justice.

They are not gathered as spiritual vigilantes nor are they gathered to destroy one another, but they have gathered in the Rest of the Lord as an expression of the inner covenant of the Lord. It is also a word which may also have reference to matrimonial harmony. The use of the form *shebeth (tbf))* in my view could be seen as a reference to the Sabbath where the brethren gathered and all the tribes came together in unity to worship and to praise the name of the Holy One. There is another word which occurs here which is actually a phrase, *gam- yachad*, "together as one." It is the idea of the unity which grows from the unified nature of Divinity. This unity is very important for creating an atmosphere of effective prayer. The LORD is one; therefore, we are one.

The Lord affirms this and clearly makes a big deal on this issue of unity for effectiveness in prayer. He says in Matt. 18:19 Jesus said, "Again I tell you that if two of you on earth *agree* (united as one) on anything you ask for, it will be done for you by my Father in Heaven. For, where two or three come together in my *name*, there, am I with them." God the Father and His Son Jesus Christ will join you in any prayer where there is agreement or unity that is prayed in the Name of Jesus. You say, "How do I create this unity?" You can do it simply by focusing on His Name. Jesus Himself said that He would be with you in that moment of that prayer. The Lord Jesus Christ is attracted to the environment of unity and agreement in prayer. Our agreement with Jesus needs to work out into our agreement with one another, especially when we pray. If there is agreement, He not only prays with us, but through us thus making our prayers more effective. If He joins us, then all creation under the authority of God joins us also. It means that our prayer has the capacity to by-pass every created obstacle for the Lord of Creation is in agreement with us. This plural "you" conveys the idea that God delights in agreement and unity among His people. The Lord Jesus Christ in His intercessory prayer for the church makes mention of this unity of the believers four times and bases these mentions on the agreement between Him and the Father. John 17:11:

And now I am no more in the world, but these are in the world, and I come to thee. Holy Father, keep through thine own name those whom thou hast given me, *that they may be one, as we are.* John 17:21 *That they all may be one;* as thou, Father, art in me, and I in thee, *that they also may be one in us:* that the world may believe that thou hast sent me. John 17:22 And the glory which thou gavest me I have given them; *that they may be one, even as we are one:*

We must be in agreement with one another. Agreement is the turning over of the will to the fulfillment of the things being prayed for. Because God gave us free will, he does not delight in violating it our agreement then affirms the purpose of God in creating us free will agents. Prayer of agreement is one the highest expression our Divine nature and expression of freedom in the Spirit. To see the power of agreement, read the following passages: Genesis 11:1-9, Matthew 18:19-20, Exodus 17: 8-13, Psalm 133:1-3, Acts 4:23, and Hebrews 10:24-25. The prayer of agreement is not a forced conformity of thought but a willing desire to see God's goodness manifested in the life of someone. It is so powerful because here we become less self-focused and seek the good of the other as God seeks our good. We throw our will into the pot so to say for the good of the other. Its power comes from the fact that it gives purpose. Biblically, the prayer of agreement is when two or more people come together and agree with one another and with the Word of God that something specific will be done. People that do not worship God or indeed worship Satan can also stand in agreement and see power released (Genesis 11:1-9).

God has given power and authority to the Church, and when we stand together in unity we can see more of God's power released (Matthew 28:16-20). Unity is standing together with one purpose, sharing a joint vision and trusting God's Word to be fulfilled. We need to appreciate the power of unity if we are to see God's power released through our prayers.

ATMOSPHERE OF FAITH BIRTHS EFFECTIVE PRAYER

Prayer demands an atmosphere of faith. There is such a thing as the prayer of faith as used in the book of James. This environment is one that invites God and goes over or rehears what God has stopped doing or is unwilling to do. Rather it rises above the circumstance and changes the atmosphere with radiating optimistic expectation and places godlike demand on God's power and ability. This belief in the desire of God to move on behalf of His children is so burned into the spirit and the atmosphere so that those who pray can taste and see what it is that they are asking to God for before they receive it. While Jesus often berated His disciples for lack of faith, it was not so much that they could not muster enough faith within themselves, rather the fact they were in an environment charged with faith by the presence of Jesus but were oblivious to it and choose to create an antithetical atmosphere. The verbal request, gratitude, and the songs and praise are all meant to create an atmosphere of faith, which makes it possible for our request to become manifested.

That faith which is ignited in the soul of the soul of the believer by the light of grace; art which through the evidence of the mind, fortifies the heart in sureness of hope removed from all self opinion, which shows itself not in inclining the ear of hearing but in contemplating with spiritual eyes the mysteries hidden in the soul, those graces, concealed from the eyes of the sons of the flesh, and revealed by the Spirit to those who feed at the feast of Christ . . . .(**Philakolia: Directions to the Hesychasts**)

In an atmosphere charged with faith it is easy for even the most spiritually weak to receive. This is why great outdoors evangelistic campaigns see more miracles than churches. The evangelistic campaign atmosphere is charged with faith—intense expectation and anticipation. In Mark 11:24, Jesus says, "When you pray, believe that you receive ... and you shall have ..." when you believe, you form an environment for the manifestation of the request or creates a space on earth in which Heaven can be manifested. Not to believe God is to create an environment in which God is not "comfortable" but absent. Because it is God who will give you your request, the atmosphere must be one in which God can come to stay.

One of the atmospheres conducive for the presence of God is that of faith. For it is written, "Without faith it is impossible to please God, for that cometh to God must believe." (Heb. 11:6) So a refusal to believe that God has given it to you makes your environment non-conducive for answered prayers. Faith is a spiritual thing seeking a place, so in praying we need to be in the Spirit. We have to have faith to have. **Hebrews 11:1: *"Now faith is the substance of things hope for, the evidence of things not seen."*** The place of prayer, our lives or our church must first be saturated with faith for God's gift to be substantiated or evidenced in those contexts. Faith is activated when we stand and speak in an atmosphere immersed in the Word of God. Faith comes by hearing and hearing by the Word of God. Our desires can be incarnated from the spiritual into the natural when we allow the Word to birth faith. Walking the environment and speaking the Word of God will change the vibration of the area so that we can decree what is needed within that context and it will come to pass. (Mark 11:12-14; Mark 11: 20-25; Luke 7: 1-10; James 5: 13-18; Matthew 9: 18-26)

Creating a faith environment happens when in our interior we develop an unshakable *confidence* in God's willingness and ability to answer prayer. We have a triangular unshakable relationship between us, Jesus the written Word and the written Word of God which becomes a square of faith as we take the over the environment where we are to pray. Because the prayer of faith is a call for the Word to be made flesh in our immediate circumstance, we must have a clear picture of the incarnate Christ. True prayer of faith is calling into effect John 1:14. It is calling for the physical tangible manifestation of the spiritual realities into the material realm. The faith environment is created through our confidence on God's Word. The woman with the issue of blood (Matthew 9) created an environment in herself so that in the midst of the crowd she could touch Jesus receiving her health. Her inner resolve and focus on Jesus released for her the environment of her healing even in the press of the crowd. You can create an environment of faith by making positive Word confessions into the atmosphere until it is saturated with faith.

AN ENVIRONMENT THAT BIRTHS EFFECTIVE PRAYER MUST BE ONE OF LOVE

In love is God found. Love is the whole law. Anything not done in love is not of God. With the Holy love one taps into the highest level of Divine energy and joins force with God to affect self and others. This world can only be changed and God's Will can only be done if you we are filled with the love of God. It is because the love of God in Christ Jesus has been shed abroad in our hearts that the Spirit is freed to energize our weakness. In this love, energy flows and God gives knowledge and insight into the supernatural that is then expressed for the deliverance of our brothers and sister. He searches our hearts, knows the mind of the Spirit, because the Spirit intercedes for the saints in accordance with God's Will. From this love, comes our real power. This holy love knows the heart and mind of Christ because it is who He is. By this love our spirit knows what is happening to other saints and moves toward them with compassion. So when we are praying in love, the power of our prayer is multiplied many times by the very nature of God. The thing about love is that like air it does not choose who can or cannot breathe it. Love carries the Christians' prayer into part of the world that needs God to intervene for them. The believer filled with the love of God and love for human beings affects life at a much deeper level. Love interrupts the negative flows and infuses the life of God into our situations.

If we are filled with the love of God, our prayers will be different and more effective. Right now those of us who believe that we are to pray must tap into love. So much intercession has been informed by hurt and anger that it is little wonder why our prayers are often hindered. But holy love does bring us to the fullness of life in the body of Christ. Love has great authority to empower our prayers in a manner that our hearts has not yet received. When prayer is bathed in the environment of holy love, we are enabled to do God's work effectively on earth. Part of creating an atmosphere of love is to be a covering for those who have transgressed to seek to minister the love of God instead of repeating the issues until the body is divided and the unity that is so necessary for prayer is sundered. According to Prov. 10:12: "Hatred stirreth up strifes: but love covereth all sins." Wherever there is strife, there is hatred at its roots no matter how it is painted, whether as prophecy, righteous indignation, speaking my mind, or standing up for what is right. Hatred is what stirs up strife and hinders prayers, especially those that are geared toward the healing and deliverance of people. An atmosphere of love is not one where we shout out our love for God but one in which genuine Divine love flows from us to others even our enemies. I am at loss in understanding how we can stand to pray prayers of hatred couched in the so-called warfare and still expect our prayers for our personal healing to be answered. The atmosphere in which we pray must be charged with love both for the God and for our neighbor.

Mark 12:30-31:

30 And thou shalt love the Lord thy God with all thy heart, and with all thy soul, and with thy entire mind, and with all thy strength: this is the first commandment. 31 And the second is like, namely this, Thou shalt love thy neighbour as thyself. There is none other commandment greater than these.

Jesus Christ speaking in John 13:34-35 says, "A new commandment I give unto you, That ye love one another; as I have loved you, that ye also **love one another.** 35 By this shall all men know that ye are my disciples, if ye have love one to another."

The measure of this love is not our feelings, ideologies, shame or our guilt but the love, which Jesus Christ Himself had and has for us— "as I have loved you." Why is it that whenever Jesus opened His mouth miracles happened? The love of the Father was manifested in and through Him. He is Love incarnate. Why are millions flocking to Him even now? It is a response to the story of His love. In fact Jesus says that as His disciples whatever we ask the Father in his name the Father will answer. Yet here He says that we are His disciples, *"if ye love one another."* We are not candidates really for answered prayers if we do not love one another. You want to look for reasons why so many prayers we pray in church is not answered? Here it is, the absence of an environment of love. In John 14:17 Jesus says, "These things I command you, that ye love one another." He also says in John 14:5 "If ye love me, keep my commandments." The new commandment is this: LOVE. If we can cleave to love, if we can love without pretence cleaving to what is good, how much Godly energy and power will flow in our prayer meetings. Paul puts it this way "Be kindly affectioned one to another with brotherly love; in honour preferring one another. In Rom. 13:10 he says, "Love worketh no ill to his neighbor: therefore love is the fulfilling of the law."

If we are to pray as Jesus prayed and be saturated by an atmosphere of answered prayers, we need to walk in love, as Christ loved us. It must be a love which will lead us to give ourselves up as He gave "himself for us an offering and a sacrifice to God for a sweet smelling saviour." Love is God saturating the atmosphere of prayer. Let's look at some of these passages of Scripture and see how important love is for creating an atmosphere of effective prayer. Here are some of the things that love does that it makes one of the most powerful ingredients for creating an atmosphere:

1 John 3:14: Love infuses prayer with life.

"We know that *we have passed from death unto life, because we love* the brethren. He that loveth not his brother abideth in death."

1 John 3:23-24: Love creates a habitation in which we dwell in God.

23 And this is his commandment, that we should believe on the name of his Son Jesus Christ, and love one another, as he gave us commandment. 24 And he that keepeth his commandments dwelleth in him, and he in him. And hereby we know that he abideth in us, by the Spirit which he hath given us.

1 John 4:7-12: Love is the key to Divine knowledge.

7 Beloved, let us love one another: for love is of God; *and every one that loveth is born of God, and knoweth God.* 8 He that loveth not knoweth not God; for God is love. 9 In this was manifested the love of God toward us, because that God sent his only begotten Son into the world, that we might live through him. 10 Herein is love, not that we loved God, but that he loved us, and sent his Son to be the propitiation for our sins.11

Chapter Six: Atmospheres of Effective Prayer

Beloved, if God so loved us, we ought also to love one another. 12 No man hath seen God at any time. If we love one another, God dwelleth in us, and his love is perfected in us.

1 John 4:12-21: Love is the principle of perfection creating boldness even in the face of judgment.

16 And we have known and believed the love that God hath to us. God is love; and he that dwelleth in love dwelleth in God, and God in him. 17 Herein is our love made perfect, that we may have boldness in the Day of Judgment: because as he is, so are we in this world.18 There is no fear in love; but perfect love casteth out fear: because fear hath torment. He that feareth is not made perfect in love. 19 We love him, because he first loved us. 20 If a man say, I love God, and hateth his brother, he is a liar: for he that loveth not his brother whom he hath seen, how can he love God whom he hath not seen? 21 And this commandment have we from him, That he who loveth God loveth his brother also.

These are the several things that make love an ingredient that creates an atmosphere for effective prayer. You too can have a powerful and effective prayer life if you can create these atmospheric conditions.

PART 2

THE ALCHEMY OF
THE LORD'S PRAYER

CHAPTER SEVEN:
GOLDEN CORD

KEY 1: RELATIONSHIP

Matt. 6:9-15: "After this manner therefore pray ye: Our Father,...."

Relationality is the primordial knob on which all destinies in the universe turns. "Our Father" activates that destiny and turns the knob of the universe to its fulfillment. That is why Jesus mentions God so many times as "Father." It was to activate his destiny and turn the knob of the universe for its release and fulfillment. The word "Father" as referring to God occurs 126 times in the gospel of John alone. To show its importance for prayer Jesus uses it six times in His intercessory prayer. Jesus taught this prayer to us this way because His primary relationship with God was that of Son to the Father. When Jesus calls God Father, He does not do so to suggest that God created Him and then adopted Him rather He does this by insisting that He is generated by God as God's internal and eternal seed. When Jesus says "Father," He sees as the complete embodiment of glory and the giver of glory. In calling God Father, He sees God as the keeper of those who believe. He implies that "Our Father indicates that God is the source of Unity." In His prayer, He implies that the problem of the world is that they do not know God as Father and righteous keeper of those who believe in Him. The world does not know "Father" because they have do not have the Spirit of the Father. At the onset of this prayer, the Master teaches His disciples to tap into that primordiality. That which is not in relationship

93

ceases to exist. Relationship is the DNA of existence itself. To exist is to be in relationship. In the Fatherhood of God we connect to the source and this blessing is rained down upon the children. As the heavens send down rain upon the earth, so the Father rains down His goodness upon those who call out "Our Father." This relationship is always implied and many places explicit in the Scriptures.

When God created Adam, according to Genesis 1, God formed man from the dust making him a result of God's active craftsmanship. The purpose for Adam's creation as articulated by God Himself in Gen. 1:26 was intrinsically Divine and could only be carried out by one who was more than a material fabrication of Divinity. In Gen. 1:26-28 we find the intent of relation and communion leading to the idea that God wanted one who shared not just in creation as other created things did but one who carried within them the essential nature of God with the capacity to soar to the heavens and the capacity of descend to hell and the ability to make decisions and carry out activities that could affect the relation of the earth to both. Thus we read:

> 26 And God said, Let us make man in *our image*, after *our likeness*: and let them *have dominion over* the fish of the sea, and *over* the fowl of the air, and *over* the cattle, and *over* all the earth, and *over* every creeping thing that creepeth upon the earth. 27 So God created man in his own image, *in the image of God* created he him; *male and female* created he them. 28 And God blessed them, and God said unto them, Be *fruitful*, and *multiply*, and *replenish the earth*, and *subdue it*: and *have dominion* over the fish of the sea, and over the fowl of the air, and over every living thing that moveth upon the earth.

In Gen. 2:6-7, we are then shown that Adam is more than fabrication mechanical pottery fashioned by God as we read, "And the LORD God formed man of the dust of the ground, and breathed into his nostrils the breath of life; and man became a living soul." To make sure that man was more than a mechanical entity and could go on to live as a dynamic spiritual being who shares intimately the nature of God, God placed a living soul into man making it possible for man to be the one upon the earth capable of manifesting the very life of God. This idea so fascinated Luke that he ends his genealogy– of the Lord Jesus with the phrase, "and Adam the son of God." God was longing for Father Son relationship when he created Adam. That intention of God is reactivated in Christ who now calls it forth from within us by telling us to pray "Our Father." The entire objective of what God does, we read from the lips of God, turns on relational communion and calls for intimacy with God. In Torah we read in Deut. 14:1-2:

> *Ye are the children of the LORD your God:* ye shall not cut yourselves, nor make any baldness between your eyes for the dead. For thou art and holy people unto the LORD thy God, and the LORD hath chosen thee to be a peculiar people unto himself, above all the nations that are upon the earth.

All of God's demands and dialogues presume that human beings can be children of God, dedicated to Him and inhabited by Him. In Ps. 82:6 we read, "I have said, Ye are gods; and all of you are children of the Most High." We read in 1 John 3:2, "Beloved, now are we the sons of God, and it doth not yet appear what we shall be: but we know that, when he shall appear, we shall be like him; for we shall see him as he is."

Fatherhood and Heaven typifies the relationship of seed to the seed bearer and the location of the seed bearer. Fatherhood is a primordial relation in which the child, son or daughter realizes that there is a fundamentally non-severable inner connection between the child and the source of their being. God, as the bearer of the seed called Adam, transfers the Divine DNA, if you may, to the seed. Acts 17:28-29:

> 28 For in him we live, and move, and have our being; as certain also of your own poets have said, For *we are also his offspring*. 29 Forasmuch then as we are the offspring of God, we ought not to think that the God-head is like unto gold, or silver, or stone, graven by art and man's device.

The child by virtue of being in the Father's nature carried the possibility of the nature of the Father in seed form and ergo has potentially the character of the Father embedded in them. This line of prayer puts the believer above principalities and powers. Yes, though we are created, yet by virtue of this Father-child relationship we move beyond the realm of mere creation to intimate sharing of the nature of God. There is a difference between fabrication and being begotten. We are begotten of God. This affirmation of God as Father serves notice to all of creation, angels demons, principalities things above, things below, things to come and things past that we are not like them. We are intimately linked with God and have God's heart open to us and His power is available to us without reserve. God is our Father.

This relationality is the basis for the release of power and presupposes that God is intent on intimate relation with those who call God Father. It is the release of freedom into the beloved, which provides a place from which they like Archimedes can move the earth around on its spiritual axis point. It is the true inner signification of our souls' highest moments in substance of divinity. Rather than being a declaration of want, it is declaration of fundamental relationality serving as launching pad for our taking our place in the royal activities spoken by the mouth of God at the creation of Adam. Dominion rulership, authority, fruitfulness, multiplication capacity, all presumes this fundamental relation to God not just as Creator but also as Father.

We have a tendency to understand this relationship as negative relation wherein God bullies us into doing what God wants us to do with threats. But Jesus made this Father-Son relationship primary in His life, teaching, activities, death and resurrection. In Jesus' prayer in John 17, Jesus uses word "Father" at least four times to refer to God. When this relationality is foundational, we no longer live under compulsion but in true freedom that allows us to come into the fullness of what Adam was created for, which has always been in God our Father. Here the point is that it is impossible for us to be independent of God. Even our negative choices are made in reference to God and, therefore, must face the nature of the God in whom they are made. This relationality then means that every prayer is an

96

affirmation of communion with the ultimate substance of the universe. Those who do not pray or do not believe in its efficacy are usually those who refuse this relational communion with the eternal for one reason or another. Some declare their independence from this relational communion because of upbringing; some because of what they consider failure on the part of God as Father; others because of the failure of an earthly Father. But this does not take away from the need for this relational communion which serves as the fulcrum for the turning of our human bodies', soul's, and spirit's cry to the heavenly sphere.

True prayer is only possible here, in this place of relational communion with the Creator, in His Fatherly outreach toward our inner man. This cannot be discarded, it cannot be marginalized nor can it be ignored. It is the ground of what James calls "effectual and fervent prayer of the righteous." Without it, prayer becomes a program that is void of any power. It is by means of this relational communion that good success in prayer is guaranteed. What a marvelous manifestation of glory when one begins to grasp the awesome and powerful potential of our prayer growing out this intimacy with the God our Father. Those who do not have knowledge of this intimacy cannot pray, really.

In this relationship the Face of God by the brooding Holy Spirit flashes forth into the face of the dark of deep waters of our needy soul, calling us out and causing there to be light, generativity and fruitfulness. This flash of the Face of God into our soul, enabled by the intimacy which we have found with God through Jesus Christ, moves us to join in the battle for the world's soul. In His flashing intimacyy, we see through eyes enlightened with God, feel His heartbeat, and desire what God our Father desires for this world. This relational communion encompasses and makes available to us the full panoply and possibility of Heaven's solution into the temporal circumstance of our lives.

We live in a time when those who have had pathological experiences with their earthly fathers and who see relational communion as being fundamentally problematic want us to forgo the pleasant experiences we find Jesus having with the Father and join them in decrying the Fatherhood and intimacy which this brings to us prayer. But if we are to pray effectively, we cannot use the pathological experience of human beings as the basis for judging our relationship with God as Father. This relational communion is primordial, primeval and fundamental. This present tendency to exalt bad experiences over good and to make it the spring-board for spiritual understanding must cease for prayer to become effective. For the power of prayer to be manifested, God's desire to be in relational communion must be seen as a substantial and pragmatic good. The psalmist said, "my Adonai (YHVH) is good and there is no unrighteousness in Him." Now this relationality is not some idle sentimentality subject merely to our whimsical view of what is good from human feelings but an intimacy which accepts all that happens within the God into whom we have entered. This intimacy causes us to know that God relates to the whole universe even in their falleness and misery in love and seeks to have a relationship with them. Thus, out of the inner heart of God's love to which the believer is related flows prayer that seeks to manifest the heart of God into the world. In this Divine intimacy we receive the compass of eternity for navigating times and seasons in which we find ourselves. With this intimacy we avoid crashing into the black hole of existential despair. Relational communion is not a program. If we make it into a program we miss the mark and in fact make our prayers ineffectual. The truth is that for too long we have programmed God out of prayer. So then rather than being a dance of freedom it has become a bondage to pattern and plans. It becomes an unwilling cross that we carry. And no unwilling cross ever led to salvation. It is out of this relational communion that life–giving prayer dialogue arises Here our thought, speech and action carry God into various human contexts of needs. Not only is our progeny Divine and are we related to God as Father in a fundamental way, our location or position is with Him. When we move from being the image of the man of dust, which is Adam, we are changed into the image of the Son of God and thus we bear the image of the Heavenly Man.

When we pray "Our Father" we call on this relational aspect of God. We activate the compassion of God for us when we suffer as it is written, "As a Father pities his children, So the LORD pities those who fear Him." (Psalm 103:13) God shows compassion to His sons. In the book of Exodus chapter 4 we find the reason why God felt such pain at the suffering of Israel, for God says:

22 And thou shalt say unto Pharaoh, Thus saith the LORD, Israel is my son, even my firstborn: 23 And I say unto thee, Let my son go, that he may serve me: and if thou refuse to let him go, behold, I will slay thy son, even thy firstborn. Ex. 4:22-23 (KJV)

It is this relationship that led hwhy (YHVH) to be gracious unto them, and to have compassion on them. His regard and respect for Israel cannot be separated from this claim which God makes of them as sons. **(2 Kings 13:23)** It is this Fatherhood of God that causes and activates compassion on us. "Our Father" is an inner cry to experience compassion and pity of God. Just as children are often helpless so we find ourselves often helpless, in life situations. But when cry "abba, abba" we activate God's bowels of compassion. The Hebrew word used here is *rahamim*. Compassion is stronger than sympathy or empathy. As we find in Exodus, this fatherly compassion on the part of God is what gave rise to the active involvement of God in the deliverance of Israel from the bondage in Egypt. If as Thomas Merton said, "The whole idea of compassion is based on a keen awareness of the interdependence of all these living beings, which are all part of one another, and all involved in one another." Then God as Father is the ultimate expression of compassion, for in Him we all live, move and have our being. He is the fundamental source of universal interconnection. This fatherly compassion is what gives rise to the care that God gave Israel in the wilderness. In another passage of Scripture, this Father/son relationship between Israel and God is reiterated.

"The LORD your God who goes before you will Himself fight on your behalf, just as He did for you in Egypt before your eyes, and in the wilderness where you saw how the LORD your God carried you, just as a man carries his son, in all the way which you have walked until you came to this place." (Deuteronomy 1:30-31)

As a Father, he will fight for them and carry them along when the way is long and rough as God did in the wilderness. When Moses wanted to see God in God's essence after proclaiming His Lordship, God opens up the description of this character with the word "compassionate" the Hebrew *rahum* which in the Septuagint is the word *oivkti,rmwn (oiktirmon)*

I LXT **Exodus 34:6** kai. parh/lqen ku,rioj pro. prosw,pou auvtou/ kai. evka,lesen ku,rioj o` qeo.j oivkti,rmwn kai. evleh,mwn makro,qumoj kai. polue,leoj kai. avlhqino.j

hw"ëhy> hw"åhy> èar"q.YIw: éwyn"P'-l[; hw"ïhy> rbo[]Y:w:
`tm,(a/w< ds,x,î-br:w> ~yIP:ßa; %r<a,î !WN=x;w> ~Wxßr: laeî

Exodus 34:6

In many of the English translations, the flow of the passage is short-circuited. Rahum and oiktirmon are translated as merciful rather than compassion. But when we look at the original, the flow makes perfect sense. Compassion serves as the springboard from which "ele ee *moon*—"sympathy," macrothumia—"longsuffering," "polueleos—"expanding mercy or plurality of mercies" and alethinos—"true dependability." All these grow from the Father=child relationship which this prayer evokes in this simple phrase "our Father." So the text should read: "And the YHVH passed by before him, and proclaimed, YYY, YYY Elohim, compassionate, sympathetic (gracious), long-suffering, ever expanding in mercy and full of truly dependable." When we speak of God as Father, these are the characteristics that should come to mind.

When we pray "Our Father," we activate the grace of God. Here acknowledge that we as children have no deserving work or act which should endear us to Him except that He calls us His children. Grace is what allows us to get mercy which we do not deserve as God based on our relation to Him as Father holds back from us the judgment that we deserve. In mercy the Father forbears and does not inflict harm thatwe deserve because of our willful provocation. Though God has power to inflict harsh punishment yet because of His mercy He withholds it. Though we often offend and set ourselves as adversary against His Will yet He expands His mercy toward us.

As Father, God has covenant with the children. This covenant in based on His person and not necessarily on our ability—though our faithfulness to Him makes it easier on us. As Father He makes promises and keeps them. As Father, he searches and finds His lost children and even when they have sold themselves to the enemy He pays for their redemtion. He is the Father who redeems the children as the fathers in Israel were told to redeem their first born children from the curse of the death of Egypt. As Father, God provides a place of refuge in Himself for those whom He calls His children. His overflowing mercy is ever present to forgiveness to the erring children who return. His goodness and mercy are tied together forever. As Father, God will defend and require justice at the hands of those who mistreat the children. Yes, God is Father. This fatherhood is nowhere made more clear that in the person of Jesus Christ His son. When we say, "Father," we enter into the same relationship that Jesus had with God, the Father.

"Our Father" activates our total inheritance. For it is written in **Ephesians 1:11:** "In Him also we have obtained an inheritance, being predestined according to the purpose of Him who works all things according to the counsel of His Will." This inheritance is sealed until we take possession of it; but only when we as children understand how to offer praise and glory to the Father does our inheritance emerge from its hidden place. We cry "Father" so that we might see with eyes of the Father and feel with the heart of the Father. It is only by this "crying Father" that we come to know what the hope of our calling is. The riches of the glory of God's inheritance for the saints is hidden in this simple formula "our Father." It is as Father, not just a Creator, that God made us partakers of the inheritance of His Light. God is the Father of light and we cannot inherit this light until we are birthed by, in and through this light. It is only those of us who have been called sons—children—who will receive the promise of the eternal inheritance. **We are told in 1 Peter 1:4** that our inheritance which the Father gives us is "incorruptible, and undefiled, and that (it) fadeth not away, (it is) reserved in Heaven for us." Since God is our "Father" and we do indeed cry Father, we are no longer bondservants, but sons; and if we are sons, then we are heirs through God. **Galatians 4:7:** If we say "Our Father," then all that belongs to God now is open to us even the most valuable of all His possessions, His Son.

"Our Father" activates not only one's relationship with God but it underscores for us the fact that we have a fundamental connection one with another. We are part of God's family. In God as Father we are interrelated through Jesus Christ who serves as bringing together of both. Not only are we related to one another, we affect each other by our being. This relationality means that we cannot act as if we are isolated and alone. This relationship with another calls forth care. This care grows out of love and compassion. Thus, the nature of our Father is the compass by which we locate ourselves relationally in the world. When our interconnection with one another is understood in the context of "our Father" it becomes the key to the transformation of the world. The authenticity of our existence is measured by the way we relate to other in the context of this "our Father." There is no way of getting around the fact of our interrelatedness that flows from this line of prayer. Our destiny waits impatiently for us to come to the awareness of our interrelatedness. It is only in relationship that we reach our fulfillment. Romans 8:19 tells us that all creation awaits the revelation of relationship— "the children of God." This sonship relation with God is also the interrelation of human to human.

When you and I pray "Our Father," we invoke the relational principle which is called the fruit of the Spirit. We read:

22 But the fruit of the Spirit is love, joy, peace, longsuffering, gentleness, goodness, faith, 23 Meekness, temperance: against such there is no law. 24 And they that are Christ's have crucified the flesh with the affections and lusts. 25 If we live in the Spirit, let us also walk in the Spirit. 26 Let us not be desirous of vain glory, provoking one another, envying one another. Gal. 5:22-26 (KJV)

The Spirit-filled life is a life of relationship. Love is about relationship to God, self and others. Joy is the response of our whole being to the interrelated web of human experience with exuberance and optimism which encourages others. Peace is ability to be at one with the self and to connect with other human beings without violence to self, to God, or the other. All of this fruit is activated when we pray to God who is Spirit as Father.

In conclusion praying "Our Father" opens two portals for us to relationship with the Godhead and with one another. The greatest example of this is the incarnation of Christ. We find in Him relationship with and with man. Relationship is the key to the universe and to individual destiny, and its most effective key is call out "Our Father."

CHAPTER EIGHT

GOLDEN CORD

KEY 2: HEAVENS

"Which Art in the Heavens" in the Greek reads, [S] *Matthew 6:9*
pa,ter h`mw/n o` evn toi/j ouvranoi/j

In the Torah, the word for "Heaven" is the fourth word of the text. So in the beginning God created the heavens. The Hebrew word for "Heaven" is always in the plural *mym;v:h+* in the TNK. The use of the plural suggests that the idea was to include the vast expanse of space as the realm of God's activities. It would include all possible galaxies and star systems. There are scriptural suggestion that there are at least three heavens, for we read that Paul knew someone who was caught up to the third Heaven. Some of the Jewish non-canonical books such as the apocrypha of Levi and Baruch speak of five heavens. We also find in the Ethiopian book of Enoch the idea of a seven Heaven. This is more likely to have been derived from the idea that earth was created according to the patterns of the Heaven in six days, and the seventh day is the day of the Lord. In later times some have even suggested that there are twelve heavens since the children of Israel are to be used as the measure of what God does with the universe. No matter how many numbers we assign to it, the truth is that the Heaven of the heavens are not enough to contain the infinite God. That notwithstanding, I subscribe to the Einsteinian idea that God is the ever expanding universe. God filled the vast expanse of the universe and that God is the principle of their very expansion.

But the Scripture, especially in the New Testament, subscribes to the idea also of single Heaven. That single Heaven Jesus refers to as "*a place.*"—The place where the throne room of God is located and from where God judges the world. It is written in Romans chapter 1, "the wrath of God is revealed from Heaven against all ungodliness. . ." There is also Heaven as paradise. But this is believed to be the paradise that was on earth but was transported away to another part of the universe until man is redeemed and comes to maturity. But it seems that paradise is just a part of the heavens not all of the heavens. Furthermore, Jesus speaks of a house, in John 14:1. Later on in the epistles Paul speaks of a city, and in Revelation there is hardly any reference to the plural concept of the heavens.

The word for "Heavens" *ouranois* in its plural denotation convey two points that are important: its complexity and the simplicity of its function. The word for, "heavens" *ouranois* (a dative masculine plural) conveys the idea of the Father continually seeding the dark edges of His creation with new possibilities and inhabiting it. In that sense it carries with it the very nature of the one whose location it is claimed to be. This Heaven, as the one who inhabits, is infinite. It is not so much a place as it is an organism whose complexity and simplicity befits the one to whom this prayer is offered: "our Father who art in the heavens…." No simple description can give an adequate idea of it. When the heavens open even in the most limited way, their visual effects cannot be neglected for they "declare thy glory" as the psalmist says. Heaven is the building up of all the external and inner hope to which all human action points. It is the intervening idea that impacts our choices and allows us the believers to adapt to the various circumstances with joy. It is the finality that brings together all human plans with a view to a Divine end. So then Heaven is regarded as the reward to all the labor of the pilgrim workman. The reality of Heaven leads us to outward forms of behavior reflecting the central personality with whom we identify when we say, "our Father." Heaven is shown with increasing clarity to us as our allegiance to it is carried by strong faith. There is mysterious imagery with which the Bible defines heavens.

According to this prayer and many other passages of Scripture, the heavens belong to God. The vast expanse of infinite space is where the Divine creativity is at play. Clearly the vastness of these heavens is far too difficult for creatures to handle. This "heavens" is regarded as the abode of God and the emerging dimension of God's work. There is no particular point from in the heavens to point at God for He is at once everywhere present. He affects the heavens as a King seated on His throne affecting it entirely as His Kingdom. When we consider that Solomon said Heaven is considered the habitation of this One who we call Father we must also take into the consideration that He is larger than the heavens. Though they are myriads of heavens yet this ONE God YHVH whom we call Father rules over all of it. Thus, no matter where we find ourselves in space or time, we find ourselves in the presence of our Father. His voice is heard in the heavens of the heavens pushing creatively at the edge of nothing. If it be true that "the Heaven of the heavens cannot contain" our Father, then it appears that we are sons make our abode beyond the stars as we enter into the heart of the God we so lovingly call Father. This description is metaphorical and is meant to give us the understanding that God's power is loftier that we can grasp. By saying Heaven, we acknowledge that we are connected to all of creation. (Gen. 24:7) In this we declare that we are not bound even now by the materiality of our existence but that our spirit can soar to dimensions and realms hitherto unknown by human scientific research.

Heaven is the prototype, the archetype of the all the ideas corporal and incorporeal—joys, happiness, pleasures and fulfillment to which human beings ever aspire. Man on earth is measured by the forms which are according to the worlds not made with hands. It is as the prayer says, the habitation the Father's essence and therefore the full embodiment of all the benefits which the Father is willing to bestow on the one who is son. When sonship is recognized, we are raised up and conducted from earth to Heaven. I speak not merely of the Heaven of the afterlife but Heaven that is apprehended and appreciated in the daily flow of our earthly life. God draws us up from this world to Himself. God shows Himself to us and we are able to behold God's glory. In the eyes of those not born from above, this is impossible but for those who have been born from above, we read, "they shall see the Kingdom of Heaven." Heaven is accessible to them because they have the

Spirit of the Father which can carry them upward not by mere intellect but by the kindling of the fire of the Holy Spirit which is them. Heaven, as it is ensconced in the microcosm of the earth, is revealed to them here and in their spirit they ascend as John ascended on the Lord's Day. (Rev. 4:1.) Heaven is to be construed in this way: it is the place of truth. It is the place of the birth of spirits. It is the place from which we are clothed with power, for it is written: "you shall receive power from Heaven when the Holy Spirit is come upon you. It is the habitation of power, authority, rulership, dominion and thrones. It is a place of ever-flowing love, for God is love and necessarily so for in Him all men are loved without partiality. Heaven is a place of diligent devotion and worshipful attention. Heaven is the place where the fragmented relationship of man, God and the world is reversed and submitted to the one eternal will and agency of the Holy Spirit. No more clandestine intervention of false imagination and the bad will of a mind possessed with a false grasp at supreme authority over all. In Heaven where the Father makes His abode, the imperfect give way to the perfect, for those who are here reflect the true likeness of the Deity they call Father. There is in Heaven an unbroken flow of virtues from the same Being.[7] For clarity let me list again the ideas of Heaven which we find in the Scripture.

1. The vast expanse of the universe which according to modern science has many systems coming to life and some even dying. This has innumerable galaxies some have never been discovered because man has not left this galaxy though he has been able to peer into them through the telescope. All of those systems are included in the plural reference of the Bible to the "heavens." In this Heaven, **Ouranios,** we have what we call nested heavens interweaved with one another in a web of interconnection. This interconnection and nested web is due to the fact that all the heavens are created by One Being our God. The heavens are the expanding created order of space and referred to in the plural, but what may not be obvious is the fact that when speaking of the new Heaven and the new earth, the Targum which is the Aramaic text of the Hebrew TNK uses the singular Heaven **shamaya** **(ay"m;v.)).**

107

at'd:x] a['ra;w> !ytid:x] **ay"m;v.** yrEb' an"a.h' yrEa. ᵀᴬᴿ **Isaiah 65:17**
`ble l[; !q's.t;yI al'w> at'y"m;dq; !r"kd:yI al'w>

The same usage is found in the Greek New Testament in **Revelation 21:1**

Kai. ei=don **ouvrano.n** kaino.n kai. gh/n kainh,nÅ o` ga.r prw/toj **ouvrano.j** kai. h` prw,th gh/ avph/lqan kai. h` qa,lassa ouvk e;stin e;tiÅ
"And I saw a new Heaven and a new earth, for the first Heaven and the first earth were passed away and there is no sea"

In the above Greek text, the first use, *ouranon* is the accusative masculine singular and the second use, *ouranos* is the normative masculine singular. My intention in pointing this out is to show that the second usage of word "Heaven" in the Lord's Prayer is a reference to a particular place but the first has to do with all that is beyond the realm of the earth. I am suggesting that it is not all of heavens that will be discarded but the Heaven that has to do with the earth. This is probably referring to our solar system.

2. We also know that the word "Heaven" can refer to the sky which we see which serves as the covering of the earth. This Heaven is nothing but the clouds and the atmosphere which includes the ozone layer which as we are being told by some scientists is depleting. So when we say "who art in the heavens" we are not referring to some kind of sky god. Neither are we talking about archons and angels who traverse the sky or even in the sun or the constellations but about God in whom all "live move and have their being."

3. Heaven can also refer to the realm of paradise or the Garden of Eden which was taken up to a different region of the universe after the fall of man. We know that God met Adam in the Garden which the Lord planted on earth. In that garden Adam was expected to do the Will of God as it is done in the specific Heaven that God built. When man fell, God caused the garden to disappear. There are many Jewish legends that say God took the Garden to another dimension of

the heavens. This Heaven was specifically prepared for the man in fellowship with the Father. We shall deal with this Heaven when we deal with the key of the will in prayer.

4. Heaven can also have specific reference to the city which is part of the Eden that is also referred to as Heaven. The Bible calls it the New Jerusalem and insists that it comes down out of Heaven from God.

Revelation 3:12: He that overcometh, I will make him a pillar in the temple of my God, and he shall go out thence no more: and I will write upon him the name of my God, *and the name of the city of my God, the new Jerusalem, which cometh down out of Heaven from my God, and mine own new name.*

Here is a Heaven, "new Jerusalem," coming out of Heaven from God. Heaven coming out of Heaven which comes from God. What a wonder. So then we see the New Jerusalem is in Heaven which is in God. At least in this case we find two things nested in God. I do believe that there are more things in the heavens nested in God than we can imagine.

The two heavens mentioned in the Lord's Prayer portend two realities. This first mention of Heaven, *ouranois,* in the Lord's Prayer in the plural is directly in contrast to the second mention when we read, "thy will be done on earth as it is in Heaven *(ouranos)*." I submit that the difference is this: when speaking of Heaven as the home and place of rest for those who have acknowledged and accepted the fatherhood of God, the singular is used and the plural refers to the whole of Heaven as God's creative domain. It is where God continuosly displays His creative energy and infinite imageries of his beauty. We may even say that God is experimenting with kinds of interrelated beings. We read in **Ephesians 3:15,** "Of whom the whole family in Heaven and earth is named."

When we say "who art in the heavens," we speak of the all inclusive presence of our Father and all the beings who may inhabit other spheres. There is not a place in the universe or as some scientists are suggesting "multi-verse" that is not ruled and controlled by our Father. There is not a race of beings that do not come under the authority of our Father. Here is the reason for the plural heavens. It puts in one swoop in relationship with the whole universe in its present form and its becoming. Put in Pauline terms, Romans 8:38-39 (KJV) expresses this concept clearly:

> 38 For I am persuaded, that neither death, nor life, nor angels, nor principalities, nor powers, nor things present, nor things to come, 39 Nor height, nor depth, nor any other creature, shall be able to separate us from the love of God, which is in Christ Jesus our Lord.

CHAPTER NINE

GOLDEN CORD

KEY 3: HALLOW THE NAME

"Hallowed be thy name."

One of the first things Moses asked God was "Who shall I tell them sent me?" God gave him three forms of His name as a way to deal with Israel and with Pharaoh. When YHVH appears to Moses, He says, "I am the God of your Father, the God of Abraham, the God of Isaac and the God of Jacob." (Ex. 3:6) He calls this name a memorial. That is a name that sets up territorial claim. In further conversation, YHVH (LORD) tells Moses what this name entails. It entails Divine care, Divine concern for the human condition. It entails liberation and providence for the oppressed. When Moses presses in verse 13:

13 And Moses said unto God, Behold, when I come unto the children of Israel, and shall say unto them, The God of your fathers hath sent me unto you; and they shall say to me, **What is his name?** What shall I say unto them? 14 And God said unto Moses, I AM THAT I AM: and he said, Thus shalt thou say unto the children of Israel, I AM hath sent me unto you. 15 And God said moreover unto Moses, Thus shalt thou say unto the children of Israel, **YHVH, the God of your fathers, the God of Abraham, the God of Isaac, and the God of Jacob, hath sent me unto you: this is my name forever, and this is my memorial unto all generations.** Ex. 3:13-15 (ASV)

God gives His names and appellation as instrument of transaction for Israel in the midst of Egypt. I AM—that is, the Becoming ONE—is given as a name that produces within the individual and the community a response of anger as on Pharaoh or of hope and possibility as in the Israelites. It is a key for unlocking the awareness of those who say it or hear it. It evoked in Moses a rekindling of the hope for liberation. The name is capable of evoking variety of responses, but there is only response that will unlock its potential for those who call themselves sons. It is the response of faith. As a key for unlocking awareness, it raises the consciousness of the one who enters into it to a heavenly level. When this name is grasped, suddenly activities, events and symbols take on deeper and larger significance. It did for Moses and the Israelites. It was the Name that made all the difference for Israel and still makes the difference for us who believe. When Jesus teaches prayer, the places he phrase "hallowed be they NAME" in the first triangle. So, what is it supposed to do for us?

This phrase "hallowed be thine name" does three things. It a request that our contexts bow to the name of the one we call Father. It is an affirmation of God as intrinsically holy. We declare the holiness of God's name and command the sphere in which we live to be brought into alignment with the holiness, power and glory of the name. It is a declaration of right as those born of God. To say, "hallowed be thy name" is to require that all existence come under the dominion of man, compliment the Creator. It is true that the location for hallowing God's Name is not specified. However, everyone and everything in the universe must come under His authority. We, as those assigned by God to be His representatives, must pay God this compliment, that He is the Lord God and that His name is the instrument for manifesting substantive good in the universe. David understood this and used this reverential intimacy with God to insist that all creation "hallow the name of God" by continual praise of the Name. "Let everything that has breath praise the Name of the LORD."

The Name of God carries the identity of God and displays the power of God. This hallowing of the name of God means keeping the identity and power of God as the Lord God intact in our minds and our hearts. One of the commandments given to Moses by the Lord reads, "Thou shall not take the name of the Lord thy God in vain." Taking the name of the Lord in vain is the cousin of materialistic idolatry in which we make our creation or even things created by us to become objects of our worship. Simply, this name is not to be attributed to anything or anyone other than God the Creator of the world. Hallowing the name of God then means that verbal idolatry must be eschewed. In its place must be put a continual affirmation and protection of the reputation of God. To hallow then is to make God's reputation great at all and times in all places, no matter where or with whom we may be. In this line of prayer, we command that the identity and reputation of our God and Father be revered and remain sacrosanct in the world.

This respect of the name of God comes from the fact that we know that this name of God is the house in which God's power for us dwells. If the name is made unholy, then we cannot expect a clear flow of the power we seek for the transformation of our circumstances. There is loftiness to the name of God which causes one who is in that name to rejoice and to bring joy to the world. To hallow the name is to take the responsibility for the sanctity of that name in the realm of life that has been entrusted to us. The name of YHVH services life and regulates the power and structure of cosmic relationality. When the name of our God is hallowed, either in its spiritual sense especially in the manifestation of God as Man in Jesus is used, there is no withholding of God. There is no withholding of intimacy to those who know the name. The writer of Proverbs says, "The name of the Lord is strong tower, the righteous run into it and are saved." That name in its holiness is the weapon for penetrating all spheres. By this hallowed name we prevail against all the wiles of the enemy. In this Name is the principle that helps keep relationships and lives from disintegration. If we want to experience the power and holiness of this name, our being must be saturated in the name. We can do this by praying the names of God prophetically. When we do this, we evoke all the powers of God.

The name of the Lord cannot truly be hallowed where the name of the Lord is not called. That is why it was important that after the birth of Enoch, according to Genesis 4:26, *"men began to call on the name of the LORD."* In a sense it can be read: "men began praying the name of YHVH." Calling the name of the Lord is vital because it distinguishes the righteous from the unrighteous. The Hebrew *wayiqra* from the root *qara'* (kaw-raw') is rooted in the idea of engaging a relative or the king by name or using a horn to call them out so as to properly address them by name and by title. This call is not just the yelling out of name but carries with it the mood of deference. Many times the Bible uses the phrase "call on the name of the Lord" as a euphemism for prayer. There had been six generation of fear for the name. Adam, having been kicked out of the Garden, could not call the name without fear and shame; but in the seventh generation men began again to pray and seek God's presence. So indeed we can say that men began to pray the name of the Lord. In some cases it may mean to cry out the name of the individual or even preach the name. In many African cultures, which would have been similar to that of Israel in this regard, an individual wanting the audience of a famous man will begin by declaring their name with words that denote the fame of such person. In fact a host may lavish such call out names upon his guest who has been invited, mentioning his/her accomplishments and given him/her new names in his/her proclamation and pronouncements that made their renowned public to those who may not know. In this case anyone challenging such proclamation will force the receiver to defend his honor.

We also read that Abraham, in Genesis 12:8, moved "to the mountain east of Bethel, and he pitched his tent with Bethel on the west and Ai on the east; there he built an altar to the LORD and called on the name of the LORD." He was not mainly calling the name but declaring the holiness of the LORD and thus was also sanctifying the land for the Lord God by placing the name of the Lord upon it. Through that calling on the name of the Lord, the land and atmosphere carried the renown of the God of Abraham and echoed it back when the children of Abraham came back. In another place (Genesis 13:4), he came back "to the place of the altar which he had made there at first. And there, Abram *called on the Name of the Lord."* The reader may note the fact that in many cases the calling of the name of the Lord is done where altars were present or being built—thus making it an anchor of prayer. The principle of holiness is in the name of the Lord. When we call on the calling of the name of the Lord, holiness is released. We call upon the name of the Lord in truth and so hallow the name of the Lord. This call implies a dependence upon the Lord. Because this calling of the name of the Lord is tied to the hallowedness of the same name, the law was given in Exodus 20:7: "You shall not take the name of the LORD your God in vain, for the LORD will not hold him guiltless who takes His name in vain." The calling of the name of the YHVH implies what Schleiermacher calls absolute dependence which forms an ultimate concern.

In Kingdom prayer, the phrase "hallowed be thy name" is an imperative to the universe to keep the name hallowed but also an implicit commitment on the part of members of the Kingdom not to misuse the name of the Lord. The misuse of the name will constitute a breach between Heaven and earth. Conversely, the correct use of the name constitutes a connecting of Heaven and earth. Because the name of God carries the identity of God, its misuse will not only defame God but will rob creation of its sustaining power. If God's name is not hallowed or deliberately misused either as curse upon others or the oppression of others, there is a tragic interruption of the commerce of the supernatural in that sphere. The misuse of God's name usually ends in some form of exploitation of the weak and marginalized because the broken reverence for the Name is the result of broken fellowship with the owner of the Name. Since God works effectively in the atmosphere of trust, this becomes the breaking of trust between God and the person, place or sphere in which the name of LORD is not hallowed. Praying the name of YHVH is a way to build trust and faith.

The effectiveness of the ministry is based on this hallowing of the name of Lord. In Deuteronomy 18:5, speaking of the Levites Moses says, "For the LORD your God has chosen him out of all your tribes to stand to minister in the name of the LORD, him and his sons forever." (See also Deuteronomy 28:10) This means that effective ministry is carried out only in the context of the hallowedness of the name of the Lord. Only when one serves in the name of the LORD God can he or she stand there before the LORD. Both prophet and priest must carry out their task in the name of the Lord for their work to be effective. When a prophet speaks, he must do so in the name of the LORD not in the prophet's own name or the name of some other entity. The name of the Lord carries the seed of prophesies to its fruition. Here is why the prophet must not speak falsely in the name of the Lord because the prophet's false speech dishonors and defiles the name in which he or she speaks. What sets the believer apart from the unbeliever is that we are called by the name of the LORD. This name into which have been baptized exudes the majesty and glory of the Lord and causes those who see us to experience nature of God. They may become afraid of us because of the name or be drawn to us because of the inherent majesty and holiness of that name. For this reason Moses says in Deuteronomy 32:3: "For I proclaim the name of the LORD: Ascribe greatness to our God."

This line of the prayer is so important because the name of the Lord is a battle sword by which we overcome. 1 Samuel 17:45: "Then David said to the Philistine, "You come to me with a sword, with a spear, and with a javelin. But *I come to you in the Name of the LORD of hosts,* the God of the armies of Israel, whom you have defied." The name of the Lord God our Father brings Divine offering into our lives and enhances peace. Out of that name flows blessing for the people of the LORD of hosts. The name is the source that births the stones that build the altar of lives. It is this hallowing of the name that holds the seed of our victory. Nowhere in the Bible is this victory in the name more pronounced than in Psalm 118:10-12; 26:

> "10 All nations surrounded me, But *in the name of the LORD I will destroy* them. 11 They surrounded me, Yes, they surrounded me; But *in the name of the LORD I will destroy* them. 12 They surrounded me like bees; They were quenched like a fire of thorns; For *in the name of the LORD I will destroy them.* . . . 26 Blessed is he who comes in the name of the LORD! We have blessed you from the house of the LORD."

One of the ways in which we hallow the name of the Lord is to sing as David said in Psalm 7:17: "I will praise the LORD according to His righteousness, And will sing praise to the name of the LORD Most High." The name deserves trust, remembrance, reverence, kingly glory, and declarative praise of the children of Zion. It is the majestic embodiment of splendor. So "Praise His name O servants of the LORD. Praise the name of the LORD." Hallowing the name is speaking well and saying with David, "Blessed be the name of the LORD, from this time forth and forevermore!" (Psalm 113:2) Salvation finds its ground and process in it. When we take up the name of the Lord, we take up the cup of salvation. It is by taking up the holiness of that name that we go up to the LORD himself and perfect our testimony in Israel. The holiness of the name engenders thanks to the LORD. To show that the name of the Lord is not distinguishable from the Lord Himself, the psalmist in 124:8 says, "Our help is in the name of the LORD, Who made Heaven and earth." Joel 2:32 says, "And it shall come to pass, that whosoever shall call on the name of the LORD shall be delivered: for in mount Zion and in Jerusalem shall be deliverance, as the LORD hath said, and in the remnant whom the LORD shall call." This is not just a onetime shouting out of the name but a continuous calling; of the name, in a sense it is to have the name of the LORD as our song. Yes indeed when we are in danger or dire need, we call out the name and we are delivered. I have had so many experiences in my Christian walk where just to call on the name of the Lord has wrought great deliverance.

When I was a young pastor in Jalingo in the Northern part of Nigeria and I was only 19 years of age, I saw the name of the Lord work out great power. No one told me that miracles did not happen. On several occasions I had encounters with people who practiced the witchcraft and deep devilish incantation. In one particular occasion, after witnessing to a man and his family, the wife and some of children gave their lives to Christ. The man with candor told me, "Tonight we shall see if what you preach is real." I taught he meant that he was coming to church that night to witness the power of the Lord. He did not come to church that evening. But in the middle of the night with all my doors and windows closed the man was in the room. He said to me, "Today you die and let's see if your God can deliver you." Immediately I began to sense the life going out of me. From the deep recess of my being I began chanting the name of the Lord Jesus Christ. He placed his hands on my mouth to keep me from making a sound. The name of the Lord whirled in my innermost being until like a flash of light it came bursting forth out of my mouth: "Jesus, Jesus, Jesus Christ, Son of God Savior." It was like beautiful Gregorian chant welling up in my soul and coming out with a powerful sound; it pierced the whole room and the man left the room as darkness disappears in the presence of light. The next morning he was moaning and crying on how he lost his power by attacking me in the night."

There are many incidents in which the Name of the Lord has been invoked and has wrought great deliverance in my life.

Once I had such strong urge in my spirit to sing the name of God for over two hours and ululate that name. I was caught up in the heavens and saw visions of wondrous things. When I left the house that evening armed robbers were waiting for me. With calm and ease I stood there and looked at the two men I could sense no fear but the presence of the Lord God into whose name I had been immersed for hours was so real. These two men with their weapons looked steadily upon me and their faces became pale and they took off running as fast as they could.

Whatever we need, whatever the situation, we can change them by immersing ourselves in the Name(s) of the Lord. We are saved not just because we say the name of God once, rather because we continually pray the name of the Lord and are hidden in that name. We have been baptized into the use of the Name. It is our birthright as sons and daughters of God to call on the Name(s) of the Lord. It is not my way to tell these things but I will tell one more and that will be it for this book so as not to take away from the Lord and the message of the book.

In 2007 while preaching in Lagos Nigeria, I had spent about five hours in prayer using various methods such as contemplation, meditative, mystery (praying in tongues) and the later part just chanting the Names of God and all the titles of the

Lord Jesus Christ. That evening at services, I had the church chant and sing the name of Jesus as we showered Him with titles befitting His Kingship. In the midst of the ululation, my eyes were opened and I saw companies of angels beautiful and radiant and some fearful. I remember saying to the church, "What are these angels doing here?" I was so caught in the glorious manifestation of Heaven I must have seemed out of it if I was not in Africa. After the service, still inebriated by the powerful presence of the Lord, we went into the car with a pastor George, his wife and another young man, Humphrey who helps me when I am in Nigeria preaching. They were all from Christian Pentecostal Mission headquarters in Ajao Estate Lagos. They were to take me to a hotel near the church. I was still chanting the name of the Lord. I found myself chanting quietly "Yod Heh Vav Heh and then Yeshua moshieny." At one moment I told the driver I did not like the road he was taking but he said it was okay. In fifteen minutes or so we ran into armed bandits with all sorts of weapon. They stopped the car and shot their guns into the air. Then they commanded everyone to get out the car but I sat there calmly as I was caught up in the beauty of the name of the Lord. Suddenly one of the bandits got angry and began to shout, "I am going to blow your head off." He placed the gun into the window upon my head as in a flash I saw the same angels I had seen at the church. He opened fire, but, to glory of God, he fell about fifteen feet away from the car. Everybody thought I was dead. The pastor's wife shouted "They have killed Bishop." But I responded "I am all right." The bandits panicked and began shooting into the air. I remember muttering, "Lord Jesus release them before they hurt anyone and they took off in a jeep, taking all my documents and all my money. That whole night I praised the name of the Lord; the next morning my documents were found intact.

The name of the LORD is strong tower. When we pray "hallowed be thine name" we should proceed to hallow the name and saturate our being and atmosphere with the name of the Lord. Be like David when you take up the cup of salvation, call upon the name of the LORD and hallow it. When you offer the sacrifice of thanksgiving, call upon the name of the LORD and hallow it. In proclaiming that God's names, you build a fortress around yourself and your family. When we sing, speak or even mutter the name of the Lord from our heart we attribute value to the Name and in so doing we release its inherent power. It is by calling the name of the Lord that we are saved from our enemies. (Psalm 55:16; Psalm 86:7) In the day of your trouble call on the name of the Lord for He will answer you.

HEBREW	ENGLISH	MEANING AND USE
*la	EL	The strong one. Should be used sparing alone because of its tendency to attracts the gods of the nations because the term is common for all that may be called God in all the world
mhla		God in all His Trinitarian majesty. Used to invoke the plenitude of Divine powers. Powerful as Name of agreement especially when used as YHVH ELHM. God in all His Trinitarian majesty. Powerful as Name of agreement.
iynda	ADNY	Lord, Master, a term for the rulership and mastery of God over all circumstances and being. Used more than 300 times the Bible. When used in combination with ADNY YHVH, it can really mean LORD of Lords. But also powerful to create unity where there is division among God's people.
Ydef la o yduf yx la	EL SHADAI	God all-sufficient; used to strengthen Abraham. (Gen. 17:2) Lord of the plenitude of all life.
hwhy	YHVH	The ineffable name of God. The root combination of all life as proceeding from God. The Self-Existent source of life.
Hyha rva hyha	AHIH ASHR AHIH	I AM that I AM; the name Divine deliverance from bondage revealed to Moses.
Hary hwhy	YHVH YRH	The Lord of provisional insight—who shows His people how to find provision in tough times. (Gen. 22:14)

Ysn hvhy	YHVH NYSY	The Lord who is the flag of victory in battle. The flag that remains forever standing—this is a battle name of the LORD dealing with particular battles not general war.
apwr hwhy	YHVH ROPHE	The LORD, the remover of diseases. To remove disease plagues and sickness.
Vdqm hwhy	YHVH MQDSH	The LORD of who sets apart in purity—the Lord the purifier, the sanctifier, able to make even the most unclean clean. While denoting holiness of God's it denotes God ability and power to make holy.
MWlv hwhy	YHVH SHLVM	The LORD, our fulfillment and wholeness. This is God as the source of the welfare and safety of His people.
H[r hwhy	YHVH ROEH	The LORD who is Shepherd, nurturer and guide, protector in a land of my vulnerability. (Ps. 23)
Wnqdc hwhy	YHVH TZDKNV	The LORD, our righteous balance in the scales of justice and mercy. (Jer. 23:5)
Hmv hwhy	YHVH SHMMH	The LORD who is ever present. Wherever you go HE is there. (Ezekiel 48:35)
Twabc hvhy	YHVH TZBTH	The LORD of Hosts is the LORD of the innumerable armies. This is the name of the LORD as it relates to war not just one battle.

Hawfy YSHVH JESUS
Given by God as source of Human salvation
Matt. 1:21;
Luke 1:31
This is the Name of Supreme Salvation given humankind
Acts 4:12
A summary of the Names of God in One. It is Above all Names named in Heaven, on earth, underneath the earth
Phil. 2:9-11
Wherefore God also hath highly exalted him, and given him a name which is above every name:10 That at the name of Jesus every knee should bow, of things in Heaven, and things in earth, and things under the earth; 11 And that every tongue should confess that Jesus Christ is Lord, to the glory of God the Father.

In our prayer life, the best way to hallow the name of the Father is to honor the name of the Son in whom the Father has implanted all of His Names and the functions of the Divinity in humanity. Many in the post-apostolic church used to chant the name of Jesus all day and reported tremendous experiences of grace through Jesus' name in prayer.

CHAPTER TEN

GOLDEN CORD

KEY 4: KINGDOM IMPERATORS CALL FORTH THE KINGDOM

Jesus told us to say *"Thy Kingdom come."*

evlqe,tw h` basilei,a soth the word "come" is translated the Greek *elthetow* which is an aorist active imperative third person denoting that it is a command, so it should read as an apostolic supernatural command to manifest the Kingdom of God in the context within which we find ourselves. This does not remove the call for the eschatological manifestation of the Kingdom of God. But if this statement is true that the prayer in the Greek speaks imperatively, something like this, "come, the Kingdom of you." We must then command the coming of the Kingdom by our faith. If indeed what we bind on earth is bound in Heaven, then we owe it to what we believe to speak imperatively that theKingdom of Him whom we serve be manifested in every sphere to which our King sends us. This must be our primary aim as it relates upon the earth. The primacy of the Kingdom of God cannot be overstated. In all that the Lord Jesus did, the Kingdom of God was primary. According to Matthew 6:33 and Mark 1:14-15:

> Now after that John was put in prison, Jesus came into Galilee, preaching the gospel of the Kingdom of God, 15 And saying, The time is fulfilled, and the Kingdom of God is at hand: repent ye, and believe the gospel.

Not only must we pray this imperative, we must make this an imperative lifestyle not just an imperative speech. We are told by the Lord Jesus Christ in

Matthew, "But seek ye first the Kingdom of God, and his righteousness; and all these things shall be added unto you." The Kingdom lifestyle is God-oriented and Christ-centered and Holy Spirit propelled and saints propagated. The Kingdom is life liberated from the false consciousness of cosmic materialism. It is supernatural and immortal life infused into the earth realm. It has its foundation, of course, in God whose desire is for us to participants in it. The Kingdom of God is not the domain of one particular group of people, but the diffusion of the name and nature of God into the world through those who believe in God's Son. When the Kingdom of God comes in any form, the old way of man vanishes and as Paul says, "behold all things are become new." The Kingdom is not a mere marginal insertion into the problems of those who find it or are born into it. It is the very constituent of their being in the world.

The Kingdom that must come is the structure by which the entire intents and purposes of God flow into manifestation. Kingdom is a barriers overcoming process. The coming of the Kingdom causes a face-to-face engagement with the structures and processes of the cosmos in light of the purpose of God. As we command the emergence of the Kingdom and respond honestly to its manifestation, we move toward the purpose for which God created the world, which is that the Kingdom of this world would become the Kingdom of our God and of His Messiah. But to see the Kingdom there has to be a transformation of affection from mere Eros to Agape. Part of how the Kingdom is manifested in our consciousness is by our praying it into our own being.

The Kingdom is the purification, illumination and beatification of the universe by the full presence of God. In the Kingdom, our beings are infused with glory through the Christ encounter. We preach up the Kingdom until the incarnational principle enters into our being and allows it to become manifest through us to the watching world. The Kingdom is not achieved by us but comes by direct Apostolic-prophetic appeal to the Will of God in Christ. It comes from God and is revealed within the web of human relationship as it becomes undergirded by God's love. The purpose then of the Kingdom is the restoration of dominion, subduing power

124

over the earth, ruling authority, Divine fruitfulness and multiplicative principle, and the replenishing capacity of humanity as the image of God upon the earth. The vitality of the coming Kingdom for which we pray can raise up new life which expresses itself in appropriate Divine forms. It is also by prayerful participation in its dynamic structure that we open its citizenry continuously to move toward what Teilhard de Chardin once called "the Omega point." The Kingdom for which the apostolic-prophetic voice calls refuses to be held captive by human institutional traditionalisms. Neither can it be overtaken completely by meat and drink and by belly-oriented emotional sentimentality, rather it bends toward righteousness, peace and joy in the Holy Spirit who is its propelling agency.

This Kingdom ought not to be confused with the church in its current institutionalism. The church as an institution like other institutions sometimes seeks to circumvent the Spirit that birthed it, to obliterate its dynamic mission for the maintenance of the status quo. Systems are created that deny the promptings of the foundational Spirit. But the call for the Kingdom to come is a challenge to such fossilized systems. The Kingdom is the spiritual force of the supernatural invading and transforming materialistic and naturalistic tendencies, which have arisen in the course of time by those who have lost its first dynamic sense. Being spiritual and dynamic, the Kingdom does not allow for total self-isolation but demands a multifaceted responsiveness to God as God continues to be revealed in the Word and the world. There is within us the Kingdom flow—the need to break out of old forms, de-fossilize and unthaw congealed forms that have taken over the church. This Kingdom for which call we apostolically and prophetically is constantly discarding old wine skins and old wine taste for new wine skins and fresh wine flowing from the innermost chamber of the Holy Spirit. It is in search for a form ready for its manifestation and use. We read in the KJV, "thou has prepared a body for me." I believe it should be read, "you continually prepare a body for me" The Kingdom suffered violence and the violent took it by force until the time of Christ. From the death of Christ, it does not arbitrarily impose itself upon the will of others but rather it signals Divine intentionality to the space, place and people who are called to embrace and respond to it in love and freedom. It is not propagated by fear and violence but by righteousness, peace and love. So if we are to pray this "come Kingdom of yours," we must overcome our fear of the surging waves of new becoming and respond without reserve to the dynamic urge and agency of the Spirit of that Kingdom.

Every structural flow purporting to be a manifestation of that line of prayer, "Thy Kingdom come," must be tested following John injunction, "try every spirit to see if they are true." The Kingdom is not of the world, therefore, we should not try to conform it to the worldly system nor use the world's system as the primary means to assess it. What we call lack of order by the system of the world and unconventionality by the status quo convention maybe the Spirit's Kingdom dynamic refusing to be hemmed in by natural man into old wine skins. We may not know "whence it cometh and "whither it goeth" (John 3), as the Master said, "Yet, blow, it must and flow, it must. "If we discern and follow its currents, we would experience its power. The Kingdom is always searching for appropriate forms of expression; we should be open to be formed into that which is appropriate for its manifestation at every given epoch.

To call the Kingdom, "come Kingdom of you," we need to ask the hard question of religious, political social-cultural ideas, forms and structures. If we watch the Master Jesus Christ, we notice how He called these institutions to answer the tough questions concerning the mind and purpose of God. When religion, society, or culture offered answers that had nothing to do with the Kingdom of God and the move of the Spirit, He called them to account and offered new ways of the world and people that liberated from false religious consciousness. In His interaction, we see that the Kingdom is usually unconventional and on the margin of institutional conventionality, religious systems and traditions which men have made for themselves. Such institutions and systems even traditions have made themselves enemies of spiritual renewal by unbiblical conservatism and ungodly liberalism. Both are sterile ideological systems of materialistic conventionality that have no true openness to supernatural manifestations which Christ intended for the church. The Kingdom calls us to move beyond these systems into the heart and purpose of God for the world. If we want the Kingdom to manifest in us and around us with power, our prayers need to be seasoned with the consciousness of the Kingdom. When we call "come, the Kingdom of yours," we are calling for a confrontation of powers and dialectic engagement of wills within the sphere in which we seek to see the Kingdom come. It involves casting out the devils and structure to which they have attached themselves, be it in community, clan or person. We know then that our call for the manifestation of the Kingdom of God is heard when we are able by the power of the King of our Kingdom to cast out devils. We read in Matthew 12:28: "But if I cast out devils by the Spirit of God, then the Kingdom of God is come unto you." The very personal aspect of this concept is also revealed in the following passage, Mark 9:47: "And if thine eye offend thee, pluck it out: it is better for thee to enter into the Kingdom of God with one eye, than having two eyes to be cast into hell fire." It is only by praying the Kingdom that we cast out the all that has sought to usurp the place of the King our lives.

Calling on the Kingdom to come is to call for change in the fundamental mode by which we transact relational business in the world. The world says make it easier for the rich and the famous to enter; "bring them in, bring them in," it cries, "but keep the needy outside." The Kingdom turns that upside down and says in Matthew 19:24: "It is easier for a camel to go through the eye of a needle, than for a rich man to enter into the Kingdom of God"—an offense to the present greed peddlers in the name of the Gospel. The world system insists that the self-righteous, the prosperous and the arrogant are going to inherit the world, but the Kingdom says, "The publicans and the harlots may actually go into the Kingdom of God before you." The world system says, "let the adults stand in the way of children, abort them because they are mere inconveniences; and make them second class citizens in the Kingdom of man and of God." The Kingdom of God says in Mark 10:14: "Suffer the little children to come unto me, and forbid them not: for of such is the Kingdom of God." The world system says, "Get yourself together and straighten up before you can come to our god and inner circle." The Kingdom says, "come unto me all you that are weak and heavy ladened and I will give you rest." The King says, "I will make your yoke easy and burden light." The world system is full of disease but the Kingdom of God for which we call comes to bring healing. The King of this Kingdom sends His emissaries with these words: Luke 9:2: "And he sent them to preach the Kingdom of God, and to heal the sick." Luke 9:11: "And the people, when they knew it, followed him: and he received them, and spake unto them of the Kingdom of God, and healed them that had need of healing." Luke 10:9 "And heal the sick that are therein, and say unto them, the Kingdom of God is come nigh unto you." Religion and its system say, "We will put obstacles on your path to the Kingdom; the Kingdom itself says, in Mark 12:34 clearly "you are not far from the Kingdom of God." The world is filled with hate but the Kingdom for which we pray, comes in love and brings love. The transformation of the worldly consciousness to God consciousness marks the coming of the Kingdom of God. The Kingdom comes to us as a Divine mystery spoken among the mature and speaks wisdom. God is our Father, God's name is for us, and this Kingdom is from God. We cast our Father's word-seed into the ground that the world might live through it. It is a Kingdom of life, peace, grace, love and righteousness and all who stand within it shall not taste of death, because they have seen the Kingdom of God come with power and glory within their sphere of living.

Because the Kingdom is an inner principle, it must begin in inner motion flowing from the depth of the heart of man. It must issue forth from the heart the place of which the Scripture says, "Are the issues of life." Thus, when it comes near ,there is a revolution in the heart of those to whom its draws near. This is why Matthew 3:2 says the Lord came "saying, Repent ye: for the Kingdom of Heaven is at hand." When we begin to pray "come Kingdom of God," we in fact stir up repentance toward the Kingdom of Heaven begin to be moved by its urgency. Repentance was preached based on the nearness of the Kingdom of Heaven. Human beings need to understand the bankruptcy and ineptitude of spirit in which they live. The Kingdom calls us to become poor in spirit. This understanding of poverty is Kingdom principle that reverses our bankruptcy and ineptitude into blessedness and thrusting us into the possession of the Kingdom of Heaven. This poverty must be evidence by the motion to repentance that in a sense draws the Kingdom, by Divine magnetic impulse into the innermost being of man.

This calling forth of the Kingdom is meant to fortify us for righteousness so that we stand even when this repentance leading to righteousness causes us to be persecuted. When we imperatively call the Kingdom, we state that we will do so by more than words. By being fortified in suffering for righteousness, we not only possess the Kingdom of Heaven but we call it forth into the lives of others even if they hate us and pour calumny on us. Our prayer for the Kingdom breaks through the command centers and strongholds of the enemy and teaches men to open up for the entrance of the Kingdom of Heaven. So by our prayer, we command and teach the necessity of the Kingdom of Heaven for human greatness. Calling the Kingdom is of itself a stance of righteousness since the least of the Kingdom of God is more than the greatest prophet of the law. This Kingdom consciousness causes the imperator to exceed the scribes' and pharisees' purported righteousness and causes those who call for it to live life being saturated in their whole being with the Kingdom of Heaven.

We call forth the Kingdom because we desire that people enter into the Kingdom of Heaven and do the will of the Father. The will of the Father is to "believe in the one whom He has sent." When we say "come Kingdom of God," our voice reaches to the East and West, North and South and shall sit down with Abraham and Isaac and Jacob in the Kingdom of Heaven. We proclaim the Kingdom of Heaven and command the world to respond to it. Our voice rings among men and women to raise a great host baptized into the Spirit of Christ and making the least of them greater than the enemy of faith. This "thy Kingdom come" is God's answer through us. In our calling forth of the Kingdom through Jesus Christ, the mysteries of the Kingdom of Heaven are opened to those who seek them. Jesus Christ tells us that "The Kingdom of Heaven is likened unto a man who sowed good seed in his field." Our prayer in this vein is like seed poured forth into the ground of human hearts.

Calling forth the Kingdom, we put into practice Matthew 13:31. In this simple line: "thy Kingdom come," we carry the Kingdom of Heaven like a grain of mustard seed sowed into the atmosphere and into the field of men's heart. By it we leaven the whole world with Kingdom vibration and harmonize God and humanity and human beings to one another. The Kingdom of Heaven is full of treasures, hidden and prepared for joy of the world. Our voice is needed. We must pray "thy Kingdom come." By this we call forth merchants with the heart to seek its goodly pearls at all cost. Reader, cast your Kingdom prayer like a net into the sea and gather of every kind fish. This is the command of the Lord.

Humility is an inner vibration in those who pray this Kingdom. By this we do not mean a beggarly attitude in prayer, rather a proportionate view ourselves in light of grace. Matthew 18:1: "At the same time came the disciples unto Jesus, saying, Who is the greatest in the Kingdom of Heaven?" Matthew 18:3-4: "And said, Verily I say unto you, Except ye be converted, and become as little children, ye shall not enter into the Kingdom of Heaven. 4 Whosoever therefore shall humble himself as this little child, the same is greatest in the Kingdom of Heaven." This inner vibration of humility is reiterated in Matthew 19:14: "But Jesus said, Suffer little children, and forbid them not, to come unto me: for of such is the Kingdom of Heaven." When we pray thus, we call it forth for our King. We call forth all creation as His servants to account. (Matthew 18:23.) Call it forth laborers by this prayer. (Matthew 20:1) In this prayer we call forth His friends to the marriage feast of the King's beloved Son. (Matthew 22:2)

Praying "thy Kingdom come" or "come Kingdom of you" means, for the average person, the alignment of the subjective feelings, emotions and sensations to the ideal world of Heaven. It means walking in the Spirit and inclining the hope of one's being towards Heaven. The Kingdom calls us to move our body, power of mind and all its potential into becoming the arena of Divine activity. In the Kingdom our common duality is transcended. Praying this prayer with our whole being can cause us to experience, going in and out a variety of dimensions of reality. In fact the Kingdom shakes our rationalistic perspective for it calls us to transcend our mechanistic view of the world and to enter into spirituality that meshes the boundary of the world. Jesus' statement, "except you become as a little child you cannot enter the Kingdom of God" calls you to open up your inner imagination to infinite possibility beyond anything you can even comprehend. This metaphorical transcendence reverses our static universe and does not set well with our adult rationality. We see this in the response of Nicodemus: "How can a man reverts to his mother's womb and be born again?" The Kingdom of God that we call to be manifested on the earth as it is in Heaven at once shakes our view of reality. It turns upside down our criteria for accepted acceptability and puts in its place and offensive idealism. This principle is carried futher when Paul said, "there is neither Jew nor Gentile, male nor female, slave nor free" and I will neither rich nor poor. Now if the Kingdom removes the demarcation fixed by men upon themselves and upon others, it causes those who have come into its purview to move into faith lifestyle. It means us thats in the Kingdom things are not judged by our opinion or even experiences but by God's purpose and end goal.

When the Kingdom comes, the spirit-body problem is solved, the Heaven and earth problem is solved; the male-female problem is solved and the God-man problem is solved; the issue of exterior-interior is solved because the Kingdom is the restoration of the harmony of the universe as God intended from the beginning. As for the external internal problem, the Kingdom that is coming is already inside the believer. Jesus said, "The Kingdom is within you." The one who is bale to pray, this is one who has received the Kingdom in whom there has been what the Bible calls reconciliation. In his life the fullness of God dwells and its Divine character and kingship is carried about by such a one. Although this is hard for some to believe, the Kingdom is in person as he or she receives it. It is quite obvious that the Kingdom of Heaven, of God, will not come into our natural realm unless it first comes into human being.

There is a profound difference between the life of one who believes and accepts this Kingdom in its fullness from one who sees the Kingdom merely as what appears at the end of life. To be engaged by the Kingdom of God as revealed in Christ's and now revealed in us is to realign us with God's intention for creation. The Kingdom that comes to earth as it is in Heaven is a Kingdom of communion.

This communion as John states in first John is between us the Father, the Son, the Holy Spirit and each other. It is the removal of enmity both Divine and human. If indeed in Jesus Christ this Kingdom has been revealed and He is the living Word who structures this Kingdom, then our path must follow His example. In order to speak meaningfully of the Kingdom we must ask: How and when has it been seen? And for all us who believe, this how and when is answered in the "who" of Jesus the Christ the Son of God.

If the Kingdom is embodied in the person of Christ, then the purpose of the Kingdom is also manifested in what he can to do and does do. The Kingdom comes to Earth's as a way to deal with the dehumanization of sin and the entrapment of man by evil. If indeed the Kingdom is embodied in Christ, then our being in Christ puts us in the heart of the Kingdom. The Kingdom as I have said is a fellowship with its root in God's love. Its source is God from whom it springs. The very atmosphere in which it thrives is the love of God, His righteousness and His peace. When love reigns on earth, the Kingdom move becomes irresistible and irreversible. Because the Kingdom is a Kingdom of love grounded in the love of God, it has sufficient power to conquer the innate selfishness of human hearts. In speaking of the Kingdom Paul said, "The Kingdom of God is not meat and drink but righteousness peace and joy in the Holy Ghost."

We can list several things which are part of the Kingdom into which we enter when we pray this prayer:

(1) It is a Kingdom of truths, so we open up and enter dimensions of truth;

(2) It is a Kingdom of faith, so we enter dimensions of faith that brings release;

(3) It is a Kingdom of grace, so we enter into dimensions of grace-filled walk;

(4) It is a Kingdom of holiness so we open up to ourselves power to walk in holiness;

(5) It is a Kingdom of wisdom and revelation, so we enter into vistas of revelation hitherto unknown;

(6) It is a Kingdom of righteousness, so we become the righteousness of God;

(7) It is the Kingdom of peace, so have peace;

(8) It is a Kingdom of Divine exuberance, so we live in joyful exuberance;

(9) It is a Kingdom of dynamic power, so we receive power over all the powers of the enemy;

(10) It is a Kingdom of His love, so we manifest love for one another and for the lost;

(11) It is a Kingdom of His life, so we live life more abundantly;

(12) It is a Kingdom of His glory, so we move from glory to glory; and most of all,

(13) It is the Kingdom of God our Father, and we are children of God.

So when we pray, "thy Kingdom come" or "come Kingdom of yours," we open up to an indwelling presence that aligns us to all of the above. The entire concepts as articulated above are embodied in God's Son, Jesus Christ. These are wave patterns of the Kingdom of Heaven as they are manifestation on the earth and in the lives of those who pray for the Kingdom to come.

The Kingdom comes through Divine communication and is manifest wherever there is a communicative process of the Kingdom. The Kingdom that we ask in prayer to come to earth is not some sort ethereal occult communication, rather it is a communication from the throne room of God which influences through and through the live of those whose souls have been invaded and transformed by the idea of this Kingdom. Jesus put it this way, "Seek ye first the Kingdom of God and his righteousness and all these things shall be added unto you." The Kingdom coming to earth is to enhance God's influence and prestige by recounting all the marvelous works and qualities, which God has manifested in the house of His creation.

There is also another side to this which in our coming to the Kingdom allows us to enhance our influence in both spheres. It enhances our personal attributes, revolutionizes our disposition, imports at our disposal supernatural resources both in terms of or enhanced health, emotional strengths and spiritual insights. Furthermore, it enhances the strength of our will in the expression of its moral and social strengths. It is not uncommon to see those who have been regarded as non influential after coming into the Kingdom gaining a level of influence that is neither due to the level of their education, pedigree or hard work but mainly due to the connection to the Kingdom. This Kingdom flowing influence in many cases has enhanced property holdings and certain knowledge in the broad sense which has no other reference except the Kingdom to which they have been connected.

Because the Kingdom changes human disposition, it lends itself to the transformation of the familial consciousness as well as the tribal consciousness of those it has affected. It does so because, coming from Heaven and manifesting in the material world, it brings with it new set of interactive systems responsible not to the earthly arena but to a Kingdom far more superior than anything less and other. Its point of view is motivated by a deeper and higher dimension of thought and imagination grounded in God. By saying these I do not mean that the Kingdom is merely for peddling influences and prestige but rather that its power is so strong and so irresistible that those who embody it have an influence disproportionate to their social status and number. Though we pray for the Kingdom to come to earth as in Heaven, the Kingdom cannot be an earthly Kingdom. It must be a heavenly Kingdom. The Kingdom of this world cannot just be the Kingdom of this world. It must become as we read in revelation, "the Kingdom of our Lord and of his Christ." Here we must take warning: We cannot reduce this Kingdom to mere human ideology. This is why the Kingdom is an object of prayer—so that it remains in the realm of Divine sovereignty, holiness and majesty.

Of course the Kingdom coming to earth and the Kingdom of this world becoming the Kingdom of our God entails the usage of every dimension of human existence as communicative instruments for the glory of God. Again herein lays the danger that so easily besets man. The danger is that the Kingdom would become human economics, human education, and human media mongering, human social uplift, human religious systems, human prejudice aimed at protecting human greed, arrogance and partisanship.

Being conscious of the Kingdom through prayer helps us develop a new attitude of introspective spirituality which helps us discover ourselves as we are, the real we rather than received set of systems given to us by people who want us to avoid examining ourselves from the Divine perspective of the Kingdom as fully expressed in the person of Jesus Christ. The Kingdom is man's origin and destiny. It is in the Kingdom of God that the true nature of human beings is revealed. We pray thus because the Kingdom is the necessary and sufficient condition for discovery of who we are. We cannot be truly sincere about who we are all until the Kingdom comes into our lives. The very nature of the Kingdom that we call generates a type of virtue contrary in its essence to the unnatural ways of doing things to which we are so accustomed. Jesus Christ devoted His lifetime to outlining of the Kingdom. Anyone who wants honestly to see the Kingdom on earth will do well to recall that without Christ in the human affair any Kingdom building is doomed to failure. It manifestation will always escape human grasp as long as they hold to a false idea of God, self and the world. Praying "Kingdom come" is a way of facing the fact that this Kingdom which is coming to birth on the Earth stems from within God's mined in eternity and is manifested in and through us upon whom the fullness of time has come. This Kingdom is being made manifest as we welcome the disciplinary impression of the Holy Spirit upon our mind, soul, spirit and body. And as we open up to this move of the spirit over the waters of our chaos, the Kingdom of light closes in upon our portable lights and the connecting causes and explosion of light in the universe. We then move from one state of being to another. Our words communicated in the sphere of the Kingdom of God pierces to all the dimensions. It does not just lead to introspection, which causes change in our person but also changes everything we touch. "Thy Kingdom come" is not merely a gassing of ourselves, rather it is a focus on God and His glory which exhausts us of ourselves and causes us to lose all carnal capacity for false relationships with the world, with God, and with other human beings. We are transported from narrow, deformed, defensive stance against God to enlargement of soul and openness to the inexhaustible depth of God.

When the Kingdom comes as we pray, it commands an entrusting faith that throws us completely into the unsearchable abyss of divinity. This coming of the Kingdom into the Earth calls forth an expansion of time and space and in actuality an expansion of emotion and intellect resulting in an expansion of care. That expansion of care develops in us a stance that warrants our confidence in the possible transformation and remaking of everything. From its perspective, our rambling life suddenly takes on illuminative excitement; and the contradictions, or seemingly so, become reconciled. The Kingdom remains a mystery. However, when it has come into our lives, we tie into the one who is an unfathomable mystery whose Spirit elucidated and clarifies it within us. The fact that the Spirit of God who has delved into our innermost being takes rule and dominion over us opens our eyes to see His story as our story, our lives as the Kingdom in motion. So to pray for the Kingdom to come on earth as it is in Heaven is not a mere pursuit of a chimera rather it is a taking hold of the things, which as the book of Hebrews says, "cannot be shaken." (Hebrews 12) The Kingdom in its coming inscribes in us knowledge of the sameness of God and of His Christ not contradicted by the artificial ebb and flow of worldly illusions. The Kingdom, which comes on earth as in Heaven, comes spontaneously and infuses spontaneity so that the man of the Spirit, like the wind cannot be predicted. This is what makes the Kingdom and its movement, so humbling and overwhelming to those who have found it or have been found by it. To those who have not found it, it presents a level of confusion and unnerving which they cannot explain. Oh, but its discovery—for the person who has called out truly, "come Kingdom of you," and has tasted its beauty—it is sweeter than honey in the honeycomb. Just by praying this prayer, we are in the presence of a force so loving, so caring, so compassionate and so sweet and flowing into unending joy.

Living in authentic joy or peace or righteousness is not possible without the coming of this Kingdom. To say "come Kingdom of you" is to ask for the incarnation of the Word. It is a call for God to assume the form of this created world. To say this prayer is not just to believe in the present age as inhabiting God's possibility but see the possibility of its eternal transformation. Saying "come Kingdom of God" is to reject the structures of human ideology as the norm of things and to infuse the world and ourselves with Divine sound and thought and to activate the Divine DNA so that the present gives way to something completely new. The Kingdom is not rules, moralities, legal systems or rituals which turn us into automatons and self-righteous sleep walkers deprived of Divinity, rather it is the intentional illumination of our darkness with its contrary-light. It is only here, in the coming of the Kingdom, that true creativity, love, evangelism, prophetic utterance, apostolic move, pastoral spirit and pedagogical zeal flows into us and our world. What is the Kingdom? Is it not the infusion of Divine Word from eternity into our present? The Kingdom, as Paul tells us, is not just words but the acting out of God as love. Only in the Kingdom can we know God. "Thy Kingdom come" is the best place to begin for him or her who seeks to know God and to obey Him. It is the linchpin of authentic prophetic imagination.

For those who are so the bent on what they say is "real" we insist that the Kingdom is real in the sense of being rooted in the ultimate. Its realness really, has nothing in common with worldly realism. It is not what we call real in our superficial materialism. In fact our illusive reality directly contradicts the reality of the Kingdom. One of the first ways in which the Kingdom for which we pray contradicts our idea of what we call real is in the fact that it is a spiritual Kingdom. Here again is the truth that the current church—Babel with its materialistic pretentions—does not want to admit. In fact the modern church is so bent on condemning the spirituality of the Kingdom as being "merely" spiritual, as if the "Spirit" can be called "mere." Our world reality is meat and drink but that is not the Kingdom reality. We are told, in no uncertain terms by Paul, the Apostle, that it is "righteousness, peace and joy." The reality of the world is sin, war and sadness or pretentious joy. The vision of the Kingdom resides in the "Spirit," not the banal conversation of self-competing egos and material measurements that are not directed to the person of the Son of God. It is not escape from "reality," whatever that may be, but the insertion of Divine reality into the "unreal" world of human illusion. Another contradiction is that in this Kingdom into which we are called "walking by sight" is contrasted to "walking by faith."

Now this "come Kingdom of yours" is a call to the transcendent level of life to reach out to us and awake us from our sleepwalking nightmare. Once we say this prayer, we either consciously or inadvertently accept that our so-called reality is a nightmare from which we cannot wake ourselves and thus stand in desperate need of a transcendent wakeup-call. We cannot undo the ravages of our greed, lusts and materialistic delusions. It will take a spiritual revolution which unclad our rags of certainty without faith. Faith is not these worldly assertions but revelational affirmations which contradict the so-called rational course of things. Again I must reiterate that the life of faith is expressed completely and perfectly in the contradictory life of Jesus Christ. Contradictory, not in character but in contrast to what the world considers important. Being God, He became man; being rich He became poor; being eternal He subjected Himself to time; being Lord He became a servant; being Life He died; being Holy He became sin. To call the Kingdom to come into our lives and into our world is to set us up for trouble with the world. In this sense many of us are not in the Kingdom. It has not come to us. The world is too comfortable with us. Rules, regulations, moralities and laws cannot bind the Kingdom. In fact where it comes as we see in the life of Jesus, it messes with the so-called standard of righteousness which we have set up in the name of God. If this is not so, then we must look to furnish a reason why Jesus Himself and almost all who followed him died at the hands of the world because of their belief in God. All of this is summed up when with all of our hearts we pray "thine Kingdom come."

CHAPTER ELEVEN

GOLDEN CORD

KEY 5: ALIGNING WILL TO WILL ON EARTH AS IT IS IN HEAVEN

"Thy will be done in earth, as it is in Heaven." Matt. 6; Luke 11

How do we unlock the floodgates of Heaven and allow to the Kingdom to manifest on earth in our earthen vessel here and now? In this chapter, we focus on the will as a way to propel us into effective prayer. The human will serves as the transitional key for moving the sound of Heaven to the earth. In the lower sphere it also serves as the key which allows or disallows the influence of others in our lives. It is through the act of the human will that what is in Heaven is translated into the earth realm—what is God is transmuted into what is human. By key of the human will, the blessings of Heaven are trans-located to earth or held up in the ethereal realm. Will is key to the opening of the Iron Gate for the release of the fullness of Heaven to man. Conversely, it can lock the gate and keep man and his earth realm from experiencing Heaven's fullness. So we can see the importance of this line of prayer: "Thy will be done on earth as it is in Heaven."

This chapter proposes to deal with the question: If Heaven is the place where God reigns as King and is the paradigmatic mode for the kingship of God over the whole world, what is the key that can be used to speed up that manifestation on earth and in human life? The simplest answer to this question is this: the Kingdom of God must first come into man as the model of God on earth." The Will of God must first come into the sphere of man as a being capable of exercising free will in the acceptance of the Will of God. The Kingdom of Heaven must be accepted into the heart of man so that as "the LORD is God in Heaven above, He may be so upon the earth beneath." There must be no room for anyone else to be the Lord and God. (Deut 26:15) If the heavens are the "holy habitation" from which God blesses the people of Israel and the land God has given them, so man who is taken from the earth must become the holy habitation of God. But this cannot happen unless the structures and processes of Heaven are duplicated or birthed into the sphere of humanity so that both the land and the life of man flows with milk and honey. Ultimately, man is the habitation of God, for man is made in the image of God and is intended to become like God. But for man to become truly like God, His Will must be submitted to the Will of God.

As you read the Lord's Prayer, you will notice that "Thy Kingdom come" occurs between "hallowed be thy Name" and the prophetic call for the manifestation of the Will of God upon earth as it is in Heaven. What the world lacks is the structure for manifesting the Kingdom of God or the pipelines for the Will of God to be done on earth. The problem is the misalignment of the will of man to the Will of God because man does not want to submit. The solution is in the submission and connection of man's will to the Will of God so that the Kingdom can flow freely through it to this sphere.

The Will is foundation to spirituality. The Will of God, is important for the manifestation of the Kingdom of God. For in man's willingness to do the Will of God the way is paved for the manifestation of the Kingdom of God in our sphere here on earth. This is one reason why Jesus, our Master taught us to pray "thy will be done on earth as it is in Heaven." 1 Peter 4:2 tells us that our power and effectiveness lies in moving away from the desire of our flesh to doing the Will of God. Isaiah 1:9 says, "if you are willing and obedient you shall eat of the fruit of the land." The key to our fruitfulness and abundance is in the orientation of our will. The passage from Isaiah suggests that most of our problems in the area of prosperity lie in the area of our will. If we no longer want to live the rest of our time in the flesh subject to the lusts of men, we must surrender our will to the Will of God.

140

The question then naturally arises: What is will? Specifically, "What is the Will of God? Secondarily, What is will in man? And what is the relation of the will of Man to the Will of God? How is the Will of God to be done on earth? Asking the Will of God to be done in our lives is the place to begin. "Thy will be done on earth as it is in Heaven" is one of the keys to unlock great things in this hour as it was for the Lord in the Garden. This line of prayer is sweeping and far reaching. Its power can reach into the depths and frontiers of our consciousness and self.

DEFINITION OF WILL

Definition of will in this book begins with the words used in the Scriptures. In this definition I hope to show that the will is not the same as the soul or the spirit or the emotions or the body. The will is the crown worn over the soul and the body serving as the point of contact between the Spirit of God and man's life..

The Hebrew word *ratzon* meaning "will" is the spiritual principle that serves as the valve that opens the flow of all that comes from being. It is the nerve center of the all the activities of being. It is so powerful nothing can stand in its ways when it is full of forcefulness. The will is a pervasive power over the soul that determines purpose and destiny. In a sense the will is the original or the head of the soul. It is the crown of being. The enemy of our soul focuses on poisoning the soul because he understands that is the formative instrumental flow of divinity passes. It is in our will that we as fallen man are like God. In the goodness of the will lies our connection to God. In the evil of human will lies our separation from God. Because it is at the level of "originality," it gives no reason for its existence. This is the basis of the problem which modern scientific psychology has with the concept of will. There is no explanation of its existence but it is there.

It is in the will of man that wisdom finds itself concealed waiting to flow out in understanding, knowledge and action. In the Bible the will of man is sometimes identified with heart but never with the soul. The will gives the soul "right" of existence and rite of passage to manifest its purpose, ill or good. The Bible says "guard your heart (will) with all diligence for out of it are the issues of life." Thus,

141

the will is supra-rational, supra-emotive in its nature. It serves to control and direct from above and in sovereignty over all of the soul's movements and stands majestically in its strength between the spirit and the soul and can bypass the soul to act upon the body for its own purpose. It also allows or disallows what the thought will think or what desire will desire. If in folly it may block God Himself from entrance into the life of a man. The rational mind in its entire prowess may choose, but the power to make choice and to pursue those chosen objectives rationally and to act on them by the mind and might are the prerogative of the will. As powerful as the Divine Will may be when dealing with non-rational creation, it finds itself thwarted by the sovereignty of the human will. This is seen in the fact that the Divine Will, when it comes to man, is expressed essentially in the commandments given to Israel in the Torah by Moses, the man of God. God allows the possibility that man by His Will may reject and refuse or by the same will may choose to accept and embrace. The way God phrases the commands "thou shall not" and "if you" shows that the will is at the human will is at the center of the commandments. The will of man sits in judgment over the possibility of obedience or disobedience. The commandments express the power of that will.

In the Greek New Testament, will is translated from two words; the one is the word boule (pronounced boo-lay) "volition," which has the sense of advice and by extension may imply purpose. When Stephen says, "David served his generation by the Will of God," he is speaking by of the counsel of God or God's advice. Of course God gives counsel based on His Will and purpose. The other word which occurs in the New Testament is the word thelema (pronounced thel'-ay-mah) meaning determination of the fundamental property of a thing. It refers to that which gives a thing active movement. In human beings it refers to the tendency toward choice. It is the determiner of purpose of an act. When you will something, you choose to incline something or someone one way or another. The word *thelema* which Paul uses in the "the Will of God" (Grk **thelema tou Theou**) finds its root in *thel'-o* which means to determine a subjective state that is disposed to something. *Thelema* speaks also to intention which drives certain action. It is therefore that which determines the compatibility of an act with one's nature. When one wills, one desires and in turn the willing is meant to produce pleasure in the one who wills or pain in another who rebels. Both words point in the direction of the human will and its sovereignty in human thought and actions.

The will is sovereign in man as the Divine Will is sovereign in God. As the sovereign decision making instrument in being, the will is the instrument of synthesis. The will synthesizes the "I" and the action. In it, adheres coherence of the past the present and the future. There in its freedom, possibility of being and non-being abide in their purity. It is by the will that man exists as the image of God since the fall. This is why deficiency in will results in evil action. Its nature as the synthesizing element makes the will the principle of human becoming. From its fountain the spring of righteousness bubbles up and is revealed in the life of a human being. From it may also flow the foul waters of evil that can overtake one's life. The will must be the focus of discipline, intense education, spiritual in-pouring, for it to spring forth that righteous in the sight of God. Heaven and earth, life and death, center on two words: "yes" and "no," which is the declaration of the will in its fundamental freedom. In the will lies the kingly majesty of decision, direction, destiny and divinity. This is why the Lord Jesus Christ prayed ***"Father if thou art willing, remove this cup from Me; yet not My will but Thine be done."*** (Lk. 22:42 NASV) The Lord could pray this prayer because He had spent His whole life disciplining His Will and surrendering it in every act to the Will of the Father. This is why He gave us this line. "Thy Will be done, is a vital prayer for this season.

Hidden in the inner sanctum of the will is the possibility of our sonship and divinity. Inside our will this divinity lies dormant. Dammed up in its reservoir is the Kingdom of Heaven waiting to flow powerfully into the world. Our thoughts, imaginations, reveries and visions must pass through the majesterium of the will. The will is not the product of emotional stimuli or even the flow of ideas though they may serve to strengthen or weaken it only if it so wills. The act flowing from the will of man is the supreme expression of the personality. We meet an act of will only when an action is apprehended in distinct consciousness, deliberated upon and left to be determined by the free choice not swayed by pressing emotions. The human will is intrinsically attached to freedom and intimately connected to it. Thus, when anyone asks for the Will of God to be done such a one intends to surrender to God's Sovereignty at the very basic level. In a sense, I stop pretending to be free and independent and allow myself to become dependent on God by freely submitting my will to God.

In this freedom to give over the will to God's sovereignty consists the true efficacy of the will. Freedom is at the heart of the connection of the human will to the Divine Will. The uniqueness of will is that will can have no content other than that supplied by the involuntary flow of ideas from that which is beyond itself. It is to touch this supra-rational source that we pray, "Thy will be done on earth as it is in Heaven." Since our will, content with unrestricted freedom of choice, stands as gatekeeper over all other content bearing faculty of being—owning none yet controlling all by its majesty—we must flee to a greater will. In us the will is the principle of resolution between ideas and intentions standing between determination and alteration. It is a good thing, but history is full of evidence that the human will can and has been known to gradually accumulate and diffuse itself in opposition to Divine Will. We have no guarantee that human will, left to itself in its fallen state, can always mingle together with God's Will so that they can act upon one another in harmony. No chance in a million years, except the will of man is given over to God as the Perfect Will. This is why God choose to freely allow human will the choice to come into conjunction with the Divine Will; so that by submission, submersion and willingly turning itself over to the sovereign Will of God, both can end up in the practical out-working of the Kingdom process.

The Divine Will must direct our will and limit our will even in our freedom. The limit of our misuse of the power of our will can only be occasioned by dread and reverence that comes from the fact that we have submitted and submerged our will to the greater Will of God . The disturbance of the outer world is never the limit to human will but God as God puts a limit to human will. Thus, our will is only truly free in relation to the connection to God's nature.

The internal connection of WILL to will, which possesses unlimited freedom of resolution of the battle within and without, can only come by the united stability of our personal will resting on the broad security of the foundation of Divine Good Will to which our existence and the sum of our impression abide. It is only in this link of Will to will that we find perpetual Will of God combined with the will of moral existential efficiency. Only God's Will is sufficient cause. It has the capacity to combine the manifold waves of our being in relationship with the ultimate. God's Will is the clear pipeline of communicative holy actions. The Will of God combined with the submitted will of man makes possible ideational interaction with the world that leads to righteousness and transformation. It is this will submitted in prayer to the Will of God that is the principle of resolution of our existential crises. God's Will and our will in prayer affects our motivation. If this is true, then our will must come under critical examination. But the truth is that for the sake of emotional convenience many of us do not regard our will with intense examination and thus miss how the failure or the weakening of the will may actually be a hindrance to our understanding of the motives that lay behind our actions or desires. We can become acquainted with our will by exercising keen observation of our choices and the inner processes by which they are made. We cannot allow ourselves to disregard the process of our will because the influence of our will on our mind and body requires serious attention. The work we must do on our will must focus on how we allow our thoughts to flow through the various levels of our consciousness. All that which comes in time and space passes through the channel of the will are not necessarily good for us. So we must submit our will to God by praying, "Thy Will not mine be done."

Another point about the will is this it is by the act of will that attention is given, sustained and applied to the thought life and the spiritual life. The permission of the will at the helm of human choice allows the sanctification of our acts. Due to this act of the will, it is wrong to describe the will as a blind faculty. It is fundamentally pragmatic. It, therefore, if left to itself will choose the easiest act and the quicker process without considering the impact on the whole person. Nonetheless, it is the springboard, the root from which speculative thought finds its bearing. I admit with Dun Scotus that it is an integral part of all that flows into human thought and its outcome and, therefore, rational at its very roots.

Now let's ask the second question posed in the beginning of this chapter. What really is the Will of God? To ask the question as I have stated it makes it seem that Will is a possession which God "has" as one may possess an article which one may discard when one is done with it. But that would be the wrong way to view God's Will. Since Will in God is the most universal characteristic manifestation of who God is, it expresses the very essence of God as God. It is His Will that God seeks to express everywhere in all that He does with terrestrial as well as celestial life. Will in God is indeed the creative universal element which gives purpose and fulfillment to all which exist. As there is one God, so there is one absolute WILL. The Will of God is the foundation of creation as well as the process and destiny of that created world. God's Will as the heart of nature, and ideals exist for the manifestation of the Kingdom of God. One can note the centrality of the will in the phrase, "thy Kingdom come, **thy Will be done**, on earth as it is Heaven." The manifestation of the Kingdom of God is dependent on God's Will being done on earth. It is the alignment of His Will between the heavens and the earth by the act of created beings that releases the Kingdom principle upon the earth. The Kingdom rides upon the interweaving and alignment of His Will with the wills of the beings He has created.

We know that in the beginning was the Word, but before the beginning was Will and in the end shall be Will. Will is foundational and teleological (purpose). The Word is the instrument for the expression of the Will of God. Words are spoken as afterthought. The process maybe stated like this:–Being-Will-Word-Act. The Will of God is the before and behind of creation. Thus, our perfection and wholeness is bound up with the Will of God. We can press beyond the veil of creation into other dimensions only by His Will. Human beings need the Will of God to manifest their Divine destiny. Their destiny is bound in it. They must learn to pray as the Lord prayed, "not my will but thine be done." But it is clear that man is not willing to relinquish His Will. But those who have tapped into the power of God have been those who learned to say, "not my will but thine be done. This is why Heaven was so open to the Lord Jesus Christ; He never did just what He willed, He willed what the Father willed even when it conflicted with the humanity He had taken upon Himself. The question arises: If this Will of God is so good for humanity, why do human beings insist on doing their own will to their own hurt? What is wrong with human will? Why do human beings not live out this prayer for God's Will to flow into their sphere from someplace called Heaven so that they may experience the bountiful the victorious life God has promised? Good question. The reasons stem from the condition of the human will.

THE PROBLEM WITH NATURAL HUMAN WILL

St. Augustine, one of the African fathers of the Christian Church, wrote extensively on the natural will of the human being and its problem. In the "Confessions Augustine states that the natural man has *an infirmed will.*

"For the will commandeth that there be a will—not another but itself. But it doth not command entirely, therefore that is not what it commandeth. For where it entire, it would not even command it to be because it will already be. It is therefore, no monstrous thing partly to will partly to be unwilling but an infirmity of the mind. That it doth not wholly rise sustained by truth, pressed down by custom. And so there are two wills because one of them is not entire and the one is supplied with what the other needs.

There are several things we pick from Augustine regarding the infirmity of the will. The will is not whole or entire. The will is double-minded. It is not sustained by truth; that is, the human will rises by lying to itself because it is pressed down by tradition of men. In the next quotation Augustine states that the human will is perverted and bent aside from God. In another place Augustine says that he "inquired what iniquity was and ascertained it not to be a substance but a perversion of the will bent aside from thee, O God, the Supreme substance . . . ."[10] The infirmity of the will is the unwholesome burden which humanity must bear until the will surrenders itself to the Will of God. Says Augustine again, "the virtue of that which makes the body, which becomes holy by virtue of the holiness of the *will*, the consent of the *will* to an evil deed makes it a sin." He suggests that "In the supreme Will of God resides the power, which acts on all created spirits." Augustine states further that humans "are God's enemy not through their power to hurt Him but through their *will* to oppose Him."

This line of prayer that goes directly against the deficiency of the will breeds evil. The defect of the will is its misalignment or rebellious opposition to God's Will. The natural man's will can be deceitful not only externally but harbor a subjective self-deceit standing in opposition to the life and ways of the Holy Spirit's urge. Self-will can be carnal and often opposes God. Self-direction can be self-praising and God dethroning, but this has nothing in common with the will that belongs to the Divine sphere and inter-weaved into the Will of God. The natural man's will fights with how and why the Will of God is expressed and opposes the direction and purpose Divine Will.

As the Will of God is expressed in commandments, the will of the natural man influencing the mind requires the mind to be a moral being, which it was meant to be. But it cannot because it sits in opposition to God's Will. Since the will in opposition to God acts only in its self-interest, it cannot enter into "the state of universal and disinterested benevolence." And since this is the foundation of true holiness, the will in thus rejecting it annuls the character of His heart. Since Love is the fulfilling of the law and thus the conformity of will to God's intrinsic nature, the will of natural man fails because it does choose love, but chooses to hate all—even itself in the end. The natural man's will does not choose Divine things for their own sake but wills them according to the relative or temporal value which they seem to have for him or her. The issue of will is among the foundational distinction between the spirit-ruled life and the worldly life. The natural will stands contrary to the Will of God and thus starts the carnality of the mind in which an individual must become insincere in their relationship with God and men. This will has not confidence in the wisdom or love of God. It does not believe that God is wise enough or good enough and so is afraid to pray that God's Will be done universally. Because the natural will sits in arbitrary majesty over all the issue of being blocking it from submission to the Will of God it has no right to pray, "Thy will be done on earth as it is in Heaven." It does not believe Him, therefore, any such petition is mockery of the Divine Will. The natural will is replete with unbelief and does not seek to depend on grace that makes provision but by doing its own desire it hopes to accomplish utopia upon the earth. The natural will is like the builders of Babel seeking by the power of the will to accomplish what is done in Heaven on earth. Since the will of the natural man is under girded by unbelief and not faith, its melody is out of tune. **Thelematic** (will oriented) a-synchronicity with Divinity is downright rebellion in which man seeks to be God. The natural will thinks that it is unfair for God to require them to surrender their will and heartily consent to and acquiesce to the Will of God. Since willing and doing are naturally connected, it means that the natural man has **bad will** which results in acts that offer an insincere offering that keeps Heaven from manifesting on earth. If the will is in sincere conformity and synchronized with the Holy Spirit, everything else that is under the control of the will, that is the body, the soul and all the emotions and activities must of necessity correspond with this state of the will.

NATURAL MAN'S WILL IS *WILL TO UNBELIEF*

He is inclined to disbelief, misbelieve; discrediting, discordance; infidelity to God dissension, stubbornly held opinions and passive inaction in the things of God. One way to deal with this tendency to unbelief is to pray, "Thy Will be don on earth as it is in heavens." The Lord Jesus Christ in speaking to the Father of the young man who was epileptic said, "If you belief, all things are possible to him that believes." The unnatural natural man's will is steeped in unbelief, and therefore 1 Cor. 2:14 states: "But the natural man does not receive the things of the Spirit of God, for they are foolishness to him; nor can he know them, because they are spiritually discerned." There is nothing more pervasive and fundamental to the malfunction of the natural will than unbelief. When human will is not joined with the Will of God, the dichotomy creates opposition to Divine command and purposes. Unbelief is structured opposition to Divine presentation of Himself. The will in opposition to God creates a situation where its presumption of God's lack of good will is emphasized and intentions even overshadowed by man seeking to be god over God. This deification of his personal will allows the self to act contrary to God. It believes itself to be greater bearer of good will—greater than God. Despite its limitation pertaining to its ability to move beyond its constrictive context, natural will continues to believe itself to be more interested in its own salvation than God. One of the determining qualities then of natural man's will is the insistence to walk by sight and not obey faith. One might argue that man's will is not so much infected by unbelief than it is seduced by misplaced belief allowing itself to dazzled by the illusion of its self-importance. Unbelief comes as the unwillingness to trust God's power.

Unbelief measures the power and goodness of God by the power and goodness of the fallen man. It's perception of God's power addresses itself to the perceived failure of God to act in good faith. The Scripture says, "this is condemnation that light has come into the world, and men love darkness more than light because their deeds are evil." Another passage says, "He that believes not is already condemned because he believed not on the Son of God whom He sent." There is probably no more powerful place to see the power of man's will to believe or to unbelief than this acceptance of His Son because in this it gives its assent or refusal to God's process, nature and purpose. Yes, even to God Himself. The will to unbelief does manifest itself in the denial of God as God—the refusal to assent and accept God's mode of salvation in His Messiah, Yeshua (Jesus the Christ).

The will to unbelief is not only manifest in denial of God but in the denial of God's power in practical situations such as the healing of the body or deliverance from our situation, reconciliation, forgiveness and transformative involvement of God in the plain of human existence. Spurgeon puts it this way, unbelief is:

> The Monarch sin, the quintessence of guilt, the mixture of venom of all crimes, the dreg of wine of Gomorrah. It is the A1 sin, the masterpiece of Satan, the chief work of the devil.

When we speak of the will to unbelief, we are saying that the natural man's will leans on human understanding bypassing Divine inspiration as expressed in holy writ and that which the Spirit of God calls to remembrance in the inner person. In the natural man we find the will to unbelief in the refusal to believe God's revelation about Himself but instead he makes the tainted human experience the fulcrum on which he seeks to stand and rotate judgmentally the annals of eternity. What folly—The natural man of course will not worship God fully, rather he feigns halfhearted worship to appease his conscience. Of course when we speak of the natural man, the believer who is churched may think he is excluded from such class of people.

But unbelief is not the sole possession of the unchurched half-hearted worship and halfhearted commitment to the things of God are expressions of unbelief. For if we believed what the Lord says of Himself and us, how can we be less than passionate about the things which are in the heart of God. One place of course where this will to unbelief is manifest in believers is the area of witnessing for Christ. Lack of passionate posture for the things of God can be traced in this will to unbelief even in believers. Of course this will to unbelief breeds insensitivity to the Holy Spirit. Another area of unbelief is that of worry. The will to unbelief says, "God promised to take of me but if do not do it myself God will fail me." Of course many believers will just say, "I have to do something. Yes, but worry about the future moves it away from doing something to a denial of God as God. Unbelief says, "I am my God; I make my way in the universe. God cares not for my well being. In fact, if He does, He only cares so superficial that I must augment His act for me otherwise I will find myself left in the lurch by an uncaring God." We do not say it thusly but our mode of operation leans and leads to this conclusion. Whether we accept it or not, worry and anxiety is the tendency of natural man's will to unbelief. "Unbelief leaves man's well being in own power and what a pitiable power it is. Because this will of natural man, will to unbelief, denies God His rightful place, man must try by his limited means to keep his heart. Since his being is saturated with fears and His Will has failed to take a courageous stand in God, he is now threatened with annihilation unless he finds some refuge of lies in which keep himself. The will to unbelief puts man in disadvantage for they committed what is precious and of eternal value into the transient hand of a dying god—i.e., man. Lack of faith in the God to whom every commitment is eternally secured causes natural will to be unbelief and causes one to be perpetually unsafe in his own hands.

NATURAL MAN'S WILL IS *THE WILL TO BAD WILL.*

The will in man is the key to the communicative process between the various dimensions of the human person. Where there is bad will, good dies and become evil, reason becomes arrogance, imagination becomes corrupted and action flows in the river of not-God.

In a sense then in the natural, the will distracts the mind and incapacitates reason and truncates action toward that which is good and defiles even the best of ideas by presumptive majesty. In so doing it divides itself against itself. So that

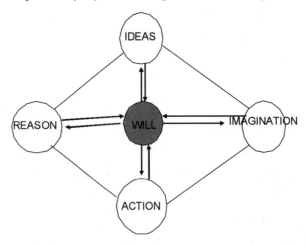

on the one hand it wills but on the other will un-wills. By what can "the whole will may be bound which before was divided into many"?[14]

It is the will to rebellion. It is from the corruption of the will of man that the works of the flesh flow. Romans 1 makes it clear that most, if not all, our sins derive from our refusal to acknowledge God as God. When the will blocks the flow of

Divine Will, the flesh turns in on itself and thus works without the aid of the animating power of the Holy Spirit. The flesh then proceed to balance evil with evil; it is unloving because God who is love is left out and this unloving nature is balanced not with good but with lack of mercy. Thus on the one side the fleshly person is not only unloving but unmerciful. The desires of the flesh go the extreme where the will has shut God out. This flesh eating upon itself leads to the depravity of the mind which then flow out in wickedness. Because the Will of God is not there to serve as closure valve, the desire of the flesh becomes greed and leads to evil acts. Furthermore, greed leads to envy and envy leads to murder. Of course envy leads to strife that ultimately leads to murder in some cases. In my opinion every human war has underlying it greed, not righteousness. Where there is strife, there is deceit. Where there is deceit, there is malice; and there also we find gossips and slanders and insolence. Paul tells us that these are the results of God-hating boastful arrogance that leads to rebellion against God constituted authorities and the invention of evil.

Finally, the understanding is darkened. This means that Paul is expanding his exegesis of corrupt human will began in the Romans chapter 1. These all led to death. The will of man then is encapsulated in death and cannot give forthtrue life in its separation from God. The descent of the will of man into death infects the soul and body of man. The will of man denies not only the glory of God but also its own glory. The will is the eye, and when it closes it turns to infernal darkness. The natural will travels away from above and abandons everything that is available to it in God. When away from God, it penetrates the depth of ignorance and darkness. Wrapped in darkness it is unable to perceive intelligently or to contemplate the beauty of divinity from which it is hewn. The corrupt will is more than just bad; it presides over infernal ignorance and fleshly works. Though it may not embody absolute corruption, yet in denying God it only finds its mystical ecstasy in concupiscence. It shuns the light and embraces destructive darkness.

Human will it its unnatural state cannot transcend its fleshly dimension. It is incapable of pure movement in the direction of divinity. The unnatural natural man's will is filled with fear, not of God but of its own demise and disappearance, ever searching but never finding itself. While the will subjected to the Holy Spirit of God brings joy, true happiness (Grk: *makarios*) and deep Divine fulfillment. The will of this unnatural natural man penetrates the body, soul and thought with not-God. The natural will *is the will to death*. It must submit to the Will of God to receive life and to be life-giving.

According to the Lord's Prayer there are two spheres in which the Will of God is to be done. The Kingdom of God is the necessary structure within which the will acts and finds cohesion and meaning, but the coming of the Kingdom depends on the Will of God being manifested through man on earth. This prayer is so powerful because it opens our inner man to the dimensions of Heaven and allows us to peer into it and see the Will of God being done and to transfer that process into our sphere.

HEAVEN: THE SECOND MENTION

This Heaven where the Will of God is done is the Heaven which Jacob saw in his dream where the ladder connected earth and Heaven. This is the Heaven of the presence of the Lord at whose feet we kneel to climb the ladder of faith. Our souls open up to that Heaven by doing the Will of our Father. Jesus told us that he is the Divine stairway—the way. Because God is our Father, the passage is graciously opened for us enter the realm where the promise of Genesis 1:26 is made manifest in our lives. Here everything is opened to us. Through our Lord Jesus Christ city, where the angels serve and angelic commerce which goes on between the upper and the lower kingdoms shall be made more manifests itself to us. So when we pray "on earth as it is Heaven" in this second mention of Heaven, we ask that God from whom Heaven proceeds should be seen here below. Since it is used in the dative masculine singular, it means to convey the idea that Heaven is the means by which God's Will is done on earth. The wide varieties of activities which take place in Heaven serve as the archetype of what must take place on the earth. The idea being that Heaven must take personal interest and become the reference point for all earthly activities. God uses Heaven as a means to move the earth to do His Will.

Heaven, according to this prayer and many other passages of Scriptures, is the place where God is and where the Divine presence is clearly manifest as far as creatures can handle it. Heaven is regarded as the abode of God, the point from which God affects the world as a King from His throne affects the entire Kingdom. Heaven is considered the habitation of YHVH. In Solomon's prayer at the inauguration of the Temple, seven times Solomon beckons YH to hear from Heaven locating God in Heaven. We must be careful here to note that in spite of the mode of speaking, Solomon also says, "behold the Heaven of the heavens cannot contain you." This makes it appear that the use of Heaven as locative for God is metaphorical and is meant to give us the understanding that God's power is loftier that we can grasp. God's presence is unhindered in its manifestation, where no part of creation... separated from God's holy presence. (Gen. 24:7) He is called "The LORD God of Heaven." It is the declarative habitat of Glory, as it is written, "the heavens declare your glory."

Heaven is the arena of the manifestation of the declarative glory of God. What is essential to know about Heaven is the fact that in Heaven the glory of God is clearly manifest. Heaven represents the clear and unhindered brightness of God's glory. In the presence of that glory celestial beings render to Him unfeigned reverence, worship, and adoration. There the renown of God is proclaimed without injury to His character by the serpent's forked tongue. From Heaven God reveals and manifests His Will through the instrumentality of the Kingdom whose subjects have no more inclination to mutiny. To God's creatures, Heaven is the sphere which represents the epitome of the ideal atmosphere that they all aspire to manifest in their temporal contexts. To lay open the Heaven is to have apprehended the place from which the fullness of all that is God lays hidden. This is what Jesus came preaching and what was established in a way by His life, death, resurrection and the Pentecostal outpouring during the feast of shvout. The part of the prayer which our Lord taught us to pray which goes "our Father which art in Heaven" is the heart of why God gave His Son and deeply relational.

155

If our birth is by the Heaven then our home even now is in Heaven though not physically. In our spirit we dwell there as often, as the King who is our Father gives us access. So when this prayer is echoed in our soul it is not just that God our Father dwells in Heaven but that we ourselves have our home with Him. (1 Cor. 15:49) In His blessedness, God our Father through our Lord Jesus Christ has blessed us not just with the heavenly birth but located us in the heavenly places in Christ. This is a choice which God makes by His sovereign Will and it is part of the foundation of the world. Until we find our location in the Heavens with our Father, the word without will remain in bondage. God loves us enough to place within us Heaven and yet to prepare a place for us to spend with Him in Heaven. One who is adapted to sonship as we have been adapted through Jesus Christ to Himself enjoys the pleasure of the Father's presence in Heaven though He remains on earth. "Who art in Heaven" is a statement not only of where God is but where we come to rest as those bought the blood and born by the Spirit. Our accepted location is in Christ who is in Heaven. (Eph. 1:3-6) This is a mystery, yet by the Scripture we know that spiritually we are located with God in the heavenlies not as equals but as sons of God's joy. For we read in Eph. 2:4-6:

> "But God, who is rich in mercy, because of His great love with which He loved us, 5 even when we were dead in trespasses, made us alive together with Christ (by grace you have been saved), 6 and **raised us up together, and made us sit together in the heavenly places in Christ Jesus**

Our Father is in Heaven; therefore, we who are now partakers of His nature have been made holy and we partake the heavenly dwelling where we sit with Christ Jesus our Apostle and the High Priest of our confession. (Heb. 3:1). When we confess Christ as Savior we, are translated spiritually to where Christ dwells. The mystery is that there is mutual relocation in which Christ moves into us and we move into Him; so that where He is, there we are also. Being children of the Father, in prayer we are in the habit of tasting the heavenly gift and partaking of the wine of the Holy Spirit. We are in fellowship with the heavens. In Heaven we are located beyond the veil which Christ through the tearing of His body had torn asunder. In fact in describing our location the writer of Hebrews says:

But you (we) have come to Mount Zion and to the city of the living God, the heavenly Jerusalem, to an innumerable company of angels, 23 to the general assembly and church of the firstborn who are registered in Heaven, to God the Judge of all, to the spirits of just men made perfect, 24 to Jesus the Mediator of the new covenant, and to the blood of sprinkling that speaks better things than that of Abel. (Heb. 12:22-24)

Gal. 4:26: "But Jerusalem which is above is free, which is the mother of us all. Thus heave is the place from which came and were we located and where we go." From the original text we see the Hebrew **hashamayim** and Greek *ouranios* are not what is used in the second mention. We have seen that its singular Heaven is not sky or the general concept of galaxies but a wonderful idea, place, goal high and Holy existing for those who have been liberated from the power of darkness and born as sons into the family of God. It is the peaceful and harmonious place where God rules without sinful interruption. It is the ultimate expression of the redeeming and preserving power of God. It is the telos, the end, and the undeviating goal of God's good will toward man. It is a gracious patrimony, which is a chief part of God's purpose in redeeming man for Himself so that man might have a place and be a place.

We ourselves being the habitation of God where God lives can find that our inner identity flows from this eternal location, a place called Heaven that is in God. There is a common confusion in common parlance of Paradise, Eden and Heaven. In the end Heaven, as we pray it, is the habitation of essential goodness; it would not be extreme to describe it as God as God is in His internal relation as Father Son and Holy Spirit. In every respect it is the summation of all that is beautiful, the culmination of sufficiency both for reason and for passion. It is that which is ever new, ever gives birth to the new earth. It is the place where love and communion are a supreme principle. Heaven is fellowship with God in all its fullness. So true believers have intense feeling of being attracted and turned toward it. So we pray "who art in Heaven" that our whole being may bend towards that place of perfection, Divine nobility, spiritual purity, continual godly delightful pleasure and unending glory which flows from our Father who is there.

In Heaven there are:

No more processes, but permanence.

No more striving after, but a beatific vision.

No more separation, but union with our Father.

No more sorrow, but eternal joy.

No more rough seas, but the sea of glass.

No more tears, but laughter and all tears are wiped away.

No more man-made temple, for God Himself is the temple.

No more sun fire burning, for God Himself shall light.

No more moon sickness, for God shall be the perfect sanity of the people.

No more wars, for the God of peace shall be in the heart of the people.

No more death, for the fount of life is there.

No more lies, for the Truth is the center there.

No more wandering astray, for the Way and the destination is there.

Our Father God is there in Heaven.

"Our Father who art in Heaven"

It is to that Heaven that we direct this line of prayer: "Thy Will be done, as in Heaven so on earth." God's Will is done in that sphere called Heaven, which is Eden which is the birth place of the New City of God called the New Jerusalem. We know that place is different from the general heavens because in the general heavens, stars eat up one another, chaos reigns and death is on every hand. The Will of God is done in this particular Heaven as we read in Psalm 148.

First is the sphere of the of Divine delight. Using Psalm 148 one may curl out the specific topography of the Will of God as manifested in praise. The Will of God in the heavens is done first in the heights, second by the angels, third by hosts, fourth by great lights (sun and moon) fourth by the stars of light, fifth by the highest heavens

158

and seventh by the waters above the heavens. The Will of God is done in Heaven according to the prayer that Jesus taught us. In the heavenly dimensions, God's Will is done perfectly. The heavens do not seek to deviate from the Will of God. The heavens and their occupants know perfectly what the Will of God is for they gaze upon the glory of God's nature daily. In this knowledge of the glory, they do not seek to deviate from the nature of God or from the purpose of God. Thus, in them they combine the nature and purpose of God in an unbroken flow and submersion of their will to the Will of God. The heights do not seek to be low. The angels seek clearly to manifest the nature of God and God's purpose, as far as we know. The hosts of Heaven do the same. The sun has never stopped ruling the day or sought to rule the night; it has remained constant in attachment to the nature and purpose to which God created it, but not by will but mechanical conformity to the laws of creation. The same can be said of the moon and the stars. Those among them that are sentient beings of course have the capacity to grow in their knowledge of God because they do not know all of God as they are not God. In their expanding revelation of God, their good will and intention is continually conformed to do the Will of God. They have passed the point of continually choosing for they have to the place of perfect conformity to the Will of God. But human beings must increasingly submit their will to God as God reveals to them greater dimensions of His redemption plan. They must choose continuously to submerge their will into the Will of God. Finney stated that "the obedience of Heaven, therefore, must keep pace with their increasing knowledge, and therefore its inhabitants must continually grow in ho-liness." Their whole being cries out "Thy will be done; Thy will alone is goodwill, O Lord of Host."

GOD'S WILL IN THE SPHERE OF THE EARTH

On earth there are twenty-four (24) spheres or location of the Will of God which represent the sphere of earthly creation. These twenty four spheres of the manifestation of the Will of God are:

1. Earth. 2. Sea monsters. 3. All deeps. 4. Fire. 5. Hail. 6. Snow. 7. Clouds. 8. Stormy winds. 9. Mountains. 10. Hills. 11. Fruit tree. 12. Cedars. 13. Beasts. 14. Cattle. 15. Creeping things. 16 Winged fowls. 17. Kings. 18. All peoples. 19. Princes. 20. Judges. 21. Young men. 22. Virgins. 23. Old Men. 24. Children.

Of these twenty-four, sixteen are aligned with God's Will but eight are misaligned with the Will of God. The last eight is Adam who needs circumcision of the heart and surrender of the will. Because Adam is king in the sphere of the earth and the cause of the sixteen elements' move from their original submission to the Will of God and thus distort their divinely-ordained purpose. People are the ones who stand in competition with the praise of the Lord; therefore, the psalmist ends the psalm with the command,

> **"Let** them praise the name of the Lord for his name alone is exalted. His glory is above the earth and Heaven." (Verse 13)

We as people must say "Thine Will not my will" in order to open up the dimensions that are hidden within this Heaven. They must **LET.** In Heaven the Will of God does not necessarily obstruct the will of the angels; so too on earth we must understand that the Will of God is not intended to obstruct or destroy the will of man, but that it is the will of man that stands often in the way of the full implementation of the Will of God within the sphere which God gave to man. The Will of God satisfies the requirement of fulfillment connected with the fact that the Will of God is good. In God, knowledge and action are intimately related. The will of man even stands against his own soul. So when we pray, "thy will be done," we prophesy our submission to God and as a result prepare our body to shift dimensions.

Will and knowledge are so connected in God because they serve as fulcrum for the turning of the wheel of Divine goodness, mercy and justice. Thus God's Will is always **GOOD WILL.** The Will of God being good will cannot allow for a mere imaginary and partial process lacking authentic and transformative acts. It must work itself out in full Kingdom manifestation and can only do so in the interim by the alignment of human will with the Eternal Will of God. If one claims to be in the Will of God, one cannot act in such a way that the interest of the Kingdom of the Lord God is denied or betrayed. Non-Kingdom acts that claim to be in the Will of God must be rejected as falsities and demonic usurpation of the Divine right by archetypal evil. Where the Will of God is present, the Kingdom of God comes. Certainly no secondary will can serve as substitute for God's Will, yet the obvious denial of the Will of God within any context can be evidence by the absence of the signs of the Kingdom of God. We need to know God's Will. The knowledge of the Will of God concretely makes possible the manifestation of the Kingdom in our daily lives and in our families, communities and world. The Will of God should not be confused in any way with the ritualized formula so common among religious people. Far from it, many of the formulas avoid the Will of God and do not seek to manifest the Kingdom of God but the emotional and sentimental Kingdom of man.

It needs to be mentioned that though there are similarities between the Will of God and the will of man there ought to be no confusion about the infinite gap that divides them. The Divine must Himself come to bridge them. Of course the Will of God as has been noted is the basis of God's absolute sovereignty over all creation. Here we enter not into the philosophical *why* of theodicy or the presence of evil in the world. Suffice it say that evil has its origin in will, but not the immediate Will of God but secondary will over which God has willfully given over to free agents. The Will of God is intrinsic to God's nature from the fundamental goodness, holiness, compassion, creativity, and all that may rightly be attributed to His character. As motivation, Will in God motions in the direction of God's glory and good pleasure. (Eph. 1)

The problem we as human being have is that our wills can never be stopped when it is in one's intrinsic will to do something. Yet there seems in our world many things which we suppose God does not will that are being forced upon God. Even though these may appear to human beings as weakness of the Divine Will and that man's will seems to supersede God's, yet it is intended willfully by God to put to shame the strong, Paul says in I Corinthians. And furthermore as believers know in some cases God allows His Will to be influenced or affected by the prayer of His human beings; so it will seem as in the case of Moses and the children of Israel, Nineveh, and others and some other instances. Yet it must be remembered that this is not a forcing of God by an external force to change but an intrinsic willing to will influenced by God in God and through God. The Will of God carries with it purpose, and this is summarized in the eternity of God in which God knows everything at once and not in succession. The Will of God is always accomplished; that of man is often defeated. His Will does not change because of the flux of time. Since God knows everything in advance, God is in the best place to deal with our confusion in time and flux and failure which our decrepit will causes us. He sees all at once.

DIMENSIONS OF THE WILL OF GOD

It is the Will of God for us to be delivered from this present evil world.

According to Galatians 1:4, Yeshua the Messiah "gave himself for our sins that he might deliver us from this present evil world, according to the Will of God and our Father." Undoubted by the Will of God is to deliver humanity from sin an evil. The story of the bondage of humanity to the shackles of evil is written on every page of Scripture and upon the scroll of history. It needs no rehearsing here— no matter what your definition of evil may be even it is wrong, for your wrong definition of evil comes from some root of evil. Deliverance from evil is so vital to the Will of God that the Lord Jesus taught us to pray "deliver us from evil." The Hebrew word *hawvy* (yeshuw`ah) is something that happens to one from the exercise of another's. Another meaning is to be saved or to preserve something from negative influence. This deliverance leads to health and provides help by saving one and attaching itself to one's welfare. The other implied meanings derived from it are to be delivered from a corner, to give someone aid in times of need, and give victory over difficult circumstances. This is no partial victory but a victory that is total and complete. It also implies prosperity or a deliverance from poverty and lack. So when John says, "I wish that you prosper and be in good health even as your soul prospers," he is drawing from the Hebrew idea of salvation as a Divine event affecting the physical and spiritual sphere of human lives. So if deliverance is the Will of God, why is everyone not delivered? Rightly asked. The key lies in the alignment of the human will and the Will of God with which we have considered at length in this chapter. Of course I am not talking of the individual will of man.

If sin is a federated issue as Paul and Augustine argued, why not will? Part of the lack of deliverance in the world can be attributed to the fact that human will is not united in alignment to the Will of God. When God speaks in the Scripture of His people, there is an emphasis on the unity of that body—this unity must be a spiritual unity which leads us to the idea of unity of will. That is why Jesus Himself says, "if two of you shall agree." At another place he says, "where two or three." The human will in its fallen natural state is self-seeking, self-deifying and antagonistic to one another, but what God intends is that the good Will of God pervade humanity in such a way that all human will joined as one begins to manifest God's good intention and purpose in the world. In Heaven there is seamless flow of the will of its inhabitants into the Will of God. There is now no friction between the Will of God and the will of the angels; hence, David says "ye angels who do His Will."

God uses individuals to activate deliverance, but the target of that deliverance is very seldom an individual. In a sense it is the will of human beings coming in submission to the Will of God, for the Will of God is deliverance that calls for the Deliverer. In Exodus chapter 3 God (Elohim) says to Moses, "I have seen the suffering of my people and their cry has come before me." The will of the people, at least a majority of them, was united in the direction of deliverance, thereby aligning with the Will of God. Deliverance is a communal and Kingdom principle. The target has always been the community. For the deliverance of the individual to be truly secured, there must be a community of delivered persons standing with the person. When God delivered Joseph the goal was the preservation of people. Genesis 45:7: "God sent me before you to preserve you a posterity in the earth, and to save your lives by a great deliverance."

In Judges 15:18 when God uses Samson, He does so for the deliverance of the people. When Samson prays we see that Samson has already began to misunderstand the purpose of God for his life and was using his deliverance as opportunity for personal vendetta. "And he was sore athirst, and called on the LORD, and said, Thou hast given this great deliverance into the hand of thy servant: and now shall I die for thirst, and fall into the hand of the uncircumcised?" Joseph's deliverance from prison would have been empty had Israel not been delivered also. Genesis 45:7: "But God sent me ahead of you to preserve for you a remnant on earth and to save your lives by a great deliverance." In 2 Kings 5:1 the target of the LORD's use of Naaman was to bring great deliverance unto Syria. The arrow of the Lord's deliverance which Elisha orders the king of Israel to shoot eastwards is directed to deliverance of Israel as people. (2 Kings 13:17) The deliverance from enemies in the Old Testament is never merely the enemy of an individual. In most cases what was at stake was the survival of Israel as the paradigm of the Kingdom of God. Individuals come as deliverer but their act of deliverance is always geared to the people as corporate entity, as we find in Esther 4:14: "For if thou altogether holdest thy peace at this time, then shall there enlargement and deliverance arise to the Jews from another place; but thou and thy Father's house shall be destroyed: and who knoweth whether thou art come to the Kingdom for such a time as this?" When we read in Psalm 18:50: "Great deliverance giveth he to his king; and sheweth mercy to his anointed, to David, and to his seed for evermore," it is to the king as the embodiment of the community.

We read in Joel 2:32: "And it shall come to pass, that whosoever shall call on the name of the LORD shall be delivered: for in mount Zion and in Jerusalem shall be deliverance, as the LORD hath said, and in the remnant whom the LORD shall call." In Joel where the deliverance starts from the individual, it ends in its perfection by being in the holy city and ending in the remnant which is the community of the preserved. Deliverance as described by Obadiah 17: "But upon mount Zion shall be deliverance, and there shall be holiness; and the house of Jacob shall possess their possessions" is territorial deliverance, resulting in territorial holiness leading to Kingdom possession. The essential task of the Messianic process is the complete deliverance of the people who enter into the messianic community. The ten sets of acts which the Messiah carries out for the establishment of the Kingdom are all about deliverance as narrated in Is. 61.

APOSTOLICITY IS BY GOD'S WILL

Apostolic ministry is the Will of God for the church, so by praying "Thy will be done," we activate apostolicity. And one cannot be an apostle except by the Will of God as Paul so often states it in the New Testament. Six times Paul mentions apostolic calling and the Will of God in the same breath. 2 Corinthians 1:1: "Paul, an apostle of Jesus Christ by the Will of God, and Timothy our brother, unto the church of God which is at Corinth, with all the saints which are in all Achaia:" 1 Corinthians 1:1: "Paul, called to be an apostle of Christ Jesus by the Will of God, and our brother Sosthenes." In 2 Corinthians 1:1 we read, "Paul an apostle of Christ Jesus by the Will of God, and Timothy our brother, We also read in Ephesians 1:1 Paul, an apostle of Christ Jesus by the Will of God, To the saints in Ephesus, the faithful in Christ Jesus." Colossians 1:1: "Paul, an apostle of Christ Jesus by the Will of God, and Timothy our brother." 2 Timothy 1:1: "Paul, an apostle of Christ Jesus by the Will of God, according to the promise of life that is in Christ Jesus."

SANCTIFICATION IS THE WILL OF GOD

The idea of sanctification is often confused with the idea of holiness in the body of Christ. But there is a difference of usage based on even the spelling in the Old Testament. The word "sanctify" is often translated in the Hebrew Scriptures of the First Covenant from the word vdq, \ \ *qadash* pronounced kaw-dash' which is a sense of causation. In many cases a human being can sanctify or make it so by pronouncement or by ceremonial cleanliness. Sanctification can even be abstractly considered though it does involve a sense of set-apartness. But it is set-apartness in which a human being can participate and often grows out the free will of the person in setting themselves or something apart to God. But God can also sanctify something by dedicating it Himself. The KJV is probably more accurate in this instance when it suggests that one can, by appointment consecrate and dedicate, a particular thing to kept as holy or by mere proclamation purify a thing or an entity. While there is no absolute distinction between this and there is separation often made between this word as the other Old Testament word which is its derivative, *vdeqo qodesh* pronounced **ko'-desh**, note the difference in spelling. This can refer to nouns, a sacred place or thing. It is never merely proclaimed upon a thing, but it is what a thing or one is by reason of its nature. The consecrated thing that is dedicated carries holiness because the God to which it is dedicated comes to take an abode in it, thus transferring His intrinsic nature into the thing or person. So in a sense then sanctification is the process by which we separated unto God, and holiness is who we are as separated persons that now belong to God. I believe that I am warranted in this interpretation by the phrasing of the verse from Leviticus 11:44:

> For I am the LORD your God: ye shall therefore sanctify yourselves, **and ye shall be holy**; for I am holy: neither shall ye defile yourselves with any manner of creeping thing that creepeth upon the earth

In 1 Thessalonians 4:3 Paul says, "For this is the Will of God, even your sanctification that ye should abstain from fornication." Our deliberate separation and removal of ourselves from immorality is in God's Will. But in some cases it is us who must separate ourselves from the context of this particular evil. In this case our sanctification exemplifies the alignment of our will with the Will of God. In Exodus 13:2, God shows Israel this by asking them to "Sanctify unto me all the firstborn, whatsoever openeth the womb among the children of Israel, both of man and of beast: it is mine." Though they are God's, yet it is the act of sanctification by the parents and the owners of the animals that set them apart for God's use. The principle of sanctification as the Will of God is also revealed in Exodus 19:10 when we read "And the LORD said unto Moses, Go unto the people, and sanctify them today and tomorrow, and let them wash their clothes.. . ." In Exodus 19:22 we read, "And let the priests also, which come near to the LORD, sanctify themselves, lest the LORD break forth upon them." It is interesting that the burden is placed on the human persons in these passages to sanctify them. This *"let,"* as I have pointed out, calls the recipient to release their will for and to the designated purpose of God for a particular item or task.

In Exodus 19:23, Moses sanctifies the mountain. In Exodus 28:41, he consecrates and sanctifies Aaron and his sons to minister unto the *hwhy* in the priest's office. Upon their consecration Aaron, as we read in Exodus 29:27, sanctifies "the breast of the wave offering, and the shoulder of the heave offering, which is waved...and which is heaved up, of the ram of the consecration, even of that which is for Aaron, and of that which is for his sons." There is nowhere in Scripture where the involvement of human agent in sanctification is more obvious that in the command which God gives in Exodus 29:36:

"And thou shalt offer every day a bullock for a sin offering for atonement: and thou shalt cleanse the altar, when thou hast made an atonement for it, and thou shalt anoint it, to sanctify it." The human being, in this case Moses, sanctified the altar and God makes it holy, if you will, God transfers Divine holiness to the altar after man deliberately and speaks to him about voluntarily setting himself apart to God. We also find this process in the Exodus 29:37 where God say to Moses, "Seven days thou shalt make an atonement for the altar, and sanctify it; and it shall be an altar most holy: whatsoever toucheth the altar shall be holy." 13 And thou shalt put upon Aaron the holy garments, and anoint him, and sanctify him; that he may minister unto me in the priest's office. Leviticus 8:11: "And he sprinkled thereof upon the altar seven times, and anointed the altar and all his vessels, both the laver and his foot, to sanctify them." Leviticus 8:12: "And he poured of the anointing oil upon Aaron's head, and anointed him, to sanctify him." It is not oil that sanctified Aaron but the act of obedience activating the oil and therefore activating Aaron.

Because sanctification is the Will of God, when we pray "Thy will be done," we call upon God to sanctify us and our world. God sanctified, as we read in Exodus 29:44, the tabernacle and the altar and the priests that ministered on that altar. "And I will sanctify the tabernacle of the congregation, and the altar: I will sanctify also both Aaron and his sons, to minister to me in the priest's office." The idea of separation is both singular and continuous for as we in several places in the TORAH God insists that Israel is continuously being separated by God unto God. Thus there is continual affirmation of the holy status of Israel in the sight of God. The Sabbath for example which Israel is commanded to keep continually is a reminder of this continuous set-apartness in which the Lord of the Universe engages perpetually in relation on behalf of Israel. Thus it says in Exodus 31:13: "Speak thou also unto the children of Israel, saying, Verily my Sabbaths ye shall keep: for it is a sign between me and you throughout your generations; that ye may know that I am the LORD that doth sanctify you." Though many times God says to Israel "Sanctify yourselves" (Num. 11:18, Josh. 3:5,; 7:13; I Sam. 16:5 I Chron. 15:12), yet in other places He says "I am the LORD which sanctifies you." (Lev. 20:8; 21:8) Several other places, especially in Leviticus, He insists "for I the LORD do sanctify . . .." (Lev. 21:15; 21:23; 22:9, 16) When God sanctifies, He so by His truth which is His Word. John 17:17: The Lord said "Sanctify them through thy truth: thy word is truth." If we move it further, the Word and truth refer to the Messiah. We also know that it is the Will of God because Jesus sanctified Himself to release truth for our sanctification. John 17:19: "And for their sakes I sanctify myself, that they also might be sanctified through the truth. This is reiterated in Ephesians 5:26: "That he might sanctify and cleanse it with the washing of water by the word." The Will of God in this regard is so strong that Jesus also sanctified us with His own blood, suffering outside of the structures of this world. He was crucified outside of the gate—putting him beyond the judgmental structures of the present age.

To drive this point home Peter makes clear in 1 Peter 3:15 that this sanctification is directed to "our hearts" in such a way that it affects willingness to respond to those who question the hope that is in us. If the way of Kingdom of God has become our structure of consciousness and the Will of God has been manifested in us, then the will gives forth meekness and fear in honor of God.

The Will of God for us is tied directly with service to the generation in which we live. It must be our prime goal that before we die that we have done what God wills for our generation. Acts 13:36 says that "David, after he had served his own generation by the Will of God, fell on sleep, and was laid unto his fathers, and saw corruption." But remember that though David saw corruption his "Seed" never saw corruption. Our serving God in accordance with His Will for us as it relates to our generation is "seed faith" if I may borrow a term from the "Faith Movement." The length of this mighty journey and its prosperous nature will depend on the alignment of our will with the Will of God concerning the generation to come. In walking in the Will of God for the generation, our own will must be open to the one who searches hearts, knows the pathway of the mind of and is able to tame it by the Spirit aligning it processes according to the Will of God.

SALVATION IS THE WILL OF GOD:

When we pray "Thy will be done," we invoke salvation. We must not fall into the temptation of thinking that praying the Will of God is philosophical of practical fatalism. Rather is it the most freeing act and creative place to be because we know that God has good will. How do we prove the Will of God? In the Old Testament the Will of God was proven in several ways. But it must be remembered that it is the revealed Will of God that was to be proven by the means which is under discussion. The written Will of God, which was the Torah, was not to be sought by any other means except the reading and inter-pretation of the text. But where the Will of God is sought regarding individual direction or even communal direction which are not explicitly commanded within the Scripture, then other means were used. For example the Will of God was never sought as to whether a murderer should be killed. But if, as it was in the case of David in the pursuit of the Ziklag murderers, there was not clear direction then God was to be sought for direction.

The Will of God can be proven. Romans 12:2: "And be not conformed to this world: but be ye transformed by the renewing of your mind, that ye may prove what is that good, and acceptable, and perfect, Will of God." The Will of God regarding temporal matters are not usually known immediately, yet by persistent pressing in on God we may be able to ascertain what God wants from us in particular situations. Paul in Romans 15:32: "sought the Will of God to brethren in Rome; he sought specifically to go in the mood of joy. 32 That I may come unto you with joy by the Will of God, and may with you be refreshed." James is even clearer about how we ought to approach temporal situations as it relates to the Will of God. James 4:15: "For that ye ought to say, If the Lord will, we shall live, and do this, or that."

Doing the Will of God when we know it is non-negotiable. We neither do the Will of God based on whose eyes are on us or for the pleasure of men but we as the servants of Christ do the Will of God from the heart not fearing what it will cost us. This line in the Lord's Prayer calls us as believers to pray for the ability to do the Will of God our Father. James 1:18 tells us that seeking to do God's Will is consistent with the fact that it is this will that gave birth to us: "Of his own will begat he us with the word of truth, that we should be a kind of first fruits of his creatures." Heb. 13:21 states it this way: "Make you perfect in every good work to do His Will, working in you that which is well pleasing in his sight, through Jesus Christ; to whom be glory forever and ever. Amen."

One can suffer according to the Will of God: Hebrews 10:36 says, "For ye have need of patience, that, after ye have done the Will of God, ye might receive the promise." 1 Peter 2:15: "For so is the Will of God, that with well doing ye may put to silence the ignorance of foolish men." 1 Peter 3:17: "For it is better, if the Will of God be so, that ye suffer for well doing, than for evil doing." 1 Peter 4:19: "Wherefore let them that suffer according to the Will of God commit the keeping of their souls to him in well doing, as unto a faithful Creator."

Doing the Will of God is the key to living and abiding forever. 1 John 2:17:

"And the world passeth away, and the lust thereof: but he that doeth the Will of God abideth for ever." Prayers are answered by God only if they are according to the Will of God. 1 John 5:14 14: "And this is the confidence that we have in him, that, if we ask any thing according to His Will, he heareth us." *Prophecy is the Will of God.* 2 Peter 1:21: "For the prophecy came not in old time by the will of man: but holy men of God spake as they were moved by the Holy Ghost."

We need to know that by praying this line of prayer taught by the Lord, we transmute the straw of the decaying effect of human will into the gold of the glory of God's Will. We see then the importance of giving ourselves entirely over to God's Will. But if our will is malformed or corrupt, we are danger of being far removed from the Will of God and carrying out that which is contrary to God's purpose. Therefore, our will needs to be formed and trained to submit and conform to the Divine Will. The human will cannot transform itself. It has no power to do so. There must be a commitment to something greater than it. Thus Roman 12:1-2 reads "I beseech therefore brethren that ye present your body a living sacrifice." How then do we renew our mind? By training our will to say without reserve "Thy will O God be done not mine."

By practicing submission to the Holy Spirit in all things, we can turn our will over to the Will of God. The first act leading to transformation and training is that of the unequivocal submission of the will of man to the Will of God. This submission of the will illuminates it and draws it into the Kingdom discursive process. The will of human being is formed, transformed and trained by this discursive process. The formation of the will is based on reflection on the information provided by the Divine concerning Himself. There is a constant of flow of communication that allow for the Divine Will to saturate the will of the man this is done through prayer— prayer is that discursive formation of the will. Prayer being a consistent exchange between God and the believer creates a cross-flow of the Kingdom by aligning Will to will. Thus then the believing community becomes the communicative community carrying with it the communicative action whose content is obvious the believer, the Word of God who is the Messiah.

By contemplating the greatness of God, our will is released to trust the Will of God. The Will can be formed also by contemplative posture. Only a being or people whose will and acts are deeply influenced by contemplative will can reach into the future and determine it by that will which has been intertwined with the Will the God. Such beings can know not only history but can produce and change history. Kingdom of God radiates from transformed will, which is also a contemplative will.

From the will having contemplative posture, there is occurring and reoccurring interweaving of the heavenly and earthly, God and human, which reaches out in productive imagination which can also be called Kingdom imagination.

By developing a visionary symbolization of how our situation can be like Heaven, we bend our will to simulate Heaven. The living impulse of the will is as a symbolizing instrument within a human being able to capture and take hold of the future in the present. Will is the principle of unity, cohesion and continuity. "the performance of an action maybe impaired by an error of the will resulting in the faulty planning and insufficient idea or else the plan maybe adequate but when the will attempts to carry out the plan some part of the body may fail to obey its command." (Ernst Cassirer 263) In a failure of will or its entropy, the failure is manifested in the movements that are made related to the desire action complex to the order of the Kingdom of God and its manifestation.

To develop a will conformed to the Will of God, we need of course to go beyond the purely sentimental entertainment materialistic Christianity that is common in post-modernity. It is the transformation of the will that enables us to participate as God intended us in the Manifesting Kingdom. It is not so much our willed effort that causes the Kingdom to manifest but the subjection of our will to the Will of God that causes an unhindered flow of Kingdom action. The impotence of unregenerate human will or carnal power is seen in the fact that man cannot bring forth pure relationship.

Will can become old, decayed, dilapidated and even fossilized so that it gives forth mainly death and destruction. But God's Will is actualized in its highest form in humanity's choice to connect with God. It is amazing to me that God deems it important for the Will of God to be manifested by connecting with finite human will. God's Will serves then as freedom and constrain to the human tendency to annul boundary and pervert righteousness. God's law is to curtail humanity's unregenerate will in its rampant sinful self-imposition upon God's world.

If a person wishes to flow in the Kingdom of God and to actively abide in its sphere, the person must develop a will bent toward transformation. The development of the will that reflects the Will of God takes disciplined spirituality and consistent practice. The training of will is more important than the training of ratio. One whose will is trained to submit is ready to hear God and see beyond the rational sphere but also able to act from a supernatural place. Because it is by conformity of the human will to the Divine Will that we come to seat in the heavenly places with Christ. Decision, deliberation, and discipline of the will are prerequisite for manifestation of the Kingdom of God. The will and the mind have a connection. The atrophy of the will leads to the darkening of the mind. The believer is told "be ye transformed by the renewal of your mind." The presentation of the body and the renewal of the mind is carried out by active involvement of the will. When the will is committed to anything the whole life begins to change to accommodate it. When the will is connection to the Divine, the foundation of former actions begin to be transformed and structure itself in the direction of the Divine. Here is where the believer is different from the non-believer: their wills are directed to opposite ends. The law of God hid the heart serves as a bridle that tames the will and brings it into subjection to the Will of God. So we choose what we see by their conformity to the beauty of the Lord so that our inner eyes may not become deformed.

The human will can be trained by hearing from Heaven. The ear is a spiritual gateway by which others enter into the recesses of our being. The Bible even tells us that faith comes by hearing and hearing by the Word of God. One of major attacks used by the enemy to infiltrate the souls of men is the audio dimension. So then in prayer we can form our will by causing ourselves to hear affirmation of the Word of God. Self-talk that puts God's positive Word into our souls can help form our will. The Scriptures tell us that "faith comes by hearing and hearing by the Word of God."

THE GOAL OF WILL FORMATION AND TRAINING

When our whole being says "Thy will be done on earth as it is in Heaven," we are ready to see wonders and signs. In this state of mind, we will every good for its own sake and according to its eternal value. Nothing more or less than this state of mind "Thy will be done" can be called true virtue. The goal of human

173

beings as this prayer suggests is to completely release our will so that God's Will swallows up our will. The "I" that stands in rebellion against the Most High must bow. If will as the instrument for our decisions, reveals our power to choose and expresses what we "we will" or "we won't" then the will becomes the power over all areas of human thought life even when the physical cannot follow suit because of impediments. We know that without the will the human person is reduced to a mere machine. The will is the instrument for thoughts; it can, if it so chooses, stymie our intellectual power and subvert the imagination of the soul and hold back the flight of the spirit to the heavens. So we must choose a will from whence flow perfect wisdom, knowledge and action. Lack of understanding and submission to the Divine Will makes a man foolish and dull. The instrument for our likes and dislikes in the faculty of emotion does distort our will. So when we say "will of yours be done on earth as is in Heaven," we are calling for God to take over our ability to express love, hate, joy, anger, tranquility and the all that we may call emotion and for His Spirit to determine its ebb and flow. It is not so much its shortage that renders man insensitive as wood or stone but its fullness apart from the Spirit of God. (Watchman Nee 1) "It is, in a word, the obedience of the will or heart to the law of God as this law lies revealed in the Intelligence. I have just said that sin consists in the supreme devotion of the will, and consequently of all the powers of the mind to self-gratification. On the contrary, holiness consists in the supreme devotion of the will, and consequently of the whole being to the glory of God, and the good of the universe." According to Charles Finney, "This entire consecration of the will to the glory of God and the good of the universe is the whole of virtue in any being, and in every world." He also reminds us that we cannot even be submitted to the Will of God nor do His Will in any moment, "especially in difficult times, we must first be practicing the remembrance of God in our lives." He insists that the human will must be trained to remember God with consistency in today's noisy world where the physical ear, spirit and emotion are continually bombarded with distraction from devotion to God. Unless the Will of God takes supremacy over the will of man, so that the Will of God becomes the will of man the whole process is futile. Jesus tell us that this is His whole purpose to do the Will of the Father not His own will:

For I have come down from Heaven, not to do my own will,

but the will of the One who sent me. (John 6:38)

He that will do the Will of God will know. One is not qualified to know the Will of God who is not already doing the Will of God. The Will of God is known where it is incarnated in the flesh of everyday action. The goal of the discipleship of the will is to make the two wills one. The two wills which are fighting in man are made one by confirming them to the Will of God. He says that it is one soul fluctuating between conflicting wills. By what I am saying I do not mean to say that the Kingdom of God will not come if men do not will it so but that its manifestation in their life and their circumstance and sphere of being is limited and they live outside of the abundant life which attends that Kingdom.

THE HOLY SPIRIT AND THE WILL OF THE BELIEVER

The fruit of the Spirit bud through the instrumentality of the will submitted to God's Will. In Galatians chapter 5 we see the difference between a will submitted to God and a working in Divine efficiency and a will working from the deficiency of human self held in the bondage of sin. Charles Spurgeon says:

"The work of the Spirit, which is the effect of the Will of God, is to change the human will, and so make men willing in the day of God's power, working in them to will to do his own good pleasure. The work of the Spirit is consistent with the original laws and constitution of human nature."

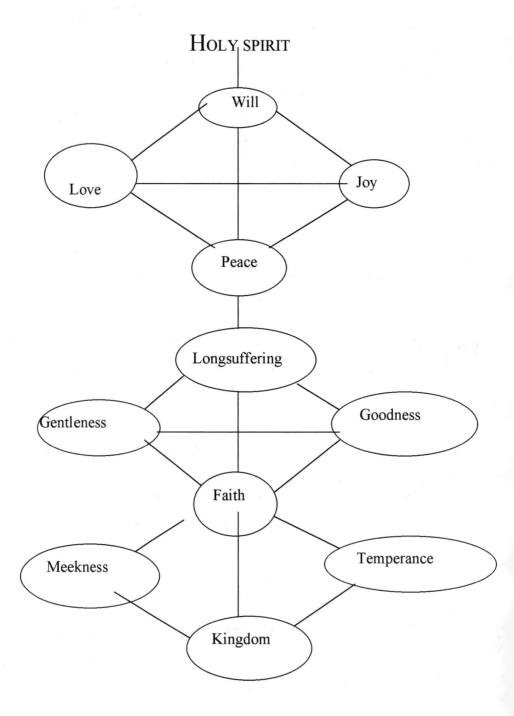

HOLY SPIRIT

Will

Love   Joy

Peace

Longsuffering

Gentleness   Goodness

Faith

Meekness   Temperance

Kingdom

In the Lord 's Prayer there is a line that reads "Thy will be done on earth as it is in Heaven." There is also a line in an old song that reads "and my will be lost in thine." The principle of will argues thus, "that unfathomable something," the principle of cohesion, the sufficient reason of all is the will. It is the inscrutable and deep secret of all causes in Heaven and in earth. It is the basis of the transformation of matter and spirit. Behind the flow of all that becomes is the will, whether it is the Will of God or that of creation. It is the alignment of will that is necessary for the manifestation of the Kingdom. All the inner and outer workings of the Kingdom of God are grounded in the Will of God. But the question becomes what is the Will of God?

To begin with the question "What is the Will of God?" demands that we define will as it occurs both as an intrinsic nature of God and as it works in God's creative outreach. In Eph. 1:11 we read, "In whom also we have obtained an inheritance, being predestinated according to the purpose of him who worketh all things after the counsel of his own will."

Will raises the question of faith at its most foundational level. There is a sharp distinction between knowing the Will of God and doing the Will of God. Or there is ideationally a distinctive difference between the intrinsic Will of God known by God and the Will of God as man sees it and seeks to work within it. In most instances the two wills are incompatible seeing that the profound nature of God keeps man always at the minimalism of knowing God as God. But there is an incompatibility of will which results from the stark opposition which flows from man's degeneracy and natural deficiency resulting from the fall. The fall away from God places the will of man always in opposition to the Divine Will until it is regenerated by the infusion of the Divine Will activated by the indwelling presence of the Holy Spirit. Man cannot know that Will of God and still believe that anyone other than God does the perfect Will of God. There is no human will strong enough to comprehend within its willing the Will of God. However, that does not mean that there is no communicative possibility between the Will of God and the will of man. In fact God seeks to communicate His Will to human beings in such a way that the Will of

God becomes the Will of God but not vice versa. When any one insists that their personal will is the Will of God, they have crossed the line from humility to self-deification. The recognition of how far our will is from the Will of God is the beginning of wisdom and sets us on the path of Divine knowledge.

I have a growing impression that many people who mouth the Will of God do not really mean to know the Will of God or to do it, rather it is a way of imposing their own will upon the will of others. In fact in so many lives, including the lives of those of us who claim to be followers of Jesus Christ, the Will of God is nothing more than "shibboleth" for dividing us from those whom we dislike and wish to do away with an excuse for our rebellion. If the Will of God is as important as we have claimed it to be and as I believe the Bible teaches, knowing and doing it becomes the primary priority of the church and of all human beings who claim the Name of Yeshua our Messiah. On the other hand if the Will of God is not important and to know or to do it has no priority in human life, then the world simply is a tragic place and there is no higher place from which human transformation can come. If the Will of God is merely something that we use to make us look good in the face of accusation by others, then it fails to meet the criteria for that which is the Will of God. Will belongs to the very essence of what it means to live move and have being. For God and for man it is the ground of the recognition of the true nature of a being. It is necessary condition for the ideation, formation, and manifestation of whatever is spiritual in the material world. It is the principle by which nature expresses itself and finds inner and outer fulfillment. God's Will offers the only way to stand against the distortions of thought and action so common among human beings. In a worlds of flux and impermanence, will offers conditions of stability and truth here and now. By will, the man and the world in which he lives is sustained and comforted through heartaches and disappointments. By will, control of nature is set and escape is possible from the cycle of bondage into which human beings are caught. There are two ways to approach the discussion of will. We can either approach from the perspective of what the Bible teaches about God or we may approach it from the dimension of man.

CHAPTER TWELVE

GOLDEN CORD

KEY 6: ACCESS TO PROVISION OPENING THE GATE OF SUPERNATURAL PROVISION

"Give us this day our daily bread."

Whenever I have been in dire need, I have taken this line and meditated on its many possibilities. Often I have received miraculous provision as I have focused on this simple line. Once I was caught up to the other realms and saw the immense provisions and upon returning to myself within a few hours had the provision I needed for the work to which the Lord had called me for that time.

ACTIVATING HEAVEN'S MANNA

Praying this line opens dimensions of provision. This day from the Greek word *semeron,* pronounced say'-mer-on, which is seen as a neuter adverb meaning *"this day"* and sometimes might refer to the night currently from which the day is birthed. It can also mean *"now"* this present moment. This provision is birthed from the dark of the night. This idea seems to grow from the fact that as God called the light from darkness, so now out of the night of need the light of provision is being birthed. Isa. 45:3: "And I will give thee the treasures of darkness, and hidden riches of secret places, that thou mayest know that I, the LORD, which call thee by thy name, Am the God of Israel." This "give us this day our daily bread" recalls the manna in the wilderness which came in the night and was manifested in the

179

morning. Ex. 16:11-18: "And the LORD spake unto Moses, saying, 12 "I have heard the murmurings of the children of Israel: speak unto them, saying,"

At even ye shall eat flesh, and in the morning ye shall be filled with bread; and ye shall know that I am the LORD your God. 13 And it came to pass, that at even the quails came up, and covered the camp: and in the morning the dew lay round about the host. 14 And when the dew that lay was gone up, behold, upon the face of the wilderness there lay a small round thing, as small as the hoar frost on the ground.

Though this was a response to murmuring and not prayer, yet it serves as the archetype for Divine provision for a person or people in need.

When God moves in provision, He allows us see through our circumstance in the night. Such provision is meant to call us to speak to one to another in praise to praise. This bread which the LORD hath gives us is more than what we eat but we receive in order to resource the Kingdom. This supernatural provision is more than drops of blessing; it is a gathering shower for every man according to the need for their influence and effect on the Kingdom of God. This Divine provision is prepared in the secret place of God according to the number of your days. Everyone involved in the Kingdom of God for God and His glory will have his or her tents overflowing with supernatural provision. It would not be just for you. Even your children, oh Israel of God, will gather more and not less. You shall mete it with a heavenly measure and even that which you have not gathered, much and over-abundance, shall flow from the supernatural provision to you. They gathered little shall remove all lack. They shall eat, everyone according to his eating, and have more to give away.

The word *"day"* is used in Scripture to represent an age or a particular generation. Supernatural provision can be generational. God causes supernatural provision to flow from one generation to another for those who are positioned for it by the covenant. It can also mean always and forever. In this line of prayer, we place our provision out of time unaffected by seasons, wars or physical geography. If this prayer is a Kingdom prayer, then all that is written within it must be connected to the longevity of the Kingdom. We read "and of the increase of his Kingdom and peace there shall be no end." The idea then is that there is a continual birthing of provision from the fecund womb of eternity for those who are in the Kingdom of the Lord of God.

Supernatural provision is always new and is not tied to past considerations of the need. Occasionally, it may seem that Divine provision has been depleted because our need is so acute. But the logic of Divine provision is that Heaven's resources are superior and does not suffer the fate of time and flux in which our perceived need appear. Our inner tensions, as regarding supernatural provision and pseudo moral uneasiness and self-rejection which yields to futility, must give way to a sense of the adequacy and limitlessness of Divine provision laid up for us in Heaven storehouse. And by Heaven I do not mean a location out of reach in this life but a realm concurrent with this one into which the child of God can reach for God's provision. This is not a cry for provision but an affirmation of the willingness of God to meet us at the point of our need. There is not a place of more intense self-doubt for many people who do the work of God than the area of material resources for the work. Note that I did not say God-doubt but self doubt. Supernatural provision as we have seen in the case of Israel can and does bypass our obstinacy, self-rejection and self-doubt to create an immediacy of hope and to materialize in the now what we have so often pushed into the future because of our misguided false humility. At this moment God is seriously committed to our progress and adequacy and wants it reflected in our life daily. The Divine provision that flows from this Kingdom prayer, as we see from Israel's supernatural provision in the wilderness, is evening and morning manifestations. That is when we have the strength and when our strength is weak. Evening represents the closure of the day. It is our entrance into a time of night in which we can neither see in the natural because we are not awake enough to fight or fend for ourselves. It is a time in which one may be haunted by imminent sense of emptiness. But in that season God reemerges riding on the wind of supernatural provision. God perceives the confines and the limit of our ability at such times, and rather than judge us God opens up the flow of eternal possibility invigorating and inspiring new vistas of providence that remove the deadening effect of want and need which has attempted to limit progress of our redemptive history. When we pray "give us this day," we include all that has been said above and more.

Now this provision is not just for some of God's children and is not dependent on the mood swing of man or woman but given to all flesh because of what happens in eternity and made flesh in the life, death, burial resurrection and advocacy of Jesus Christ our Redeemer. Provision grows out of the eternally enduring mercy of God.

In blessing Asher, Jacob says in Gen. 49:20: "Out of Asher his bread shall be fat, and he shall yield royal dainties." So the idea of bread is not just so that one fills one's belly with the husk like the prodigal in the swine pit but that one will become royalty before God who causes there to be an overflow. This supernatural provision symbolizes not just the vision of God to His people in time of need but the dwelling of God among His people perpetually. By this provision we arise and return from the far country of our resource exile. Supernatural provision is the LORD visiting the people with the release of Heaven's resources. It is a sign to the believer of God the Father mercifully lending eternity's fruitful bow into his/her life. This supernatural providence is directed to the heart of God's people to make them drunk with the wine of gladness. It is meant to cause their face to shine with the oil of the Lord's anointing. This supernatural bread strengthens the believer's heart. This provision is not because we are wise or so strong, not even because of our depth of understanding, not because of our righteousness; it is the favor of God freely flowing to us.

The next part reads "our daily bread" and offers us insight into the principle of provisional grace for which this prayer is intended. The word "daily" from the Greek *epiousios*, (pronounced ep-ee-oo'-see-os) could mean "tomorrow's" which offers not so much a prayer for tomorrow's provision but the acknowledgment of the future as already manifest in God. With God all that every day holds is already perfected. However, what is interesting is that Greek scholars seem to think that it is derivative of the present participle feminine. This will then mean that we speak forth in the belief that every day, today and tomorrow are pregnant with all that we need to thrive. The solutions to our need are pregnant and waiting to be birthed into whatever day we enter. The idea is that of the primary presupposition of Divine superimposition of provision in all of time, place and relation. Because of the relation, providential distribution flows from the Father over us so that we can find full rest. The enemy finds no point with which to point an accusing word toward God. So if this text is read in that way, then what we speak into existence in this prayer is the provision of God above and beyond what we think, ask or even need. The exemplification of this prayer in its fullness seems to me to be the miracles that Jesus Himself did. We read:

Matt. 14:16-21

16 But Jesus said unto them, they need not depart; give ye them to eat. 17 And they say unto him, we have here but five loaves, and two fishes. 18 He said, "Bring them hither to me." 19 And he commanded the multitude to sit down on the grass, and took the five loaves, and the two fishes, and looking up to Heaven, he blessed, and brake, and gave the loaves to his disciples, and the disciples to the multitude. 20 And they did all eat, and were filled: and they took up of the fragments that remained twelve baskets full. 21 And they that had eaten were about five thousand men, beside women and children.

In the passage we see that the time is important because it was evening, which is the extreme of the day; we also note that they were in a wilderness place where they could buy no food. It is interesting that Jesus lets them follow Him into the wilderness where they would have to look to Him for sustenance. But what is important here for our point is the fact that there was an overflow enough for the next days.

This provision stands strong against attacks of the enemy, who comes to steal, kill and destroy; and as long as it stays tuned with the realm of God's glory nothing touches it beside the ones who have charge of it. But this bread must come from the Father. He it is, who must give us this day. Note: not this night but this day. The simple indication is that it must be bread received in the light of God's presence and not from human avarice or selfishness. If you will recall, the first temptation of Adam and Eve was the temptation of bread to which they fell and the first temptation of the Lord in the wilderness was to receive bread apart from the generosity and kindness of the Father. The bread must be given by the Father and not taken from another by force. It must not be conjured up magically from hell or by violence it must come from the hand of the Father of light from whom all good gifts come.

"Therefore I say unto you, Take no thought for your life, what ye shall eat, or what ye shall drink; nor yet for your body, what ye shall put on. Is not the life more than meat, and the body than raiment? 26 Behold the fowls of the air: for they sow not, neither do they reap, nor gather into barns; yet **your Heavenly Father feedeth them. Are ye not much better than they?** 27 Which of you by taking thought can add one cubit unto his stature? 28 And why take ye thought for raiment? Consider the lilies of the field, how they grow; they toil not, neither do they spin: 29 And yet I say unto you, That even Solomon in all his glory was not arrayed like one of these. 30 Wherefore, **if God so clothe the grass of the field, which today is, and tomorrow is cast into the oven, shall he not much more clothe you,** O ye of little faith? 31 Therefore take no thought, saying, What shall we eat? Or, What shall we drink? or, Wherewithal shall we be clothed? 32 (For after all these things do the Gentiles seek:) for your Heavenly **Father knoweth** that ye have need of all these things. 33 **But seek ye first the Kingdom of God, and his righteousness; and all these things shall be added unto you."**

Note the passage above says: "your Heavenly Father feeds" and "your Heavenly Father knows." That is a key for belief in God's ability and desire to meet the need of even the least of His creation. Releasing himself to pray "give us this day our daily bread," the believer transports himself to stands on the holy hill of God where the streams of provision are in constant flow. Our security and safety from the dread of lack and famine is assured in the Kingdom hills. Let the world worry about drink, food and clothing, our thoughts and our will remains focused on the structure and flow of the Kingdom of God. Even when the warriors and chariots of the incessant need come charging through the valleys and hills our lives, we will simply take a firm stand and focus our whole being on the Kingdom of God. In the focus of my thoughts to that Kingdom whose eternal content is the righteousness of God, I align myself with the flow of supernatural provision. In this way when things increase, one's heart is not set on it.

The source of provision is God and its location is the Kingdom and the key to unlock it is the righteousness of God. The righteousness of God which we seek, that unlocks the provision, is Jesus Christ our Lord. He is the key of the Kingdom. He is the righteousness of God we are commanded to seek. He Himself said, "I am the door by me if any man enter he shall be saved, he shall go in and out and find pasture." (John 10:9) The ordinary principle of daily provision means more than just food to eat. It is the flow of abundance in which God secures our whole life in the Kingdom reality. Really, in the flow of abundance we do not need to raise chariots of war to go and get what God has given us. The sample of the continuous provision of God based on the absolute move of God and not merely on the sword of man is reveled in several provisional miracles of the Bible. It is not that we come charging through hills, the fields and the valleys with our sword and spear to take our provision. God simply ask us to take a hold of Him and come to the hills of his provisions. He tells us that He prepares a table even in the presence of the enemy. When the enemies of our provisions come, God will return and re-supply ours troughs with His abundance. He has lifted up His voice and His hands to Himself and has said many things regarding our provisions to us and this exemplified in the Scriptures. When the children of Israel went out to gather their provision or increase had not thing to do with their physical ability to gather much; in fact, God made sure that they got this as clear as possible.

185

Ex. 16:18: And when they did mete it with an omer, he that gathered much had nothing over, and he that gathered little had no lack; they gathered every man according to his eating.

Before entering the Promised Land, God takes the time to let the people know that He will be the security of their provision and that they must understand that the abundant overflow they were about to experience was not the result of their own power.

Deut. 8:7-13:

7 For the LORD thy God bringeth thee into a good land, a land of brooks of water, of fountains and depths that spring out of valleys and hills; 8 A land of wheat, and barley, and vines, and fig trees, and pomegranates; a land of oil olive, and honey;9 A land wherein **thou shalt eat bread without scarceness, thou shalt not lack any thing in it**; a land whose stones are iron, and out of whose hills thou mayest dig brass.10 When thou hast eaten and art full, then thou shalt bless the LORD thy God for the good land which **he hath given thee.** 11 Beware that thou **forget not** the LORD thy God, in not keeping his commandments, and his judgments, and his statutes, which I command thee this day: 12 Lest when thou **hast eaten and art full, and hast built goodly houses, and dwelt therein; 13 And when thy herds and thy flocks multiply, and thy silver and thy gold is multiplied, and all that thou hast is multiplied.**

This section of the prayer is to keep our heart from being lifted up to the LORD, and to keep our wandering minds from forgetting the LORD our God who constantly brings us, pulls, us out of the wilderness of lack and furnishes us with abundant supply even in the midst of our enemies. Though we have been led through that great and terrible wilderness wherein there has been fiery serpents, and evil scorpions, and drought, yet God has poured out water for our thirsty souls and provided bread for the hungry. For Israel, God is one who "brought forth water out of the rock of flint and who fed them in the wilderness with manna which their fathers knew not that He might humble them, and that He might prove them, to do them good at their latter end. So, why pray this prayer? Is it to remind God of the need for supernatural outflow? Absolutely not. Rather, it is to keep our heart in check and remind us of God as our eternal source. No matter how resourceful we are, we cannot give ourselves life nor can we provide ourselves the strength to get wealth and provision. So this prayer is not begging God but a placing of fence around the heart so that we do not fall into what God warned Israel about. Guard it so that you do not get to the place where you:

. . . . say in thine heart, My power and the might of mine hand hath gotten me this wealth. 18 But thou shalt remember the LORD thy God: for it is he that giveth thee power to get wealth, that he may establish his covenant which he sware unto thy fathers, as it is this day.

When it comes to provision, we should not be just be ordinary men and look at things from the material perspective alone. If we are going to enter the dimension of supernatural provision we must see with the eyes of the Spirit. We ought to be aware of the weakness of trusting in our natural resources and concluding that our provision is a result of our physical strength or even our spiritual qualities. Truly our help in the time of need is not us but God who in His grace and in His indescribable love pours them out as He wills. God wants us to taste and see. Ps. 34:8-10: "O taste and see that the LORD is good: blessed is the man that trusteth in him." We need to know that loving and serving the Lord is not in vain, no matter what things may look like. The Lord has not called us just to suffer with Him but also to reign with Him. Thus the plea "O fear the LORD, ye His saints" is followed with "for there is no want to them that fear him. The young lions do lack, and suffer hunger: but they that seek the LORD shall not want any good thing." "There is no lack to them that fear him" is then qualified by the fear of the Lord and the goodness of God. Again this why the prayer begins with "Our Father" and then proceeds to speak of His Kingdom at its very inception. The idea from the beginning of this prayer is that we approach God as loving Father but also fear

Him as the King who wills to protect His domain from the impact of the negative influence of unrighteousness. He will go to war for the citizens of His Kingdom. What He does not withhold from those that fear is not just anything but "good things." The very idea of the Good is God. Thus what we ask for when we ask for bread is not merely material provision, even though God will give material things to its fullest, but what we ask for is God in all of God's fullness. The daily bread as supernatural provision is truly good. It is a manifestation of God in our life's circumstance. Even material provision is a physical taste of the Good as God. Provision to the believer is the bread that comes down from Heaven. It is a gift given from God. There are two parts to provision as there are two parts to the week in the Hebrew calendar. The first part is the six days of Creation and the second part is the seventh day. The six days are the days of human labor, but the seventh day is the day of Divine Rest. It is a day in which we receive from the flow of eternal satisfaction. Provision for the six days have to do with the labor and sweat of man mixed with the grace of God, if you will; but the seventh day is God's alone. In Ex. 23:12, we read: "Six days thou shalt do thy work, and on the seventh day thou shalt rest: that thine ox and thine ass may rest, and the son of thy handmaid, and the stranger, may be refreshed."

It is the day of that bread which man, no matter how much he labors, cannot receive unless it is given to him from Heaven. It is bread eaten in and for the refreshment of the soul. In this Sabbath of provision, God reveals the equality of all. This heavenly time called Sabbath is the place of the release of your abundance. In restful trust you and I open the gates of supernatural provision. In this dimension there is ample supply for our need. Supernatural abundance in supply for our need in that day is equally present for all human beings. "As it is written, He that had gathered much had nothing over; and he that had gathered little had no lack."

Fall back on God for your provision in these times of need. Fall back on the blood for protection in this period of turmoil. Rather than being afraid of the menacing winds of our time, stay constantly in His presence and you will receive into your life the infinite flow of this supernatural provision and power. Whether afternoon, evening, or morning the good news is that everything is provided for you. So this provision is all-inclusive...this prayer is not just for the bread that goes into the mouth. God is faithful to give full provision in all areas. "Give us this day our daily bread" includes also the provision of healing. Our Lord Jesus intimated that healing is bread for the children. Said He, "it is not meet to take the bread of the children and give them unto the dogs?" Many times the bread of the mouth is not sufficient for the soul of man. God has proven faithful in meeting the needs His children—be it physical, psychological or spiritual. When we are sick, we have an emergency room for our healing in the presence of the Father.

For a long time I tried to separate this provision of bread from bread. In other words, I did not see that the bread is all-inclusive. The essence of this bread is that it brings with it the healing of our physical body. The fact that God wants us healthy must be taken seriously. For some time, many in the church did not reach out in faith for healing. But God is provider both of meat and perfect wholeness. The prayer taps into the possibility of immediate change, by the power of God, in the life of the person who prays. Praise the wonder of such a God whose name many times meets us with the bread of life. When we pray "give us this day," we immediately cause our inner being to turn its gaze from the natural to the supernatural and to depend entirely upon God as our source for bread that sustains the physical strength and bread that sustains health in all dimensions. Bread (all bread) is the heritage of the Son of God who said, "I am the door: by me if any man enters in, he shall be saved, and shall go in and out, and find pasture." (John 10:9.) In this prayer for bread we have an extraordinary entrance into an extraordinary sustenance. It is a call to have open eyes in the realm of the Spirit. While this may lead us to the recognition of our weakness and our inability to use our natural resources to overcome the vicious cycle of famine and loss and locust, grasshoppers and cankerworms, yet it not meant to place us merely as helpless victims in the face of our need. It is meant to secure our sense of the all-sufficiency of God toward us.

THE BREAD AND MANNA SYMBOLISM

When Moses was admonished to build the Tabernacle, he was instructed to gather a pot of the manna that fell from Heaven and put it into the Ark of the Covenant in the Holiest Place. This was a symbol and reminder of God's supernatural provision for them through the wilderness journey. Praise God! When God trains us for a particular work, we may find ourselves often where we are forced to trust God alone for our daily provisions. In this way God gets us acquainted with the keys for entering the dimensions of supernatural provision. When the terrible day comes, we must be able to tap into a greater realm for our provision. It would not do to hoard earthly provisions, as has been the custom of men in times of famine. There is a lesson to be learned in the way God provided for Israel in the wilderness, for Elijah in the days of famine and how the Lord Jesus provided for the people in the desert. It is not those who gather much that will be protected but those who through it all purpose in their hearts to trust the Lord. It is those who choose to walk by faith and not by sight that will thrive. Pray this line as an acceptance of the grace of God and pledge to depend upon God and not natural resources and abilities.

Those who have not learned to pray this line and to make it part of their daily meditation find themselves buffeted by forces of the worldly anxiety. Being filled with anxiety and fear, they put pressure on God's people to walk by sight. They become more concerned about personal survival and protection of their inordinate lifestyle instead of building faith and trust in God. As you pray this line, your inner man will become more aware of God's Divine provision and goodwill to you, Mount Zion, the city of the living God, the heavenly Jerusalem and not Edom for your provision. It is not a coincidence that this line of prayer comes after the line "thy will be done on earth as it is Heaven." It is God's Will that heavenly provision be made manifest on earth for God's children. It is also not an accident that one of the major temptations of Jesus in His wilderness training was about bread. Heaven's provision is always bent toward us but must not be forced by carnal processes. The question is, "Have we developed the discipline necessary for God to put them into our hands?" This prayer line is a check on greed and our often misguided attempted to use God's resources to lift ourselves over others. The fact that "day" is used twice in this line as I have said before means that provision is about human intimacy with God. During the first twelve hours man pretends to be his own provider. During second twelve hours of the night most men are asleep unaware of their earthly possessions. Even men who do not believe in God must depend on providence to keep them safe half of the day. This could be the reason the manna came by night when Israel was asleep to show that God is the one who gives this day, the bread for the day.

Today we are being called to transition from the six days of human labor to the seventh day of Divine rest. In this Sabbath we cease from materialistic strivings and enter into the rest of our God. In this rest our daily bread becomes the responsibility of the one we call Father. Our food and clothing are the responsibility of this one whose image and likeness we bear, whose dignity, honor and glory we worship and adore. For us who are God's children, there are different types of bread available to us.

THE BREAD OF LIFE–JESUS CHRIST AS BREAD

When Israel was in the wilderness, they ate manna which God gave them— bread from Heaven. Jesus insists that He was the bread. In John 6:32-35:

"Jesus said unto them, Verily, verily, I say unto you, Moses gave you not that bread from Heaven; but my Father giveth you *the true bread* from Heaven. 33 For the bread of God is he which cometh down from Heaven, and giveth life unto the world. 34 Then said they unto him, Lord, ever-more give us this bread. 35 And Jesus said unto them, *I am the bread of life*: he that cometh to me shall never hunger; and he that believeth on me shall never thirst."

He says that Moses did not give the bread from Heaven. It must have been shocking to the people that the bread which their Father's ate did not come from Heaven. It was a shadow of the true bread. God is the one, not Moses, who gives the true bread, which is the Son, to Moses. The Master insists that if that bread was from Heaven, the abode of the Father, they would have not died in the wilderness in disobedience as they did. John 6:48-51: "I am that bread of life. 49 Your fathers did eat manna in the wilderness, and are dead." This line also calls up participation in the life of Jesus Christ. Jesus is "the bread which cometh down from Heaven that a man may eat thereof and not die: "I am the living bread which came down from Heaven: *if any man eat of this bread, he shall live forever:* and the bread that I will give is my flesh, which I will give for the life of the world." When He taught us to pray "give us this day our daily bread" He was placing us in a position to have access to His life as our sustenance for eternity. It this phrase we activate our access to the life of God within our own being. This bread keeps us from falling into death as the Israelites did in the wilderness. It empowers us to faith and obedience. He is the bread of healing. He is the bread of fellowship that binds he brethren in Divine unity. He is the bread of forgiveness. In communion He is the physical bread sustains our natural body. Whatever Christ is as the living Word, He is also **The Bread of the written Word of God.** The bread is also the written Word of God which carries revelation for our daily journey. In Jeremiah15:16 we read, "Thy words were found, and I did eat them; and thy word was unto me the joy and rejoicing of mine heart: for I am called by thy name, O LORD God of hosts." So when I pray the "give us this day our daily bread" I reach for the internal life of God and the revelation that is seeded in the written Word.

CHAPTER THIRTEEN

GOLDEN CORD

KEY 7: FORGIVE UNTYING THE GORDIAN KNOT IN THE CORD

12 And forgive us our debts, as we forgive our debtors.

The crisis of offence has so saturated the body of Christ that it has become the Gordian knot that has wrapped up human believers in so many arena. Everybody seems offended by someone. Jesus addresses this issue in many passages of the Scripture in His teaching.

This prayer of forgiveness is not concentrating on our own failings but focuses on perception of the failings of others and its effects upon us. Here the formula for untying this Gordian knot is given in the Lord's Prayer. The measure of forgivers is not the infinite nature of God but the human being in the context of our own act of forgiveness. The prayer of forgiveness is not just us asking God to forgive our sins or daily failings; it is more than speech, and "it is act." Here prayer becomes act and being, not mere words. We are answered as it relates to forgiveness according to our actions not according to our request. There is a measure and it is us. While man may not be the measure of all things "he is the measure of his own forgiveness." "This act" is in itself a prayer that resolves the crisis of his failings and conflict with divinity. In this act of forgiveness as prayer, we bring to God our modes of reacting towards our brothers' and sisters' wrong doings in to the presence of God and He measures our actions back to us as harmonic resolution or disharmonic condemnation to our own dilemma. This acting towards our brother is our prayer coming from within and teaches us to treat our brothers, friends, enemies as embodiments of ourselves and as the answer to our own prayer for forgiveness at all times in the eyes of Heaven. It is as though the brother that offends us with whom we have to do is the context in which the loaf of bread that becomes our life is baked. Our basic instinct is to tear into our brother, friend, enemy in such a way that their longing for life is cut short ending in the eradication of their hope and possibility. In this simple prayer act of forgiveness, the person is presented to us as ourselves—"for with what measure we measure, the same shall measured back to us."

You are the measure of your own forgiveness though you are not the measure of your salvation.

You are as free as you let your brother be; you are as released as you release your brother—you are the measure, not God. How deep you can continue to experience the forgiveness of God depends on how many people you are willing to release from the grip of your inner shackle of unforgiveness. The release of power, true godly power, in our lives is very much dependent on the *aphekemical* (from the Greek *aphikemi*, "chemistry of the heart") disposition of our hearts. Our capacity to forgive gives birth to real transformation which allows the supernatural resolution of our own inner crisis. Now we each know as believers what forgiveness is because our Father in Heaven has placed before us the Son Jesus Christ as our mark of what it means. Our act-prayer forgiveness deals with the imperceptible inner influences where our criticism, judgment, condemnation and hurt churn and clutter our perception of the person as one who God loves and for whom He gave His Son as sacrifice. But by the act of forgiveness we unmask the false covering under which the enemy hides in order to attack us and make us vulnerable.

Forgiveness is redemptive because it is the supernatural resolution of what can become an eternal crisis. It redeems the one against "whom we have an issue" and sets us free from our self-enclosed hell, forming a bridge for reconnection with the other. We cannot exclude the possibility of forgiveness if we are in Christ and are truly conscious of how God redeemed us from bondage. In forgiveness then we embody God for the world—so that God can see His true reflection in us.

Many use anger and hurt as excuse to control and hold others in places of subordination but if we look carefully at this act, which is placed here as prayer, we realize how seriously God takes this act of offering ourselves as prayer in forgiving one another. Forgiveness is the act of prayer that deconstructs and recreates situations allowing us a new visional power to see ourselves from God's perspective and therefore reverse the headlong plunge of our baser nature into chaos. In the prayer act of forgiveness, we choose God in the other person no matter how far they may seem to be from Him. Forgiveness is a practice of participation with God in the healing of another and ultimately in our own healing. What we cannot achieve through vast accumulation of knowledge, we can accomplish in one moment of prayerful forgiveness.

The process of forgiveness should be understood as an act in which God heals the concrete situation through us. It is dialectically related to the act of judging righteously but its structures allow us to resolve the antithesis of wills into synthesis of being. Forgiveness is a revelational move in so far as it identifies us with Christ and allows Him to be manifest to others through us. We are bearers of God, and as bearers of God we dispense Him to our brethren and open them up for wholeness. When we forgive, we see, live and speak divinely. Forgiveness must occur, as the prayer states, because we ourselves are in desperate need of it. As we forgive, our vision is expanded. Heaven and earth nudge closer toward each other in us. Forgiveness is not the same for everyone, for everyone is not hurt the same way nor does everyone hurt the same way; but by intending and acting upon the Divine command to forgive, we all expand our horizon. God's forgiveness of our daily errors and our forgiving of our brethren's daily faults against us are made interdependent in the Scriptures. "Forgive us" cannot be separated from and cannot be said apart from "as we forgive." In the Cross of Jesus Christ, we find forgiveness but in our forgiveness we carry the cross.

Forgiveness is a spiritual attitude held in relation to God, self and others. Things that people do are allowed to impress themselves so strongly on our consciousness that they dictate our responses to things that are not even remotely connected to them in real life. We walk, talk, reflect on it until it enters deep into us and seeps into our subconscious and from there inform our instinctive responses. Our spiritual atmosphere becomes charged with the energy of the person who hurt us in the first place. When we think of them, their act, voice, and appearance vibrates through our whole person raising the negative force to higher octave, anger, disgust, shame, hate and the like. This results in clogging our soul and spiritual pathway and distorting channels to our movement in God. We cannot get to God, and most importantly God cannot get to us because we remain in the cube of unforgiveness. This can become so toxic that those who come in contact with us and even seek to help us are repelled without knowing why.

I must urge you to know how important a forgiving spirit is for creating an atmosphere of personal breakthrough into other realms—especially the realm of the true power of God. Sometimes being able to break through into dimensions of which we dream or envision is simply to take hold of forgiveness. A knot on the cord in this area will keep us from crossing over into heavenly dimensions. It will keep us tied in knots in our body and our soul. Lack of forgiveness can hinder our physical body's reconstitutive ability. It is true that lack of forgiveness in many of us is fueled by beliefs, opinions, views and ideals many of them justified by our re-ligious outlook. But forgiveness has very little to do with these. It is meant to re-lease Divine dynamism into our spiritual walk. Our desire, good intentions, godly ambitions and our desire to change the world for good can be blocked not by the devil or others but by a knot of unforgiveness on the heavenly cord of prayer.

I encourage you then to cultivate a spiritual attitude of forgiveness so that you walk constantly in an atmosphere of openness to other dimensions with the ability to see and hear from Heaven. When this is done you will find that you will attract good toward you more often than evil. The leaven of forgiveness will leaven the whole lump of your life. Conversely the leaven of unforgiveness will leaven the whole of your life in the negative direction.

UNFORGIVENESS	FORGIVENESS
Knots	Loose
Anger	Joy
Distrust	Trust
Fear	Faith
Hate	Love

We can list many things like these, but you get the point. Building up a spirit of forgiveness will free your being to forge into other dimensions. Train your heart, therefore, to forgive and train your mind to release the pain so that new thoughts, ideas and visions may flow freely into you. I personally believe that Jesus won victory over the fallen humanity He had taken upon Himself on the cross specifically at the moment when He said, "Father forgive them." Wow. The first cry that reached Heaven from fallen humanity was that of unforgiveness. It was Abel's blood crying out against his brother. Since then we have fought, maimed, decimated, and attempted to destroy each other because of this beast called unforgiveness. When Christ asked the Father to forgive those that hurt Him, He won the battle over that sinister dragon who has wrapped itself around the neck of fallen humanity since the fall. One way to deal with this is make a list of all those against whom you have something, especially the one you keep talking about and every time you think about it you re-experience the pain. Now intentionally release them and symbolically burn the list and speak healing to the situation in the name of the Lord. As you forgive and let go, you will experience the combining of the forces of Heaven and earth propelling forward to affect and influence your environment toward Divinity for good.

How many of us are like Peter in Matt. 18:21-22: "Then came Peter to him, and said, Lord, how oft shall my brother sin against me, and I forgive him? Till seven times? Jesus saith unto him, I say not unto thee, Until seven times: but, Until seventy times seven." Peter really thought, "Boy, I am doing so well," but

Jesus blew him out of the religious water. The Lord said 70x7 (140 by mathematical standards); we could say that it is closer to 144 which is the number of the New Jerusalem, the new Israel. So if Peter is going to measure forgiveness, he must measure it by how many times God forgave Israel. So if you are counting you have missed the point.

Forgiveness is the harbinger of Divine creativity. Forgiveness produces tangible transformation in the one who forgives as well as the one who is forgiven. Only the one who has experienced hurt can forgive. No one else can forgive for you. You must do it yourself. God cannot do it for you without you. You cannot hold onto the pain and ask God to forgive the person. It does not work like that. It is seed you must sow because you are going to need its harvest for yourself in the future. Forgiveness is not restricted to the act committed against you but it extends to yourself as the recipient of the act as willing or unwilling partaker in the act. Forgiveness does not co-habit with judgment in the same person for the same act. Now this does not mean that the act may not turn around and bite the doer, but it does entail that the forgiver frees themselves from being the judge of the act and releases their mind to love as God the Father loves. Now that is difficult. Yet this is what God asks of us in order to create new forms for the manifestation of our Heaven-born selves. Forgiveness, true forgiveness, flows from intimate knowledge of the Christ whom we follow. It is not just therapeutic but redemptive in that it reaches to the eternal point within us and there touches the heart of God. Jesus did not just teach this prayer, He practiced it at the most importune time—on the cross. By so doing, He took away from me any reason to hold onto my hurt.

God has given us the capacity for self-expansion into so many dimensions that our capacity to move into these dimensions and to move in them are buried deep within us and can only be activated by God's love. The more hurt we harbor, the more this possibility for self-expansion is pushed further away from our conscious reach. But if we can reach deeper through the Holy Spirit and activate this capacity by letting go of the hurt and forgiving, our Divine creativity can burst forth. Forgiveness is the only original act left for man. It is the only originality left for him in world of hurt and sin. It is his only creation out of nothing. By it he becomes new and by it he moves the hand of Heaven to make all things new. It seems clear that there are no easy steps on the way of forgiveness. But here is where our divinity is hidden and our Divine likeness still shines forth. A flood of constructive creativity overcoming the pessimistic bitter waters of life, reigniting God awareness and gracing the darkened night with its glimmering ray, that's forgiveness. Here on earth the worlds wait for the moon of man to reflect the sun of God's eternal light in simple letting go and releasing the hurt. "Father forgive them."

THE TWO LETTER MILLION DOLLAR WORD: AS

When we learn to pray, "Forgive us our sins **AS** we forgive," then we have unknotted the golden cord in its most knotty section. We cannot just pray "forgive me" and leave it at that, for that is not a prayer but a weighing down of the soul on the scale of Heaven's justice. "Forgive me" cannot be the first; the "**AS** we (I) forgive" is the first act which puts me in place of being able to ask "forgive me (us)." This putting my brothers error in my presence so as to feel it again and then to release it lets me know that depth of what I am asking the Father to do for me at least in term of my finite human ability. "I forgive you" must be the primary orientation of my being if I am ever going to reach the depth of the being I started out by calling "Father."

How do I forgive? That is the 24,000 question. By what process do I arrive at forgiving another? By what tortuous road of twisted human logic do I travel to forgive those who have hurt me? This "**AS**" scares the daylight out of me. For when I look at the "*as* I forgive," I tremble before the majesty of the King before whom I have come for forgiveness. If I must cross the threshold of Heaven and reach into the throne, I must be willing even from the cross to say, "Father, forgive them." For me to say, "Father forgive me," I must first of all from the depth of my heart forgive, for I cannot lie to the one to whom I come for forgiveness.

Forgiveness plays a considerable role in training our will to submit to God's Will and helps our soul to break through to submission to the Will of God. In performing acts of forgiveness, we set in motion processes by which a human being back into a taste of Eden's grace by doing the Will of the Father. In forgiveness, the voluntary action of our will is initiated and works independently to run the course of love. We extend our soul to abduct another person redemptively into peace and joy from an act that has served to limit their Divine nature. The thing about forgiveness is that it does not need superhuman strength or even acceptance from the person who to whom it is offered to be powerful; it merely needs the conjunction of the human will with the Will of the Father. In this seeming weakness, the will is stronger than physical force and can bridge distance and time and restore broken breaches. The forgiving person leaves an impact in the world that is eternal by extending good will to all. His own abduction from the abyss by the good will of God propels His Will. If another reaches for the forgiveness which has been offered to him, he willingly gives it. He wills the eternal hand of God to reach through him to abduct them also from their encircling darkness. This stretching out of the self to another is so clearly seen in our Master and Lord as hung dying on the cross. However, it is the result of the will of man trained to conform to the Will of God. This move to forgive is grounded in the surrender of the will of inner man as well as the world outlook to the Will of God. The one who forgives has formed a will that flows in the stream of divinity but stands firmly contrasted to the world. They have overcome the influence of the egotistic factor that rules the world. They have apprehended the spiritual world and the emancipative possibilities, which free men from the constant debt owed the cycle of anger and revenge. They have a free will because their will is interweaved with the absolute Free will of God. By conjunction of will to Will they have forgiven others. Therefore, they can cry, "AS we (I) forgive." This bending of the will toward forgiveness, releases one from the grasp of the materialistic mindset of the world. By willingly letting others be released, one is not submerged into the present cosmos but transported through the gates of love and mercy into the throne room in the presence of the mercy seat.

Lack of forgiveness is dangerous impairment of the spiritual faculty in any human being but worse in the Christian because it blurs the image and likeness of

Christ. It affects his or her ability to be a witness for the Christ who while hanging on the cross said "Father forgive them." The pattern set in this line of prayer and illustrated at that moment on the cross sets the galactic traveler apart from those who wish to go nowhere beyond their present cosmos. The forgiver may be termed excessively indulgent, compromising or in common sarcastic language, "feely-touchy," yet in truth what he or she does or does not do is not based on sentimentality but based on the objective measure of Divine Will in Christ, notwithstanding feelings, moods or needs. He or she does not lose sight of the Christ reality which has been experienced. When we lose sight of this *"As we forgive,"* we become judgmental and destructive and tend to use the law of God as weapons of our own vengeance and presumed righteousness.

Forgiveness can help organize our life, center it, and allow it to manifest its ultimate purpose which is to be like God. Here in forgiveness, freedom and meaningful actions springing from God's heart produces its fruits and forces shifts in the landscape of our conscious and unconscious. We become no mere men. Here is the key to expansiveness, modification, redirection and renewal. The greater the move to forgive the stronger the spirit and the higher the consciousness of God as God and the more open the channels of movement in various dimensions of life. Forgiveness is Divine radiance which moves us into deeper places in God which we would not have gone had we allowed our hurt to calcify underneath and become an underlying root of bitterness. It is valuable in itself and brings more good and causes growth. The very definition of forgiveness connotes growth and progress in the quality of our spiritual walk. It changes the environment for the release of God's dynamism and repairs pathways to the realms of the Spirit. The practice of forgiveness helps us to increasingly adapt our spirit and mode of thought to mind of Christ. Concepts and ideas which are so commonly accepted in our cultural milieu that have entered into us can now, by the discipline of forgiveness, either be removed or transformed to conform to the image of Christ.

CHAPTER FOURTEEN:
GOLDEN CORD

KEY 8: FOLLOW THE LEADER
SUPERNATURAL GUIDANCE

13 And lead us not into temptation.

Before we deal with this line of prayer, we need to remember that temptation is not sin in itself, rather it is the influence exacted upon one by an exciting hope or desire which is not in submission to the Will of God and does not conform to our God-given destiny. In temptation we could be led into circles of influence that cause us sometimes to contemplate or do things just because we are in its sphere. Temptation is the urge to act contrary to our ideal deriving either from self-delusion of fleeting pleasure or flattery from the enemy of our God-given destiny. We know that many things and persons can attempt to lead us astray and take us off the track of Divine good will. But to insinuate, as this passage seems to do, that God can act to lead us into temptation will meet with holy indignation and sanctified fury from the lovers of God. In fact even a biblical prophet vehemently opposes the idea that God can tempt a man "When tempted, no one should say: 'God is tempting me.' For God cannot be tempted by evil, nor does he tempt anyone;" (James 1:13) The same James proceeds in the same passage to say (James 1:14-16):

> "But every man is tempted, when he is drawn away of his own lust, and enticed. 15 Then when lust hath conceived, it bringeth forth sin: and sin, when it is finished, bringeth forth death. 16 Do not err, my beloved brethren."

202

So we know that God does not tempt us but what this passage is implying is that God can and does lead us to be tempted by the enemy so that we can be proved. Matt. 4:1: "Then was Jesus led up of the Spirit into the wilderness to be tempted of the devil." In Heb. 2:18 we get an explanation for this temptation: "For in that he himself hath suffered being tempted, he is able to succor them that are tempted." Heb. 4:15-16:

> "For we have not an high priest which cannot be touched with the feeling
> of our infirmities; but was in all points tempted like as we are, yet without
> sin.16 Let us therefore come boldly unto the throne of grace, that we may
> obtain mercy, and find grace to help in time of need."

In 1 Cor. 10:13-14, we read:

> "There hath no temptation taken you but such as is common to man:
> but God is faithful, who will not suffer you to be tempted above that
> ye are able; but will with the temptation also make a way to escape,
> that ye may be able to bear it. 14 Wherefore, my dearly beloved, flee
> from idolatry."

Could we cause God to lead us into temptation? Could it be that God leads us to be tempted but is not an active tempter because there is no evil in Him? Rather He leaves the tempting to Satan and his demonic cohorts who are habitations of evil.

Temptation does not just happen to us. They cannot be separated from other aspects of our lives. According to James they are outgrowths of our psychological landscape—our desires, moods and feelings are its launching pad. Though it is not evil in itself, it is for the tempter an important step to evil if not dealt with adequately. Victory can be achieved by accessing the power of Christ which He exercised over His own temptation. This is really a prayer to guard the heart in its innocence so that it does not become the breeding ground for our own undoing. While temptations in themselves do not constitute production of evil, we should never underestimate the power of temptation and its potential contribution to our spiritual distraction. Overemphasis on temptation can lead to spiritual and communal isolation, which keeps people from engaging the world with the power of God because of fear of falling.

But this line of prayer points to the fact that God is not interested in veering us away from temptations which we think are too difficult for us but to deliver us from its evil. When we see one that can overpower us, we cry "lead us not into temptation." We pray this also because some temptations can be distractions from what God has committed to us. Sometimes in the Authorized Version of the Bible, the Word "temptation" is used interchangeably with the idea of trials. Of course the temptation to sin is not from God. So, God does not lead us deliberately to temptation so that we might fall. This would go against the very character of God. We must make a distinction between temptation and trial for the purpose of clarifying the function and purpose of God from that of the enemy of our soul in the situation. James 1:13-18

> 13 Let no one say when he is tempted, "I am tempted by God"; for God cannot be tempted by evil, nor does He Himself tempt anyone. 14 But each one is tempted when he is drawn away by his own desires and enticed. 15 Then, when desire has conceived, it gives birth to sin; and sin, when it is full-grown, brings forth death. 16 Do not be deceived, my beloved brethren. 17 Every good gift and every perfect gift is from above, and comes down from the Father of lights, with whom there is no variation or shadow of turning. 18 Of His own will He brought us forth by the word of truth, that we might be a kind of first fruits of His creatures.

According to this passage God cannot be and does not desire to be the direct agent of our temptation by evil. But He does lead us into situations in which we are tested. The Greek word *ekpeirazo*, pronounced **ek-pi-rad'-zo** suggests a thorough test of the material of which our character is made. It does not mean that God does not know our makeup, but the Scripture insists that God proves our character by placing us in situations where we are tested and tried. God does this so we can see if we shall deal objectively with God's goodness and endeavor to keep faith with Him. Sure this scrutinizing of our being may entice us to bring accusations against God but it does not have to. For the purpose of God is to prove His glory in us, not to destroy us. This prayer is meant to keep us from avoiding the discipline of the Lord. Now by discipline I do not mean the idea of punishment that has become attached to it. Rather by discipline I mean the root idea of discipleship in which the character of the Master is formed in us by lessons and tests on the way. God as Father "disciplines us" in the sense of a course of study in His eternal principle which lead us "as dear children" to be "imitators of God." We are in school. So the trials or even temptation that God allows to be put in our way are never intended to throw us into the hands of sin or evil but to clarify for us the lessons learned from the Father's heart. They are to affirm in our hearts the words we heard in the times we spent with our Lord. "Lead us not into temptation" does not mean remove this trial from us but keeps us from falling headlong into the trap of the enemy when our lessons are tested by circumstances of life. It is interesting that James inserts the phrase "Every good gift and every perfect gift is from above, and comes down from the Father of lights, with whom there is no variation or shadow of turning." In this way it is shown that whenever God permits any trial, He does so to shine the light into our lives and to check shadow of variations which may serve to short circuit our manifestation of God's image and likeness. This examination as it relates to our relationship with God as a means of proving our character is evidenced in what God said was the purpose in putting Israel through such ordeal in the wilderness. We read in Exodus 16:4:

> "Then said the LORD unto Moses, Behold, I will rain bread from Heaven for you; and the people shall go out and gather a certain rate every day, that I may prove them, whether they will walk in my law, or no."

Even the manifestation of God to them was a test as it is said in Exodus 20:20:

> "And Moses said unto the people, Fear not: for God is come to prove you, and that his fear may be before your faces, that ye sin not."

In summarizing the journey of the children of Israel, Deuteronomy 8:2 says:

"And thou shalt remember all the way which the LORD thy God led thee these forty years in the wilderness, to humble thee, and to prove thee, to know what was in thine heart, whether thou wouldest keep his commandments, or no."

Later on in the same chapter, Deut. 8:16, Moses said God, *"fed thee in the wilderness with manna, which thy fathers knew not, that he might humble thee, and that he might prove thee, to do thee good at thy latter end."* All the trouble of the people God that is permitted by God is directed to the heart and action to reveal whether our way will be consistent with what we know and say we believe about the LORD in our actual walk.

Though the purpose of God is not to lead us into temptation, yet our response in the situation may lead us into temptation. We may respond to God with anger or become hot against God which may lead us to speak haughtily and trying to force God to prove Himself to us rather than submit our wills humbly in prayer to God as Lord. Since this tendency dwells inside of us, God then permits trial once, twice, yeah thrice. We read that Jesus was led into the wilderness by the Spirit to be tempted by the devil. This also means that God can and does intentionally take us to circumstances, atmosphere, environment in which we are tested. When we look at Jesus, the goal of God was to initiate Him into the struggle of humanity and to hone His skills for human war against the enemy. However, the Devil's temptation was to undo His character and make Him unusable by God. When our lives begin to grow and our fame is heard in the spiritual realm and our concern for the name of the LORD is recognized, then the devil takes permission to test us and to prove us through some hard questions of life.

But here is the heart of the issue in being lead by God into a place where we can be tried. God never sends us alone but sends us with the help of the heavenly city and with us a great company of Heaven, the spices of the Word, the golden nuggets of Heaven's abundant mercies and doors of escape marked with precious stones of Heaven as long as we continue to commune with Him with all our hearts. Furthermore, God leads us to the place of our trial to show us whom we will justify. If we justify ourselves in our time of trial, we have not learned the lessons of our Farther very well. If we justify ourselves, then we set ourselves to fall into condemnation. But if in the trial we justify God and maintain the perfection of His praise, then we shall be proven to be His. David knew this so he cried in Psalm 26:2: "Examine me, O LORD, and prove me; try my reins and my heart."

If God's intention is to prove us, then the prayer "lead us not into temptation" does not focus on making sure that we avoid all trouble as some modern preachers tend to propose, rather it focuses on conforming us to the image of the Son and the transformative renewal of our mind. In another place we read: "that ye may prove what is that good, and acceptable, and perfect, Will of God." (Romans 12) How do we prove the sincerity of our love in the face of human forwardness? Is it not the ability to maintain that love in the face of continuous onslaught by the opposing side? Self-examination is not enough, for in it we may even delude ourselves into thinking that we are what we are not. We need objective examination to see if we are truly in the faith. This is not to prove something to God but to prove to our own selves. This is how we come to truly know our own selves and that Jesus Christ is in us, and that we are not reprobates. Every one of us is constantly working for God or for ourselves. The proof of our work is whether it ends in bearing joyful fruits to the glory of God or seeds of praise for ourselves. Testing our work has a certain sense of "being alone," for it is not temptation in which another seeks to glory over us by our fall but is the test of what we own as ours in the presence of God. In 1 Thessalonians 5:21 we read, "Prove all things; hold fast that which is good." Testing separates the true from the false, the viable from the non-viable so that we might be able to hold the good and discard the evil.

In dealing with the issue of being led into temptation, this prayer to our Father is directed toward dealing with our desires and enticements and our bent to sin and death. Part of our bent to sin is the false consciousness which began in Adam and assumes that God deprives us unjustly of what we think is rightfully ours without our consent, He causes us to wait for a time while we on the other hand must have it now. So, instead of devoting ourselves to prayer, we let Satan use our lack of self-control as instrument of seduction, enticing us to go astray from right relation with the Father. That which has the quality to seduce us is truly given that it might qualify us for that which God holds back for a short time.

The prayer in a sense may also be directed to our tendency to tempt God. So if we are not to be led into temptation, one of the temptation to which we are praying not be to be led into is that which was so common to the children of Israel in the wilderness—the temptation to tempt God.

In Exodus 17:2 we read, "Therefore the people contended with Moses, and said, "Give us water, that we may drink. And Moses said to them, 'Why do you contend with me? Why do you tempt the LORD?'" In Deuteronomy 6:16 we are explicitly commanded, "You shall not tempt the LORD your God as you tempted Him in Massah.

Malachi 3:15: "So now we call the proud blessed, For those who do wickedness are raised up; They even tempt God and go free." Matthew 4:7: Jesus said to him, "It is written again, 'You shall not tempt the LORD your God.' " Luke 4:12: And Jesus answered and said to him, "It has been said, 'You shall not tempt the LORD your God.' " 1 Corinthians 10:9: "nor let us tempt Christ, as some of them also tempted, and were destroyed by serpents"

Leadership of God is mentioned here in a negative sense so that we would understand that we must seek positive guidance from the Lord. There are, it seems to me, several types of leadership. Speaking in Psalm 23, the psalmist says, "He leads me besides still waters. He leads me in the path of righteousness for his name sake." Furthermore, the word *"lead"* may be directed to the good or to the bad.

There is no doubt in my mind that we often come into the sphere of temptation by our desire and intentions but also that God sends us into atmosphere of trials, even temptations. (Deut. 8) It would be a convenient denial to say that God is not involved at all in our trials or that the devil is the main architect of our temptations, trials, tests and tribulations. The phenomena of temptation when experienced and overcome create a quantum leap into a higher plane of spiritual consciousness. Until we move into a different stage or phase of our knowledge and relationship with God, we tend not to see this positive side of these four T's. Temptation consciousness should not be mainly from the perspective of the possibility of **falling** but also as containing the seed possibility of a quantum rise or leap into a deeper or higher experience of Heaven's purpose. The experience of Jesus Christ our Lord seems to suggest that its structures contains a God-driven stream leading to clarification of values, deeper wisdom, greater spiritual awareness and even humility. In Hebrew we read that "He learned obedience by the things he suffered." This is ground for knowing that you and I can overcome temptations, tests, trials and tribulations because you and I possess the quality of the Divine consciousness and awareness and that God's nature that is always accessible to us in the midst of any of the four T's: Temptation, tests, trials and tribulation.[15]

Now I have said that God does not lead us into temptation. However, can God lead us into a place where the purpose is for us to be tempted but does not Himself engage in the act of tempting? There is one exception it would seem in the case of Abraham where it is written: "now it came about that after these things that God tested Abraham." The KJV uses the term "tempted." I see no reason why we as believers should not allow God the right to try us and to prove us. However, God does not test with evil intention or bad will. When God tests, it seems to be done with our good in mind though it be at the cost of something dear to us. We consider these tests evil because of our attachment to temporal things and relationship and partiality of our perspective.

What then are the spiritual compositions of temptation? What are their physical, or mental structures? However one enters, the surface of temptation is never firm. But no matter what it feels like, it is compressed and composed with possibilities of star birthing or star death. In the absence of temptation, if that is ever possible in this body, we should not read the favor of God but examine the atmosphere to see that we have not made an uncertain, destructive peace with the enemy of our soul—our comfort zone. Whether temptation is limited to human beings is not the issue. The issue is that human beings are subject to temptations and trials for the Divine purpose.

When we speak of leadership we must remember that if we pray not to be led into temptation, we are also saying that we are willing to follow that guidance which God provides. We are indeed saying that we will obey Divine guidance and follow God's leadership whithersoever it takes us. It is saying that we are willing to let go of our own vision of what is best for us and trust God. This complete trust in God means that we have come to know that Divine leadership always leads us into victory and understand that Divine leadership will always lead us into clarity of thought and vision in the end. It will lead us into conformity with the life and action of Jesus Christ. Submission to this leadership entails openness to the ever-present companionship of God's precious Holy Spirit. But it never means a life without pressure or wars. While we are to pray "lead us not into temptation," we should not become so morbidly preoccupied with fear of being led into temptation or falling into it that we cease to pray for the positive aspect. We ought to pray for positive guidance and be willing to follow that guidance for ourselves and for others. "Satan has desired to sift you," Jesus tells Peter. Yet in the next breath He says, "I have prayed for you." Even though we must pay attention to the possibility of being thrown into the atmosphere of temptation, we need to hold fast to the idea clearly written in Scripture and clearly exemplified by many faithful men and women that God does lead and guide the beloved positively in all areas of life. "Lead me O Lord in Thy righteousness," says the psalmist in Psalm 5:8. Further along he says, "lead me in you truth." (Psalm 25: 5) In Psalm 27:11 he says, "lead me in a smooth path." And again in Psalm 31:3, "lead me and guide me."

Divine leadership is a key reason for this prayer. Through this one and only negative line in the Lord's Prayer, Jesus summarizes all the positive statements about Divine guidance. There are five spectral flows of prayer as it deals with what I term the human ordeal as it relates to guidance—the spirit, the heart, the soul, the mind and the physical strength. Guidance goes in steps and since spiritual guidance is our goal in praying this prayer, it calls for fluidity, flexibility and will-ingness to see any experience of the moment as temporal and draw the courage to look beyond it based on our view of eternity. Says Paul, "For I reckon that the suf-fering of this temporal age is nothing to be compared with the glory that shall be revealed." (Romans 8) Divine guidance and leadership means that we become aware of the impermanence of the present world.

Experiences are seen as markers on the way to know God more. We are ready to let go, release and demystify any experience for the purpose of following freely after God. Any analysis of divine leadership will have to deal with the presence of the unknown and the trials that accompany it. If we do not allow that divine lead-ership or guidance does contain its "dark" uncomfortable dimension, then we tend to stumble when certain difficulties arise in paths we believe we took based on clear divine leadership. Many of us have encountered problems in divine leader-ship which in the interim—because of the dark night of our soul, the body, the mind, ear, the eyes—questions arise as to whether this is really God's leadership: "Did I really hear God right? If I hear God, why do I have all these obstacles?" Simply saying that if one is suffering it must not have been of God cannot solve the problem of Divine leadership.

Taking the view that God is causing us to be born into a different dimension in which we take hold of the beauty, glory and wonder of our Father in a greater way will help many of us deal with the shaking that comes from following God's leadership. This birth like any other birth has its pangs, blood, sweat and tears. God structured the world in such a way that because of sin we have to go through four T's to attain the glory prepared for us. The solution to the problem is not to run away or to conclude that God is not leading but to insist on following God and continuously breathe prayer for Divine guidance.

When we are being led by God who is the Spirit, many aspects of what we may seem to know in the natural are up for grabs; the purity of Divine leadership points to the yet unmanifest, unformed, unattained dimension in our lives. The truth is that usually where God leads us no eye has seen, ears have not heard, no mind has conceived, neither has it been grasped by the heart of man—including ours. So the leadership keeps us in a state of fluid openness to the Divine. In the four T's we are being melted, liquefied for reformation. In it there is a stripping of our carnality, psychical orientation in order to reformat, realign, and realize us spiritually. This cloud of unknowing leads us to where God is all-in-all and we literally "no longer live but Christ lives in us." The life we begin to live is lived not by the power of ourselves by the grace of the Son of God who has loved us and given Himself a ransom for us. The opposite of being led in to temptation is being led to what is good, right, to rest in God. There is no separation between our openness to the Spirit and the guidance we receive.

Divine leadership first leads us into the terrain of our own soul. By praying this line: "Lead us not," we will discover where our resistance to positive health or where we reject the very God whom we seek. This leadership then directionally flows through the stream of the inner structures we have developed. Thus, we may say that divine leadership takes us where our hearts has already gone. Therefore, the prayer, if we follow James, is not so much directed at God as it is directed to the structuring our inner desire and consciousness.

"Everyman is tempted when He is drawn away by his own lust, and enticed. Then when lust has conceived, it brings forth sin, sin when it is finished brings forth death." (James 1:23-24)

Temptation is not out there. The tempter is not external to us, but we are often the tempter and the tempted in most cases. Thus, this may be a prayer in which we ask God not to allow us to be drawn away by our own lust and be enticed by it so that we cannot extricate ourselves from the tangled web we have weaved. Just as temptation is not an external phenomenon separated from the inward structures and landscapes of my being, so neither can the leadership of God be completely separated from the landscape of my interiority and my willingness to be led by God into the unknown.

Temptation is simply the pursuit of our own shadows from which we seek to flee or hide. The reality of temptation is that it is my temptation not God's

212

temptation, nor the world's temptation. It is my own hidden desires pressuring me and calling for acknowledgment. When I do not acknowledge it or them and deal with it, these desires take on their own personality, which then torments me. God did not lead me into it, but since God must bring me to the place of testing so that I may know my heart truly before God, this—my alter persona—shows up so that I can deal with it and relate to God authentically. This persona which is my temptation is not in the image of God, for it is the creation of my unacknowledged and therefore my unconfessed negative desires and decisions which take me captive because they are legitimately my offspring but illegitimate as relates to God.

My temptation is my projected self, my objectified and rarefied self, which I refuse to give to God or which God will not take because I give it to Him in by the way of "the lie" not "the truth." What is the lie? The lie is that I refuse to acknowledge these negative phenomena honestly as mine and let it be seen in light of the person of Jesus Christ so that its repugnance in the sight of God may become ever so clear to me. Jesus says, "because you say that you have no sin your guilt remains." At another place John tells us this:

> "But if we walk in the light as He is in the light, we have fellowship with one another, and the blood of Jesus Christ cleanses us from all our unrighteousness. If we say we have no sins, we deceive ourselves and the truth is not in us. If we confess our sins he faithful and just to forgive us and to cleanse us from all unrighteousness. If we say that we have sinned, we make him a liar and the truth is not in us." (I John 1:7-10)

Therefore, the Divine leadership that tests the material of our making pulls us vertically, horizontally, interiorly, exteriorly to show us what our hearts, souls and spirits cling to frantically in opposition to God. Every aspect of Divine guidance is made up of God's instructions and our willingness to follow. Temptation then is not what God does to us but a matter of our total conformity to the good will of God. As the leadership of God is a spiritual action, which calls us to subordinate our baser and grosser personality traits to the purpose and glory of God, temptation allowed by God can also be seen as performing its purpose in this way. Every trial, every temptation, every test, or tribulation whatever we call it serves as mirror to what is truly important to us. In our lives, temptation appears and performs the role of, as the old song goes, consuming our dross and refining our gall. In other words no matter where we end up—whether we believe that God is behind the trial, temptation, test or tribulation—the bottom line is how we act in them depicts for us where we are in our commitment to God and His purpose for our lives.

Temptation, trial, tests, tribulations and our overcoming of them is a significant measure of the weight of glory that will be upon us in life and ministry. Our victory is measured by the depth of or grasp of the passion of the Lord Jesus Christ, who endured all these and yet came out of them faithful to the God who sent Him into the world. It constitutes the catalyst for our Christilation. Through it, we pass from one stage to another, from one level of intimacy to another. It carries with it the seed of our transformation to higher, or if you prefer, deeper levels of experience with the Divine.

This then means that all temptation is transitory and very temporal. Because it is fleeting we can rise above it and we can outlive, and in the process become increasingly competent on how we deal with it if we pay attention and follow the example of Jesus Christ our Lord. There is always an antidote to temptation. There is always something disempowering in its venomal though in our blindness and sometimes frantic panting we may not see it. If the temptation is in the area of thought, I have learned that another simple thought can displace it. If it's a word, I have learned that a word spoken fittingly can overcome it. The key is that one makes sure that what displaces the temptation proceeds from a better place— Heaven. Remember, that there are spiritual dimensions, feeling dimensions, psychic (soulish) dimensions and physical dimensions to temptations. There are certain vehicles for the manifestations of God in our lives contained in the Lord's Prayer. Above and beyond the actual temptations is the Divine design whose main aim is to reveal the splendor of our King in our lives.

To deal with this passage we need to take a brief excursion on Divine leadership.

Since the prayer begins with "lead us not into temptation," it assumes that there is a leading which we would prefer, certain guidance we would like to receive from the heavenly benefactor. Why does God allow temptation? Why does God not make sure that we never encounter it? God leads us in order to elevate us to the rock that is higher that "I" above the systems of this world and to conform us to the new nature which has been given to us in the new creation through Christ Jesus our Lord. God's leading, even though intended to raise and transport us to the heavenly places, must take us through the rough terrain of the earth in which we live. The leadership of God is separated from our concrete humanity with its embeddedness in our social-relational interactions. The function of divine leadership is to integrate in us the image and the likeness of His Son. It is leadership to the place of Divine self-manifestation through us. The end of Divine leadership is God as God revealed in us. The leadership of God manifests through all aspects of our lives. In these leadings, there are particular markers which point the way and God's presence is ever-flowing to carry us if we will let God. First of all there is aspect of it that comes intuitively by virtue of being created in the image of God and the residue of that first imprint that remains us even while we are sinners. Then there is that grown from instinct which is the quest for spiritual survival not just physical well being. This instinct grows out of the baser grosser animal nature which is directed by fear; while intuition raises a notch higher than instinct and taps into the low dimension of the soul. From that point God guides us through direct impact on our soul-psychic sphere, but all that is tied to the unrefined emotion and feelings that flow unchecked into our ego. But the Bible clearly warns us not be like the horse and mule led by brittle and harness and led about.

Everyone needs divine leadership: Divine leadership is a fundament good. We need this leadership not only away from temptation and its consequences but so that we might order our services to God aright. Whether one can be led by God, where one can be led by God, how one can be led by God depends on the depth of the commitment of the will to God. The one who submits to the leadership of God develops a spiritual mindset devoid of inner dissatisfaction and hastiness with where God has one. What does a person gain by submitting to Divine leadership? The advantage of being led by God is that it opens us up to infinite arrays of Divine possibilities and moves us quicker though not easier through the spiritual stages of life. As we experience this leadership and are moved within it, we are effectively and affectively transformed into God's visional purpose for us in His Son Jesus Christ. The result of being led is that as we allow ourselves to be thus led our thoughts and affections begin to conform to the image of God. To be led by God brings us to a state of devotion that encompasses our heart, soul, mind, spirit and body. Therefore, divine leadership is a very personal relationship of intimacy with God. As we grow in our acceptance of divine leadership, we will experience the incredible capacity to harness the power of God and to evoke that power consciously using it to affect our atmosphere far beyond our immediate comprehension. This leadership when followed puts us in direct confrontation against the systems of the sinful world. It puts the God-image-likeness in the forefront and makes it accessible to others who may be struggling in their lives with direction.

Divine leadership means and unfolding of divine direction and purpose. In this Divine leadership God works the structures our inner landscape to show us what we are truly made of. So the complex process of being led by the Spirit to the wilderness to be tempted by Satan, not by God, takes place partly in response to our own inner fears, faith, hope, and even attachments. So the temptation cannot be summative description of God's leadership, for God leads to provision as he led Abraham to the ram in the thicket. He leads to victory as he led Joshua and children of Israel. He does lead by His righteousness, though He may lead through the valley of the shadow of death. Being in divine leadership creates a sense of worth, identity and focus "as many as are led by the Spirit, they are the sons of God." (Romans 8) Since Adam, man has spent most of his time away from the Garden asserting the autonomy of his pitiful will. In this state speaking of being led by God or by man is an affront to that sense of false independence. How Adam can be led and yet remain thus is precisely the question. Divine leadership means that one comes to define their identity and purpose totally in relation to God's Spirit. This leadership means that Adam must let go and that Adam must integrally become a manifestation of the Divinity from whom he has sought so much to be independent.

The nature of Divine leadership means that God takes the lead absolutely, relationally—yes, our participation in this being led is not that of suggesting an alternative God's Will but of conforming to God's Will. The seven million dollar question is: "How do we know that we are being led by God? It may sometimes be quite formidable to find the exact flow of Divine Will; however, to follow it when it is made known and to empty ourselves into it is the heavenly million dollar answer. Divine leadership is not the mere maintenance of our comfort, equilibrium or status (quo ante) rather it is the shaking up of comfort zones, the dynamic revolution or our pneumatic geography. But there certain myths about divine leadership and hence of temptation that keep us from having victory and receiving the benefits that flow from our experiences of the four T's:

1. That God leads objectively, without our inner subjective soul and sound.

2. That Divine leadership means the absence of dialectic tension and untroubled harmony at every state and stage.

3. That evil as we know it momentarily cannot be used by God deliberately to achieve God's own end.

4. That leading into temptation and allowing temptation is the same thing.

After Jesus was tempted, gates were opened for angels to come and minister to Him. He showed that He was able to handle power. There is so much power available to us but the gates to them must remain closed because we are not mature enough to handle them. Even though Jesus was God's Son and had received the approval of Heaven, yet the powers of Heaven were not at His disposal until He proved He could handle the negative forces of the human personality.

Jesus was tempted, tested, and tried and put into tribulation many times by His humanity. It was always a way for Him to bring forth a revelation of the Word of God. And after His trial on the cross, He opened up the door of resurrection and life to others. The four T's: trial, test, temptation and tribulation are geared toward the big leap into other dimension. Each one of them is directly related to one of the four dimension of the foursquare City of God.

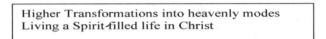

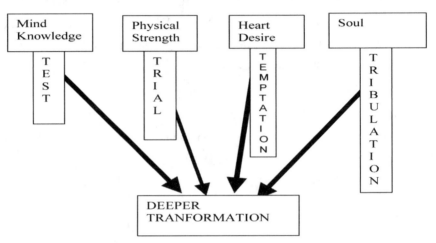

It is interesting that the passage does not say lead us not into tribulation or into trials but temptation. It points us to the commitment that places the agony of spiritual rebirth in us.

We as persons who believe in Jesus Christ cannot be separated from the profundity of inner truth that fascinates and forms us. In the four T's, especially in temptation, our spiritual agony is forced to the top of our lives as the self is plunged toward conformity with the life of the Master. Our life story must become intertwined with that of the Master; we must take up the cross. It is our cross but in a real sense it the cross of the Master. Our cross makes no sense apart from His. If, in our inner man, we recognize our deepest need of mystery of His being, His incarnation, His life, death, burial, resurrection, ascension, and continual advo-cacy, our life story will be told in the flow of greatness, and we tap into the super-natural, miracles, signs and wonders. Knowing Him, the mystery of His passion, mystical power of His resurrection, moves us to trust Him at the depth that often maybe too difficult to justify in psychological and religious terms.

Divine leadership has salvific and transformative effect. God leads us so as to change our existential situation as well as our inner landscape. In this leadership God acts in every moment to break the cycle of bondage to any time, place and tradition that blocks our view to Him and in fact makes our prayer ineffective. The idea of God's leadership is bringing together the broken and spiritual pieces caused by our blind flight into the wall of sin.

God leads in love, never in anger. In fact this part of Divine leadership calls us to be aware of the presence of God and distinguish it from the fragmentation and possible misleading of our ego or even by the demonic. God's leadership, because it is based on love, gives full affirmation to who we are. This means that God is fully connected to us in whatever space or act leads us. "yea though I walk through the valley of the shadow of death, thou art with me, thy rod and thy staff they comfort me." This love is the manifest presence of God's Holy Spirit creating an inner awareness of the Divine confidence and assurance that God's purpose in our lives will ultimately be actualized—if we hold on to the end of the temptation, trial, test, or tribulation. This love leads us to conquer every wall, every foe, every principality, and every power. This love does not mean that we will not face the foe, but it keeps us ahead in the fight. God's leadership is kind. God's leadership is patient. God's leadership is tolerant of the weakness of our immaturity. God's leadership is not easily disappointed. God's leadership exhibits concern for others. God's leadership rejoices in righteousness. God'; leadership is easily appeased. Ultimately, where God leads us to we cannot fail if we focus on His love, for love never fails. Where anger, resentment, negative criticisms, faultfinding, and intolerance abound temptation easily overcome and leadership of God has no sway. When we are led by God, the love of God, for God and for others so radiates us so that the self-worship that is at the heart of so much temptation disappears.

In His loving leadership God does not deny our imperfection but seeks by the presence of temptation to draw us intimately into Himself so that we might be changed from glory to glory. This love sets the guideline for our capacity to trust and grow until we by intimacy recover the lost image and likeness. His leading love evokes trust in us. Trusting God's leading helps us, in that it keeps our hearts from releasing the venom of unbelief that ends up poisoning us and becomes the cause of judgment as we fall headlong into temptations. Without taking hold of this love, temptation creates perplexity which paralyzes our spiritual effectiveness. But this love gives us a larger interpretive perspective of life which keeps us from over-blowing the assumed destructive impact of our temptation sphere or act. Instead, by holding and focusing on the love God, there is made accessible to us the truth about God, ourselves and the situation. It will bring our natural body and psyche to be raised with the supernatural body and Spirit. By this I do not mean the mere transmutation of our carnal desire from one level to another but the entrance of new species of desire which have their genesis in God's nature.

Temptation is an ethical phenomenon, in the sense that it comes to the whole human person and demands a choice between self and God. The choice is between the tendency toward self-deification and openness to the voice of God. The goal then of temptation is inner enlightenment which lets us know that life must be a move away from absolutes of partiality into the absolutes of the eternal against the provisional.

Every temptation is about loyalty for the believer. Josiah Royce the great American philosopher made loyalty the key ethical principle of his system of thought. It raises the question as to our willingness to completely commit ourselves to what we say believe. Though often looked at mainly from a spiritual perspective, temptation is highly practical and material in a sense in that it presents an opportunity to serve God beyond roused emotionality. In it, our will is being trained to control and self-restrain its carnality. We, as disciples, cannot be separated from the profundity of the inner truths that fascinate and form us. All our spiritual agony or joy is to force to the top the truth that lies hidden in our deepest psyche. In fact as we plunge ourselves into the Master's total life, this becomes more clear until we are formed completely into His true reflection. Our life story must become intertwined with the Master's. We, as He said, must take up our cross and follow Him; yes, though the cross is ours, in a real way it still the Master's cross. If in our inner man we recognize our deepest need of the mystery of His being, His incarnation, His life, death, burial and resurrection and ascension and His advocacy, our lifes' story will be told in the flow of His greatness and we tap into the supernatural miracles, signs and wonders. Knowing Him and the mystery of His passion, we receive the mystical power which helps us passing the darkest of moments of human life into light and abundance. We are moved to trust Him at a depth that often may be too difficult to justify in psychological terms. The temptation, the trials, the tests are all meant to bring us there. But that is only if we learn how to deal with them and ultimately overcome them.

CHAPTER FIFTEEN

GOLDEN CORD

KEY 9: CALL FOR BACKUP—DELIVERANCE

"But deliver us from evil:"

We all need the key for deliverance from evil in our lives. The question however is: 'What is evil? I define evil as anything that does not conform to the eternal purpose of God for our lives. In that sense, evil is inclusive of personal as well as communal. Some translations read "deliver us from the evil one." It is true that evil includes the a personal aspect, but the idea of "the evil one" does not appear in many important manuscripts. It is usually supplied by implication. In this passage there is a strong suggestion that evil is personal—something that we need a power larger and far more capabable than ourselves to deal with. This is based on the fact that it follows the request "lead us not into temptation." If we are led into temptation, there is a possibility that we may become bound by evil, ontological and existential, spiritual and material, in thought and action. The progression of this is not hard to find in Scripture. It is a common assumption of both Judaism and Christianity that God created Adam and Eve good. The declaration at the conclusion of the Genesis creation story: "and God saw that it was very good" supports this. The progression into evil tendency and evil action begins with the Satan tempting man to do what God forbade. The result of this was the invasion of evil into the human soul. Human beings became evil. Because of this the Bible sees the devil as the primordial root of the all of these dimensions of evil.

The word "deliver" as used in the Old Testament derives from the Hebrew root *natsal* (*naw-tsal'*) because we have what may be called root need for disentanglement from evil to which we as human beings have become intertwined. As human beings we are caught like prey in the web of the enemy so we need someone to snatch us away from this snare of his activities.

In a positive sense, it means that we are being delivered into the hands of God for safe keeping. In a negative sense, we are being delivered from the hands of our captor. As deliverer the Lord puts Himself at our disposal as the means of our escape. Without failure, the God to whom this prayer is directed will pluck us from the hands of the enemy. He is able to preserve us for Himself if we stay with Him. Deliverance also entails the rescue not just of our soul from its captor but the recovery of our God-given gifts that have been usurped by the enemy or discarded by our existential carelessness.

In deliverance, the Lord spoils the camp of the enemy and strips him of his power to hold us captive. Another word used in the Scripture usually translated "deliver" is the word **shuwb** (pronounced, *shoob*) In this case it is the turning back of the enemy in which God does not allow him or his army to transition into our territory. In this case the deliverance is done before the enemy gets into our camp. Here God goes to battle literally and figuratively and turns the enemies' plan upon its head at its starting point. This deliverance does not give the enemy the opportunity to retreat but discomfits him at the point of his intention. This deliverance means that the enemy is broken at the very point where they have dug the ditch so that they are incapable carrying out their evil design. At the very place of their strategy, they feed on their tears and lay down where their counsel for war became their grave lodge. In such deliverance God makes His people rejoice and sends weeping through the camp of the enemy. He answers again and again. All that is averse to the submission our lives into Divine intention for us is pushed back as we hone in our spiritual antenna homeward. Simply calling to mind God can carry us beyond the stronghold. Deliverance is not the cessation of troubles or even demonic attack.

Certainly evil comes our way continually but deliverance is always available. If we ask and accept deliverance from the Father He will not deny us or draw back from us, rather He hastens to fetch us home again. Bringing us back to home, that is the heart of God and keeping us from being tossed to and from by a demonic restlessness. The idea of deliverance as bringing one back again to a Divine center reminds us that though deliverance is always spiritual, it may also be directed at the perverted pull of our sinful self away from God. Often it is the recovery of something lost and entrance of holistic refreshment and relief from the Lord Jesus Christ. Rescue, restoration, retrieval, return and when possible reversal and sending back problems into nothing are the aim of this call for deliverance. The Old Testament uses the word *nathan (naw-than')* as a deep spiritual need of humanity to receive that which is given with the greatest openness of heart possible, knowing that in such receipt from God's love lies the deliverance from many evils. In calling God for deliverance, we are in a sense assigning God the task of being the avenger and healer who bestows what is due to all whom we meet. The work of deliverance means that we are also in the process of bringing forth into the light that which is hidden or held captive by the enemy. But in many cases this bringing forth cannot happen unless there is casting out. In this casting out, we must seek for the cause of the hindrance to the Divine manifestation and take charge in the Spirit of Christ and use His name to come against it. To this do we must commit our own being completely to the deliverance that the Lord Himself offers. When we consider the cry for deliverance that comes from so much of humanity, we cannot ignore the fact that God has called us to distribute this deliverance as we preach the Gospel.

Without equivocation God is a God of deliverance that we all do experience sometime in our lives. We all can and will experience it. The notion of deliverance implies that we all struggle with things or beings whose sole aim is to hinder, bind, constrict and sway us from the purpose of God for our lives. From the fall of Adam the struggle against evil has been constant. We even now are engaged in this battle against evil; we search for meaningful ways to deal with evil. Philosopher and theologians theorize and pontificate about the nature of evil and the reason for its existence. Though its nature and its source may be important, but that excursion is irrelevant to the one caught up in evil. What is vital and relevant is at the heart of this simple prayer taught by the Lord: "deliver us from evil." No amount of politicizing is going to make evil go away. No amount of colloquy is going to send evil packing from the life in which it is entangled. Deliverance is the answer. But not the way most so-called deliverance ministers think of it. These modern preachers I must say promulgate fear and anxiety not faith and confidence in the finished work of Jesus Christ on the cross. I must say again deliverance from evil is not summarized in naming and casting out demons. Casting out demons is merely an infinitesimal part of the idea of deliverance. So dealing with demons is part of a wider and deeper problem that man faces as he and his progenies are caught in the web of evil.

The problem of evil is so deep in the world that it often implicates God in the mind of the sufferer. If you have a problem with this, look at the problem of Job. In deliverance we must deal with evil as personal, with evil as social, with evil as spiritual, with evil as material deprivation, with evil as economic, with evil as political, with evil as relational, with evil as violation of human destiny. Evil may work itself from any of this place and infect the whole being. And evil does not always mean sin, though there is always sin in every evil context. However, it always has a spiritual basis and from there it works itself out into the material dimension personally and globally. The possibility of evil begins with being led into temptation. When we are led into temptation then the content of the heart is revealed in goodness or in evil. When are led and we succumb then our will which is the safety valve against the evil of others is pacified and laid dormant until we are bound by the act or the being which led us into it. The process or act of deliverance has a spiritual basis as evil does. We can deal with it by tracing the process by which our being became bound by the evil and bringing it to light, and that light is God and Christ the believer. For the same one who said, "I am the Light of the world" said with the same breath "you are the light of the world."

There is an interesting passage in I Corinthians where Paul commands the church to "deliver" the perpetrator over to Satan that his soul might be rescued. What does it mean? At least in this sense it means that deliverance is used in various ways in Scripture as I pointed out. To deliver one to Satan so that the flesh of sin maybe destroyed is based squarely on the work of Jesus Christ on the Cross—who came into the word, to destroy the work of the devil. It is by being in the Spirit that we stay delivered from the day-to-day attack which comes from our sinful self as well as from the influence of demonic powers. Our everyday must be the day of the Lord so that our flesh is saved from its encumbrance with darkness. The one deliverance minister is Christ, not man, for it is He who gave His life and in a sense still makes available that life for our security in the light. Christ is He who has "delivered us from so great a death, and doth deliver: in whom we trust that he will yet deliver us."

According to Gal. 1:4, it is He "Who gave himself for our sins, that he might deliver us from this present evil world, according to the Will of God and our Father." And there is a promise from God written by the hand of the Apostle Paul to Timothy in 2 Tim 4:18 which states it thus: "And the Lord shall deliver me from every evil work, and will preserve me unto his heavenly Kingdom: to whom be glory forever and ever. Amen." In other words deliverance is not my work but the work of God accomplished through my Lord Jesus Christ. On this side of the cross we are simply not asking to be delivered from evil. According to the passages cited above, our deliverance has been accomplished. It is a *fait accompli*. Like everything that has been accomplished in Christ for us, it can only be activated by faith and by consistent affirmation of its actuality.

Heb. 2:10-18:

10 For it was fitting for Him, for whom are all things, and through whom are all things, in bringing many sons to glory, to perfect the author of their salvation through sufferings. 11 For both He who sanctifies and those who are sanctified are all from one Father; for which reason He is not ashamed to call them brethren, 12 saying, "I will proclaim Thy name

226

to My brethren, In the midst of the congregation I will sing Thy praise."
13 And again, "I will put My trust in Him." And again, "Behold, I and
the children whom God has given Me." 14 *Since then the children*
share in flesh and blood, He Himself likewise also partook of the
same, that through death He might render powerless him who had
the power of death, that is, the devil; 15 and might deliver those
who through fear of death were subject to slavery all their lives. 16
For assuredly He does not give help to angels, but He gives help to the
descendant of Abraham. 17 Therefore, He had to be made like His
brethren in all things, that He might become a merciful and faithful
high priest in things pertaining to God, to make propitiation for the
sins of the people. 18 For since He Himself was tempted in that which
He has suffered, He is able to come to the aid of those who are
tempted. (NAS.)

When all is said and done, the believer knows that the God whom He calls
Father has the necessary knowledge and ability to deliver out of temptations and
to preserve those who cry to Him daily for deliverance. This is of course is meant
to remove the spirit of fear and cause the power and love of God to infuse the
mind and saturate the spirit and to silence shame. It is to the testimony of the Lord
that prisoners are set free so that we become partakers not only of the afflictions of
the Gospel but that we become the habitation of the power of God as was manifested
in the Lord Jesus Christ. He intends to save us and to sustain us until we arrive to
the objective for which He has called us with that holy calling. Deliverance as we
see in this prayer is not by our works but according to God's purposeful grace which
was given to us in Christ Jesus before the foundation of the universe. Deliverance
from all evil is the continuous manifestation outflow of the life of our Savior Jesus
Christ. It is simply the result of the fact that He has abolished principle of death
and has brought life and immortality to light through the Gospel in our lives.

The Greek word used here is the word *poneros* (ponhrou). According to the lexical definitions, it could mean: 1. A physical state of being in poor health that is painful, virulent and causes one serious discomfort. It is then a call for us to be delivered from sickness. We can see this in the fact that Jesus went about healing the sick. Sickness is evil. In the fact, in the Great Commission one of the marks of the Kingdom message is that it deals directly with the evil of sickness—that which attacks the physical being of man or anything that makes this body unable to carry out the work assigned to it. So when we pray "deliver us from evil" we are opening up for the healing of body from the evil of sickness which came upon it as a result of the fall. Jesus healed the sick as a way of displaying this principle of deliverance. In His healing, human beings were delivered from physical evil. In healing sickness, Jesus confronted the presence evil in illness and disease. By overcoming the illness and its symptoms, He proved that it is God's Will to deliver human beings from its evil clutches. It was a conquest over physical evil manifesting personally in the life of man. If Jesus "appeared was to destroy the devil's work" as 1 John 3:8 says, then assault on human sickness, illness and disease was meant to deliver man from the infection of satanic power of sickness over creation. The prayer "deliver us from evil" is a cry for participation in the victory of Jesus over the Satan's power in the physical life of man. "Deliver us from evil" activates the healing of all our body's systems and restores our body's healthy function. It is in a sense a reclamation and recovery of wholeness for the physical body. Healings proved that though Satan had tempted us and led to be shackled with evil God can still plunder the prison house and snatch us from his hands.

When we pray "deliver us from evil," we call forth the healing that was so essential to the ministry of our Lord Jesus Christ. This deliverance is anticipated by the line that speaks of forgiveness. The ultimate activation of this aspect of deliverance is the physical impalement of the body of our Lord on the cross, whose personal resurrection forecasts the deliverance and the complete restoration of the human body in the eschatological reign of Christ. Jesus delivered the human body from the evil of leprosy, blindness, dumbness, deafness, epilepsy, lameness, general paralysis, hematological problem, fever and death. Every healing and restoration signals deliverance from evil that has befallen the human body since the fall. (see Mark 2:1-12)

NAS **Matthew 15:28** Then Jesus answered and said to her, "O woman, your faith is great; be it done for you as you wish." And her daughter was healed at once.

NAS **Matthew 12:22** Then there was brought to Him a demon-possessed man who was blind and dumb, and He healed him, so that the dumb man spoke and saw.

NAS **Matthew 14:14** And when He went ashore, He saw a great multitude, and felt compassion for them, and healed their sick.

Matthew 15:30 And great multitudes came to Him, bringing with them those who were lame, crippled, blind, dumb, and many others, and they laid them down at His feet; and He healed them,

NAS **Matthew 21:14** And the blind and the lame came to Him in the temple, and He healed them.

2. In the social sense, it signifies the sense of being disadvantaged and marginal. Usually women, strangers and children were subjected of social evil, even to the point of enslavement. Though Jesus never engaged in a physical fight to free those who are under the evil of slavery, yet His interaction with those who were social outcasts exemplified the intent of this line of prayer. In this sense, evil is personified in human beings who use their powers to subjugate others in the social sphere.

Evil as social is not concentrated on the question of what is good for society but in seeing evil in terms of social acceptance and its impingement negatively on God's purpose for human beings. It hinders the human experience of wholeness in the social sphere. Thus when we pray "deliver us from evil," we activate our Father's power to deal with social conceptualization that deprives certain human beings of "the good" which God saw in the beginning when it is said "and God saw that it was very good." One consequence of evil as social is the processes that human beings put in place to deny the legitimacy of the existence, survival, freedom, dignity, and destiny of other human beings. In the Bible these social evils are continuously attacked by the prophets and spiritual leaders. Evil as social can take life of its own. It becomes so pervasive that human beings become active and dynamic participants. Human beings meaning well become "righteous agents" of it propagation. This line of prayer introduces into our consciousness Divine themes of alternative reality which bear the seed of transformation. It moves evil from and academic discipline into the realm of concrete action needing to be dealt with by concrete action. But this prayer does not say "help us to deliver ourselves from evil," rather it directs itself beyond the person. As it relates to evil as social phenomenon, the prayer beckons the Father to deliver us from the evil of social conformism that deadens our conscience to the wickedness of the society to which we belong.

Second, it directs itself to the realm whereby we fall into hands of a social machinery of evil patterns that we cannot escape. We ask for deliverance from being victims of such evil and then also deliverance from participating in it to detriment of our soul and that of others. One cannot pray this line truthfully and deny his own participation in evil as social phenomenon. Note the plural referent of this deliverance. Not deliver me but "deliver us." Every evil I experience or participate in catches other in its web. If it is sickness, it catches others in web of pain and suffering. In its social setting I touches not just us who are engaged in it or those who are its immediate target but it can reach into the realm of generation possibility poisoning the springhead from which the human consciousness emerges. If this bothers you, think of how we participate in the sins of Adam.

In order to understand this prayer, it is important to remember that you as a human being are caught up in a web of relationship this both temporal and eternal. Thus the impact of evil as social is both the temporal now as well as timeless space. When you pray this prayer you in that moment touch the generations that will come out of your loins. To pray it then is to lock on the ever-present fact of evil which is intertwined with human social interaction. In saying "Our Father. . . deliver us from evil," you reach for the possibility of the dissolution of the serpent's coil around the fabric of social consciousness of man. In it our Lord gives us the words for releasing man from enslavement to the merely material aspect of the universe. By it you are not trying to escape the world but rather to keep yourself and others grounded authentically "in the world" but freed from the poisonous tentacles "of the world." Again this line of prayer "deliver us" defends men against the usurpation of social forces which threaten to take over his soul. It also defends your God-given right to be here on earth. And at the same time it opens one up to plunge headlong into the goodness of the Lord in the social sphere. It about us not just about me. It would seem to me that some of the evil for which David sought deliverance were social and political evils. For example in **Psalm 7:1** (7-1) "Shiggaion of David, which he sang unto the LORD, concerning Cush a Benjamite. (7-2) O LORD my God, in Thee have I taken refuge; save me from all them that pursue me, and deliver me." **In Psalm 27:12** we read, "Deliver me not over unto the will of mine adversaries; for false witnesses are risen up against me, and such as breathe out violence." All of these are violence sanctioned by the socio-political climate in which David found himself. When such is the case, one has no other place to turn to except God. In the next verse it is even clearer. Psalm 43:1: "Be Thou my judge, O God, and plead my cause against an ungodly nation; O deliver me from the deceitful and unjust man." One of the telling examples of deliverance from evil in the social realm comes from from the story of the woman who washed his feet.

3. Political evil is of giving legitimate voice and providing legal structures for evil to express itself. When political evil expresses itself, it takes away voice and will from the people who have been impacted by social evil. There may be many examples of this but the greatest still remains the record of the children of Israel in Egypt. It begins in Exodus 1:8-22. This a clear case of political structure giving voice and structure to social unease. It beings in social jealousy and fear arousing unnecessary suspicion vs. 9: "and he said to his people, 'Behold the people of the sons of Israel are more and mightier than we. 10 Come let us deal wisely with them, lest they multiply and in the event of war, they also join themselves to those who hate us and fight against us and depart from the land.' It was common social perception that the people of Israel were taking what belonged to the Egyptians even though they lived in the ghetto of Egypt. They could not transact business freely. For the

reason they lived in Goshen was because their lifestyle and trade was deemed abominable by the Egyptians. According to extra-biblical sources, the children of Israel fought for the army of Egypt, yet the Egyptians persisted in their social evil. From this social evil the evil of political structures were set up to impose the Israelites. Structures of forced labors were set up and when that did not work political structures were set up for genocide. "The king of Egypt spoke to the Hebrew midwives, one was named Shiprah, and the other was named Puah and he said "when you are helping the Hebrew women to give birth and see them upon the birth stool, if it is a son you shall put him to death; but if it is a daughter, then she shall live." (Ex. 1:15) Later in Chapter 3 we read these words: "I have surely seen the affliction of My people who are in Egypt and have given heed to their cry because of their taskmasters, for I am aware of their sufferings. So I have come down to deliver them from the power of the Egyptians and to bring them up to good and spacious land, to a land that flows with milk and honey. . . ." (v. 7-8) The cry "deliver us from evil" set in motion the deliverance of the children of Israel from the social and political evil into which they have fallen. When we ignore this line of prayer which our Lord taught us, there arises a tendency to underrate and overlook the political evil that is visited upon other people. One cannot truly pray this prayer and condone oppression. When we pray this prayer, we move the heart of the Lord for the poor.

4. In the ethical sense it conveys the idea of wickedness, baseness, maliciousness, sinfulness, viciousness and degeneracy. Yes, even the punishment which God dishes out on man for it is he who instigated man to locate himself in opposition to God. Secondarily, human beings can be the source of the evil that befalls them, even the one visited upon them by nature. Thus a,lla. r,u/sai h,ma/j a,po. tou/ ponerou/ is inclusive of all types of evil from which man is to be delivered.

SIN AS EVIL OF HUMAN BEINGS

The first kind of evil from which we need deliverance is the one that lurks beneath our own skin. The Scripture calls it sin. It is something within us that rebels against righteousness and pushes us as human beings to destructive behaviors. It is a nature that lives in the soul of the saintliest man who has not yet met Christ. This is a cry for salvation in that sense. "Deliver us evil" for those who are not yet Spirit-born, is a cry for salvation. When we pray this as believers, we include in it all those who need salvation. Evil in this sense is not an act which we commit, have committed or will commit. It is part and parcel of who we are. In one sense, it is a cry to be delivered from ourselves. There are too many passages in Scripture that deal with the evil of human nature to bear any argument. However, since there are those who will argue the fact, we will give several quotations. When we speak of evil here we do not speak of evil as an act but evil as human nature. This does not mean that man cannot do good as seen in the temporal processes, rather it concerns the fact that when it comes to matters of, his soul's eternal value man is wholly bent on his own destruction. Here humanity is deprived of good at the very basic level. And this is what corrupts his entire activities even those considered by him to be his most sublime achievements. He needs deliverance from the evil of his own nature. "Deliver us from evil" is meant to extract man from himself and to move him to the realm of the one who this prayer calls Father. Evil as also an act as much as it is being. Here evil is human defiance of God and their quest to act independent of God's moral requirements. Evil in this sense is the subjective and objective contrariety of man's thought and action meant to contravene the relationship between him and his God. In this evil man becomes a subject without an authentic content. In this evil consists the fact that man confronted with freedom chooses chaos, bondage and hubris. Since evil in this sense is intricately tied to man's being, he positions his activities vise á vie the good as an outsider. His choice creates a sense of the impossibility of the good. The good scandalizes him, righteousness offends him, peace disturbs him and love is perceived by him as weakness. This is so much so that every good becomes even for him the necessary guise of evil. As Paul puts it in Romans 7:14-23. In the passage we find phrases such as: "I am flesh sold to sin," "I am not practicing what I like to do but I am doing the very thing I hate," "for I know that nothing good dwells in me," "I practice the very that I do not wish." In verse 20 we see these words: "But if I am doing the very thing I do not wish, I am not longer the one doing it, but sin which dwells in me." At the end of the passage Paul cries out: "wretched man that I am! Who shall deliver me from the body of this death?" It is to that cry which is within every man that Lord directed this prayer line: "Our Father which art in Heaven . . . deliver us from evil." When we pray this line "deliver us evil" we ask also for deliverance from sinful behavior and action. The Father can and desires to deliver me from wickedness, from all acts that sabotage purpose and destiny. Whatever sinful habit that has enwrapped our souls, this prayer is directed to God for deliverance from it. The Scripture lists so many sins to which man is prone that it hard to list them all. However, in one scoop we ask God to be delivered from all of them.

5. In a natural sense it conveys the tragedy that often befalls man from nature. In the natural realm evil befalls human beings. Earthquakes, hurricanes, tornadoes, volcanoes, and tsunamis are all common experiences which may be termed evil because they cause human sufferings. The convulsion of nature against the pitiful strength of man is evil and may in fact lead man to the evil of denying God. Many people have used the horror of natural disaster as reason to curse God and turn against God's children. I believe that Jesus taught this prayer because he believed that God is able to deliver from these natural disasters. He Himself affected nature in the stilling of the storm. In the Old Testament, prophets are often called to help pray to stop natural disasters or the people are called to repentance in order to avert natural disaster.

6. Judgment of God. In the Old Testament evil can denote the judgment of God upon a people or person. We find in Scripture people asking to be delivered from God's judgment. God's judgment is seen as evil because of the pain and destruction it can wreck on humanity. So when we pray this prayer, we are also praying for general deliverance that might come upon us and the world because of God's anger regarding human wickedness.

7. We also find in the Bible deliverance from devils and demonic possessions and attacks. This is obvious in the way Jesus dealt with demonic activities in the life of those He met. "Deliver us from evil" is inclusive of all the aspects and manifestation of evil in the world. Jesus in teaching us this prayer give us the key for dealing with all dimensions of evil. First of all, it forces upon us the realization of the reality and impact of evil upon our world. In this awareness we are able to ask for strength to overcome it. Secondly, it activates within us knowledge of how the Father sees evil and by this knowledge-activated inner knowledge we over place ourselves in the place of deliverance. As it is written, "Through knowledge the righteous shall be delivered."(Proverbs 11:9) Thirdly, it also allows us to submit ourselves to God in such a way that we can resist the devil and the evil which he brings into our contexts. As it is written, "submit yourself to God, resist the devil and he will flee from you."

CHAPTER SIXTEEN

GOLDEN CORD

KEY 10: RELEASE ALL TO THE ALL

"For thine is the Kingdom, and the power, and the glory, forever."

THE KINGDOM POSSESSION

Two things are mentioned twice in this prayer: Heaven and Kingdom. The Kingdom is one of the contents of the prayer. The Kingdom is the integrative principle of prayer. Its aspects are infinite. It is the single point at which all Divine purpose comes together. In prayer there is a one-to-one relation with the whole for there the integrated soul of the believer unified by his supernatural birth that communes into and participates in the Kingdom. If the Kingdom is the content, then the Kingdom needs definition and its aspects need elucidation. What is the Kingdom? Whose is the Kingdom? How is the Kingdom structured? Where is the location? When we considered the first mention of the Kingdom in the Lord's Prayer, we considered how we prophetically announce it in all our contexts. The fact that it is mentioned twice shows its importance. The Kingdom is the place from which all emanates and to which they must turn in prayer.

What is the Kingdom as it relates to this aspect of prayer? In order to understand the significance of the Kingdom force we must first grasp its source and the role of the Father to whom prayer is addressed in it. Of course God is the supreme king of the Kingdom from whom all its content flow. In Him the Kingdom is formed created and manifested. So then prayer having the Kingdom as its matrix has the

Father as its saturating focus. Prayer follows the flow of this Kingdom as it moves from His inner being of God to the world the created world. Until prayer is Kingdom saturated, it misses its purpose and is merely carnal wishes. When we pray in and through the Kingdom, we are actually interacting in the levels of God's nature and its effect upon the created world. Kingdom prayer traverses the spiritual domain in which various beings maybe encountered. For the Kingdom is not what we see, rather the most important agents are not seen and can only be tapped and revealed by Kingdom saturated prayer. Prayer links us with the Kingdom's supernatural providence. We are citizens of this Kingdom and are open to it, flowing its wealth, thought, memory, love, mercy, life and holiness into this world in which we live. Kingdom as the content of prayer works though the name of the King, manifesting through humans, seraphim, cherubim, princes, powers and angelic hierarchies and hosts—yes, and even beasts of the fields.

The Kingdom is the environment, the matrix if you will, which founds the existential universe. Authentic power flows from it. Kingdom is a tool meant to effect intentional change in the various sphere of existence. The Kingdom of God is the tool by which God intentionally effects change in the universe and it is within Himself. The Lord's Prayer states it thus: "on earth as it is in Heaven." That is why I see the Kingdom as doorway, a portal to power and to glory. The Kingdom as we can see in the parable of the Master inspires imagination and instigates an intellectual quest which will not rest until it finds the pearl of great price or the one sheep lost; the Kingdom is the seeing of everything in interrelatedness and every act in its eternal relation.

Paul tells us that "the Kingdom of God is not meat and drink, but righteousness and peace and joy in the Holy Ghost." If the Kingdom is yours, then all is yours. The Kingdom is the summary of and embodiment of what God is and thus lacks nothing since all that it seems to lack in any epoch is within its creative potential. It is an inner awareness which influences the ebb and flow of that which it comes into contact just by intending it so, by a faithful trust in God who is not just the owner of the Kingdom but is the Kingdom. If God then is the Kingdom, then we are in it and it is in us. We are intimately connected and touched by the visible and invisible realms of this Kingdom. It is a free flowing process of our spirit in the Spirit-God who is the milieu. In the Kingdom, the world is seen in its Christocentric movement in which God continuously manifests into human form. This also means that the worlds, is being seen in spiritual ways because the move from God to man suggests that the world is not as ironclad as we sometimes would like to believe. This God becoming man, this all becoming one, this infinite becoming finite, this eternal becoming temporal suggests that at the deepest level the Kingdom of God is indeed not meat and drink but Spirit flowing freely without limitation.

The Kingdom is God being released into new forms and realities for our sake and for our ability to use as a ladder toward our creativity and salvation. This "yours is the Kingdom," points to God as the spiritual matrix in whom we move, live and have being. This is the activating possibility of inward change and world transformation. The Kingdom is the essence of Divine alchemy in which God becomes man and man becomes God. In this Kingdom, there appears a Christocentric functionality that is radical for those who are in it so that "nothing, absolutely, nothing is impossible." What Christ means for the world is precisely this, that by being connected to this Kingdom with God as the spiritual matrix of all things, we can change from sinners to saints, from sick to healthy, from hate to love, from lies to truth, from mortality to immortality. This Kingdom opens us up to the very fabric of the universe and thrust us into dimensions of compassion and transformation that were hitherto unknown.

The Kingdom is deeper, higher, wider, more expansive than anything we can imagine. In it is the very seed of eternity and life. What the Master meant when He said "repent for the Kingdom of God is at hand" points to two things: First, the Kingdom is so close we can reach out and touch it; second our mindset is in the way. For us then to touch the Kingdom or to let it through, we need to restructure the birth canal of our mind. We must think from a different dimension, see from a different vantage point and create a new kind of consciousness—Christocentric consciousness. The Kingdom which is God's through our submitted human will distills the dew of life and Heaven's spectral light into the assumed concreteness of everyday life. The cry "come Kingdom" carries with it a fundamental dissatisfaction with present situation and thus makes those who are in touch with seekers, not so much of knowledge but of the life of God as it must be manifested in every dimension which they find themselves. "Seeker" is here a sense of the tapping into the expansive nature of the Kingdom which is God Himself. A refusal to be satisfied with the way things are not dissatisfaction with the life they have but dissatisfaction with the holding back of the Kingdom from its full manifestation in the moment. Here those who have tasted the Kingdom are not willing to accept anything less. It is communion with spiritual essence of the universe, and they will eat not defiled bread.

The Kingdom is the mother of manifestations. It is the source of abundance and the free flowing power to receive the universal bon. It is the wholeness and fullness of the vital force, free from fear and based on love. "The inexorable march of history drums all to God, people will spend kingdoms emerge and vanish, thrones and dominion rise and fall. The Honorable become dishonorable and a dishonorable because honorable. Where is the rock on which men may stand? Therein is the fixed point from which we may obtain a steady picture of the world. Why do the nations rage as well like the stormy sea? Mankind—from where has it come and where is it going?" (Eric Sauer *The King of the Earth*, Introduction)

While it is true God, the world and its Kingdom's vanish like the fleeting morning sun, the Kingdom of our God is an everlasting Kingdom. We read in the book of Isaiah that the increase of His Kingdom shall have no end. So when the Lord's Prayer ends with "thine is the Kingdom," it points to the Kingdom as tied directly to the very nature of the God whose Kingdom it is. The possession of the Kingdom is not motioned or achieved by the unanimity of human opinion or the convergence of the streams of human thoughts mechanically woven together. Rather, it is an unstoppable flow from the very heart of the Creator.

The possession of the Kingdom compels us to revise our hasty impressions of who we are and why we are here. In it we are called to discard the bifurcation of identity and the world in which really. The Kingdom is what resolves our conflicts with creation because it is a clear manifestation of the creator's mind. When we discover the Kingdom and know whose it is and discover God as the one who bequeaths it to us, we come to the understanding that we are intimately connect to it emotionally, morally, aesthetically, and spiritually. Those who have come into the Kingdom in this sense are they who can pray "thine is the Kingdom." Praying this section of the prayer helps us to develop an appreciative consciousness which energizes us for positive redirection of the created sphere.

We must not be tempted to believe that we can through anything in us conjure up the Kingdom and thus make it ours. It is God's. It comes from God. It is the eminent manifestation of God's essential personality. Indeed, His infinitude, the riches of this Kingdom, the immensity of all its time and space are at the disposal of those who grasp it and are willing to participate in the Kingdom.

If indeed it, that is the Kingdom, is the focal point off our freedom and our eternal establishments, then we must live in its emancipative reality now. And for this reason we can never consider our present moment not even our willed future as being shut or closed in. The Kingdom is then future that is present with us, as God is with us.

Being in the Kingdom is letting something significant and truly moving emerge from within us. It is being moved and being open to dimensions that are full of possibilities. The power of those who possess the Kingdom is measured by its capacity to sustain meaning in this life and in the life to come. As being a manifestation of God, it holds the potential of crystallizing meaning into our new and inexperienced contexts. The Kingdom, which is God's, needs no justification by the old systems of the world. Nor does it seek its reason in the flux of the merit of human feeling. It is an intentional production of God's eternal being. "Yours is the Kingdom" is a reference to God's ownership and points of the inward growth and uniqueness of its pattern. We who pray "your Kingdom come" and end it with the phrase "yours is the Kingdom," accept that we are involved in Divine environments which form the matrix for the bursting of the new humanity. In possessing it by the benevolence of its owner, we possess the possibility of a continuous experience which is nothing more than manifesting God in all aspects of the universe. The key to the Kingdom is this: God has determined to be fully available to all strata of creation. There is a statement in Scripture which suggests that though the Kingdom belongs to God, yet he is willing to give it to us. Jesus said to the disciples, "fear not little flock it is your Father's good pleasure to give you the Kingdom." In this sense the Kingdom is God's and ours. I find this intricate connection between Divine ownership and our ownership rather intriguing. For this "yours is the Kingdom" implies that if I am God's son then the Kingdom is mine too. So when we come to the end of the prayer, we come to a thorough conclusion of our place in the scheme of Divine things. It is therefore a prophetic pronunciation of our place in God and in all that God does. The power of this prophetic pronunciation "yours is the Kingdom" can only be understood if we look at the life, act, suffering, passion, death, burial and resurrection of Jesus Christ. For after Christ one cannot speak of the Kingdom as belonging to God without speaking of the Kingdom as belonging to man also whom God has brought into Himself as co-heir. Jesus said, "Fear not little flock, for it is your Father's good pleasure to give you the Kingdom." This is said without reservation. If the purpose for creating man was to give him dominion and rulership, then the Kingdom cannot be said to belong to God alone for God intended to give it man, even if that Man is the only Son of God, from the beginning.

The Kingdom of God, Jesus said, is at your door—"it is at hand." It is a Divine innovation. The nature of Divine innovation is seen in all clarity in the person of Christ who is the God-Man. In Him the reality of the Kingdom is embedded and uncovered. Through Him we see into the nature of God's Kingdom. As I said before, if the Kingdom is God's and we are God's children then the Kingdom is ours. If this is not acceptable then consider that we who are believers are now in Christ and Christ is in God. In Him, through Him and with Him, we inherit the Kingdom. The implications of these statements are far reaching. For, if we identify with Christ's life, passion, death and resurrection and He is identified with us, then our identity is a God identity. In speaking to the children of Levi God said, "I am their inheritance." So the Kingdom is not only in us but among us, through us and for us. Now by saying that the Kingdom belongs to men, we do not mean every man's but only every man who is Christ's. Though potentially we must admit it is every man's. This said, we must still remember that possessing the Kingdom is not merely an ideal or an impersonal abstraction but an actual relational interconnection of your person and my person with God. Through Jesus the "All" has become my "All." Mine too is the Kingdom, not as its originate or but as its inheritor. My prayer, "yours is the Kingdom," is the prophetic announcement of my being embedded in the King and the Kingdom.

The Kingdom is mine now although it is still waiting to be manifested. I live in it now, though I will live in it in the future. Herein is the mystery. That which is mine is still going to be mine. Why is this so? Because there are areas of my being that are still waiting to be awakened. They are dimensions of my being which shall not wake up until the last human being comes to consciousness. This completed and yet to be completed is the mystery of the King and the Kingdom. According to E. Stanley Jones, "The Kingdom is written in the Constitution of our being," yet its mysteries are yet unfolding. It is God's bequeath of Himself to us in His Son Jesus Christ."[16]

E. Stanley Jones states further that:

"When we fling open the doors of our being and let the Kingdom invasion possess us, we are not letting something strange, something alien and sinister into our being but the benevolent God whose mercy endures forever. We are letting in the very Fact for which we are made. The Kingdom within us rises to meet the Kingdom without us and together they cast out the unnatural Kingdom of sin and evil. The coming of this invading Kingdom has the feel of homecoming about it."[17]

"Thine is the Kingdom" puts a check on every human arrogation of rulership and power. After we have spoken of dominion and rulership given to human beings, talked about potentials and possibilities, theologized and divinized to the 60th million degrees, the truth remains that God rules over all. "The earth is the Lord's and fullness thereof; the world and all who dwell in it."

The Kingdom is not man's search for God, nor is it man's action on behalf of God. It cannot be said to be originated in man or to belong to man in an absolute sense. It can only be given to man—as in "thy Kingdom come." The Kingdom as God's sole possession which God either chooses to share or not to share with creatures is absolutely and unequivocally God's. Because the Kingdom is God's, man cannot progressively attain to it by changing his social or even moral order. The Kingdom being God's carries the value of God and becomes the ordering bases of all that it touches. It may be important to note that Jesus taught us to pray "thy Kingdom come . . . on earth as it is Heaven" not "Thy Kingdom come to Heaven as it is on earth." There is no reversal of this statement in any part of Scripture. Nowhere is the Kingdom said to go Heaven as conceived on earth by men and women, no matter how righteous they maybe. Rather the Kingdom descends from Heaven if you like the ladder model. It grows from God if agriculture is your thing. It flows from God if you are a scientist. It is energized by God if you have been tinged by the New Age energy language. It flows from God into the whole universe which is subject to God's sovereignty and potency.

The Kingdom is God's because God is its legitimate ruler.

The Kingdom is God's because God is its foundation and its capstone.

The Kingdom is God's because God is its creator, sustainer and redeemer.

The Kingdom is God's because, its vision flows from within the recess of His being affecting every created thing.

The Kingdom is God's because God is the Kingdom.

Because God is, if you will, without end, the Kingdom flows unceasingly until it's either realized in them (creatures) or something in them gives and they cease. The Kingdom is the presentation of God as God to creation for the complete fulfillment of God-*self* in all. When we apprehend "thine is the Kingdom" then we have come to the possession of the final good. We have arrived at that which all religious systems have sought often without success. The Kingdom as God's possession is the ultimate ideal, and to come to the realization of this connection between the Kingdom and God is the ultimate ideal, the Holy Grail that all mystics seek. The power of Christianity is that affirmation that Jesus Christ is God in the flesh, thus making Him the King and Kingdom brought to earth. It is the ultimate affirmation that the Kingdom must come from above not from below. This is the response to the request which interrupts the human claim to supremacy in any realm. The will is done on earth because the Kingdom is yours. We are forgiven because the Kingdom is yours. We forgive each other because the Kingdom is yours. We receive provision "daily bread" because the Kingdom is yours. We are not led into temptation because the Kingdom is yours. We are delivered from evil because the Kingdom is yours.

THE POWER

"Thine is the . . . power.

Power is the active force or pole agitating for the creating something out of nothing or recreation and reordering of the all things in Creation to make them manifest their Divine form. It is God's strength and ability. In God it is inherent not borrowed residing in Him by virtue of God eternal nature. When God exerts and puts forth power for performing miracles or manifest moral excellence, He does so not by our influence but as a natural extension of Himself. The Bible attributes our ability to increase riches and power to get wealth to reservoir of God our Father. Though there are innumerable powers flowing from Him consisting of myriads of armies, forces, hosts of angels and archangels and living creatures, powers thrones, dominions, yet absolute power belongs to the LORD God alone.

Power is the conductor of the motive of the person for harm or for help. God our Father makes His power available to us for good. You are God-born, filled with His might and an embodiment of His strength, if you have come into the Kingdom. You are the Excellency of God's dignity but the Excellency of power is of God and not of you or me. Indeed the purpose for which God has brought you forth and raised you up is that you might be a conduit of His power. His power is to be declared through us into in all the earth. The psalmist is very clear in Psalm 62:11:

God has spoken once,

Twice I have heard this:

That power belongs to God.

In the right hand of the LORD is glorious power which serves as the intermediary between the Kingdom and the glory. This power which belongs to God can dash obstacles to pieces to bring into manifestation everything that has been narrated as the need of the children who pray "our Father." (Exodus 15:6)

It is good that power belongs to God and not to man. Because power ultimately belongs to God our Father it can break the pride of the assumed power of men. In the presence of His power the most powerful creatures stand drained and powerless. His enemies, which often times are also the enemies of His children, melt in the awesome display of His power. In Numbers 14:17 Moses prayed, "And now, I pray, let the power of my LORD be great" and tied the greatness of this power to the mercy and graciousness of God.

Because the power is His, His name shall be hallowed upon the earth. Because to God belongs the power, His Kingdom will come. It is because He possesses the power that His Will must ultimately be done on earth as it is in Heaven. It is because the power is God's that provision will never fail those who are His. In fact in this power, God feeds even the enemies. By this power, God forgives and cleanses the sinner's follies. By this power, that is God's alone the righteous people are led in the path they should go. By this power, The LORD delivers those that call upon Him. The power of our God is not just brute force that runs over people rather it is grounded in God's nature as love and is never separated from that love for His children. It is because God loved the fathers, Abraham, Isaac, Jacob that their descendants where chosen after them and were brought out of Egypt with His Presence and might. In Deuteronomy 8:17, we are warned against the arrogant assumption that we have any real power to deliver ourselves. When we are blessed we are warned not to suppose that "My power and the might of my hand have gained me this wealth." Whatever power we have is received. We must remember it is "the LORD your God, for it is He who gives you *power* to get wealth." (Deuteronomy 8:18)

When we attribute power to God, we declare that He alone as LORD has the ability and will to judge the people based on intrinsic Divine compassion. The power of God goes out to us not to condemn us but to help us when our resources are gone; this power is not meant to bring us into bondage but freedom. It is true that sometimes God's power when displayed can strike great terror even in those whom God loves, yet we must not forget that our Father seldom shows all His power to us for our own protection. When we look behind us, behold, His power ascends and descends between the Heaven and the earth. When we have no power to flee this way or that way, we turn back on the power of the One who Source is power itself. Our LORD is a great God and has great power. In 2 Samuel 22:33 David is quoted as saying, "God is my strength and power." In 1 Chronicles 29:11: Yours, O LORD, is the greatness,

The power and the glory,

The victory and the majesty;

For all that are in Heaven and in earth are yours;

Yours is the Kingdom, O LORD,

And you are exalted as head over all.

The power of God is avenues of both riches and honor. God's power is declared to God's people so as create an atmosphere in which they may experience His works without hindrance. It is through the power of God that we as believers receive our heritage. In fact it is our calling to speak of the glory of the Kingdom and to talk of God's power. When we say as the psalmist says in Psalm 147:5: "Great is our Lord, and mighty in power." When we attribute power to God as is fitting we create an atmosphere conducive for manifestation of signs and wonders.

When power becomes our goal or motive and not a compassionate process it is easily distorted—much of the problem with human power is that it has been regarded as an end in itself—as violation of something or someone else to gain what we want. To truly deal with power effectively it needs to be seen as the process—a means to an end, the motive, the idea, the thought, and desires furnish power its ingredient for working. Every thought, idea, feeling, imagination, desire produces the power on which they travel towards their realization. Power is the tendency towards outward expression or manifestation of the inner structure of being. (Proverbs18:21) Thus "death and life are in the power of the tongue" not as its substance but as environment forming mechanism for the manifestation of life or death. When we consider the use of power to oppress as it occurs in many instances, we notice that power serves mainly to create atmosphere in which the freedom of persons are hindered by physical force which must not be confused with power as an attribute of God. The attempt to act as if the atmosphere of power is the creation of man has long since been the problem of man. This prophetic sound "thine is the power" releases energies that make the atmosphere favorable for manifestation of the works of God. When say thine is the Kingdom we make the atmosphere unfavorable for those who presume to use human power to thwart the cause of righteousness. There is no less temptation than to ascribe too much credit to the natural man and overestimating his power to lift himself. So long as we think of power as a series of phenomena tied inherently and connected to the use of force we cannot conceive the essence of power as pure activity flowing from pure being and pure intention. We must see it when attributed to God as the principle that unites and regulates the complexities of passion, thought, idea and action. When we state that "power belongs to God and to God alone," we then open ourselves up as possible agents of that power as we come to share in its endless flow from it compassionate essence to loving activity. But the problem with many of us is that in spite of our concession of this point in prayer, we still seek ways to assert human magical powers over the power of God and so get ourselves entangles in opposition to the power of God against which we cannot stand. The idea that we may participate or even be agents of this power presupposes that we are connected to God as Father and that this connection affirms our being in His being.

We need to understand that the experience of God's power is connected to love, compassion, faithfulness and God's redemptive intent. It is important to observe how the Scripture narrates the experience of God's power by those whom God chooses. How this power may affect those how are not in alignment with God differs from how it affects those who call God Father and whom God calls sons and daughter. Some people of course deem this demarcation irrelevant. But to those who pray "thine is power," we know that by His power He keeps the commitment He has made to us. It is His power that can help us but at the same time hinder the presumed power of those who are working contrary to the Divine purpose for our lives. His power is the key element in the battle that we face on our way to keep our commitment to living a godly life. Like the potential of an electrical force, the power of God can be brought to bear on our welfare in vast array of things which we encounter. This power can be destructive or constructive depending on how we connect to it. It can also be distorted by person in relationships or channeled as creative illuminative flashes of genuine divinity in any situation. This power functions as a reminder that we need not fear or feel unrelenting guilt or shame or allow condemnation to grip us so tightly that we forget the promise of the Lord's mercy to us. Remembering that power belongs to God as Father can serve to free us from so many things even the compulsion of our fallen nature. Remembering this power can cause us to summon courage in the face of danger, elevate bravery from our anxious and fearful breast, incite bold action in our timid heart and inspire faith in the face of despair.

"Thine is . . . the power" means that God is in control not merely in cliché way. God has power to, power with, power for, and power through—yes, even power in. As such, this prayer with its inner recognition is a ground for openness to life and future. When I say, "thine is the power," I raise a theme that reassures me of the glorious fulfillment of the gracious promises made by "our Father which art in Heaven." Harmful use of power cannot be attributed to God, rather His power provides positive ground for our continuous victory over the negative forces of our lives even when it contradicts our seeming sense of moral right. Power belongs to God. The acceptance of this as fundamental reality is integral to our faith and trust in God. The story of God's power in Scripture is seen in God's act of creation, continuous deliverance, sustenance and judgment. His power is revealed in His love and faithfulness, backed by the word and confirmed by miracles, signs and wonders. To speak of God's power is ultimately to speak of promise of our own protection and victory when all is said and done.

This power though belonging to God is also given to us who have received God's gift of His incarnation. "As many as received Him to them he gave the power to become the sons of God." (John 1:12) Through this power God abides with us and energizes us to change different aspects of our lives. So the power is not merely verbal exercise—but result producing—in which the sick are healed, the prisoners set free, the sorrowful drawn to joy and oppressed delivered. God's power is committed to us, but unlike His love it is not committed unconditionally. It is committed to those who have been proven or those who are being tested.

It is interesting that the Lord chooses to use the Greek word *dunamis* in this verse and not the word *exousia*, which will mean authority. Physicists tell us that power is energy exerted for motion or work performance. Power here is the exertion of energy for the continuous manifestation of the Kingdom. By "power" the Bible does not intend to convey the idea of God as an agent exercising an ability to act which has been invested within Him nor does it mean to convey the idea of coercive force. Rather God is the embodiment of the governmental origination of control and greatness and the ultimate persuasive principle toward the good. God owes His power to no superior agent, spirit or being. He is force originated, applied, productive, without inward or outward pressure. The degree to which this power is mirrored in Creation or God's children depends on the magnitude of their availability and openness to Him. "Thine is the power" denotes God's ability to put forth or exert sufficient strength, force, or energy that is equal to any situation. God's power is its own argument. God's is the power and has ability to exercise all kinds of control, authority, influence and dominion if God so choose. He cannot be circumvented. All true prayer must find the Kingdom as one point of the Divine triangle.

THINE IS THE . . . AND THE GLORY

"Glory" as used in the TNK (**Torah**-Law, **Nebiim**-prophets and **Ketubim**-writings); there are several words which convey the idea of glory. 1. Haddereth which is derived from an Assyrian root word meaning great. 2. The word Hodh which means brightness or shinning as in lightning flash. 3. Yeqara which has the connotation of something that is rare hence costly or even the result of much labor. 4. Tipharath which means beauty. 5. Tsebu taken from a Babylonian term which means something desirable. 6. Kabod which means weightiness as in value cost and ornamental. The word kabod to me as used in this prayer is combination of all the five expressions of the inner nature of God as well as the outer expression of His person. It expresses in one line the greatness, the rarity, honor, beauty, as well as the brightness of God's manifest presence. This glory when it appears in physical forms is often seen as brightness, fire, storm clouds and lightning expression of the Presence of Yahweh. To say "thine is glory" is to proclaim praise to God in the most exalted state without condition. The manifest Glory of God is result of the power moving in the Kingdom environment and stirring its potential so that its light is transferred from its hidden place to all creation. The glory of the God can startle by its appearance. The "kabod" the glory is the physical tangible presence of God. This **kabod** (glory) was seen in various forms in the TANAK and could be observed by the people as I have noted before in forms of clouds, fire, lightning and even storms. In the New Testament, the Greek word translated "glory" is *Doxa. Doxa* connotes honor, respect and beauty. When used of a person or deity it is the flow of beauty of action in any location or process with not just apparent ease but real inner attractiveness. In another sense it means to manifest authority with finesse and to do one's business with commanded poise. In my understanding, in its inner sense "glory" is the weight of righteous conviction informed by the simplicity of the good that is God. In its outer sense, it is the radiating brightness of power with God as its reference point. "Thine is glory" speaks to the idea of God being honorable and the source of abundance, riches honor, splendor, honor, dignity and reverence balancing justice and mercy. Glory rises from the subjective or hidden character of God becomes the displayed dignity His Kingship so that it can be seen. In a sense this dignity of God as King, can also be manifest in the subjects of His Kingdom as honor, wealth, fullness of life. This is the sense in which it is used in reference to great men of God in the Bible.

When we contact the glory in prayer and it becomes manifest, the results can include physical transfiguration of Creation. This we see in the life of the Lord Jesus Christ in the story of the transfiguration in the mountain. First, we see that his physical appearance changed, even His clothing became as white as the sun. Secondly, we see that there is a cut across the time barrier as Moses and Elijah appear in the midst of the glory brightness. Thirdly, there is a coming together of the revelational paradigms; Moses the man to whom God spoke mouth to mouth meets the prophets who spoke in visions and dreams and sounds, and both of them meet the Word made flesh. Fourthly, there is clear communication of God's voice—a "this is." Fifthly, the disciples saw and heard clearly. Wherever the glory is present these five manifestations are basic. Sixthly, it is this manifestation that signs, miracles and wonders flow. When Jesus says "this signs shall follow them," there is in my perspective the assumption that the glory is manifest in the lives of the disciples. The second major result of the glory is transformation of the inner landscape of the human consciousness. This we find in Isaiah 6. In encountering the glory in its beauty brightness, splendor and weight, Isaiah's soul, thought, feelings, imagination and spirit are stirred revolutionized. This inner transformation thrust Isaiah into a prophetic ministry that lasted many years and ultimately cost him his life. The third major result of this encounter is that it often opens up the flow of heavenly treasures and riches. It is said of Jacob after his encounter with the glory that he came up with all his glory meaning his wealth. Our Father Abraham also encounters the glory in his vision and at the end of his life; we read, "and the Lord blessed Abraham with everything." The glory can make one great, refine one's life and cause it shine in godly splendor. So when we pray as "thine is the . . . and the glory" we ask for the beauty of God our Father especially the beauty of God's holiness to cover us. When we press into the glory in prayer, we become saturated with the glory and thus become desirable to the company of Heaven as we become truly the abode of the Shekinah.

As it relates to social life, the glory bestows material wealth and is meant to support the Kingdom as it manifests in various places. It is also the increase of our dignity and majesty in the world as we read of Eliakim in Isaiah 22:23. The glory is the key granted to us to open closed doors. In fact the glory is the key to all the doors. There is not a door but the glory can open it and allow us in. Our soul increases in power and beauty as the glory is allowed to manifest more and more.

As we have seen, glory is not just what is intrinsic to God but is something which men and women can give to God through praise, adoration, worship and thanksgiving. This is the sense in which we use the idea to glorify God. This is why an exaggerated judgment, opinion, estimates, whether good or bad, concerning someone splendor, could be described as glorified. (See Acts 22:11) But when we say "thine is the glory" as we see here, we speak of that manifest physical radiance of hidden nature of God, the Shekinah of the Living God which manifests itself where people seek, worship and focus on the His nature. It is part of His being as God. Acknowledgment, of the glory as belonging to God in prayer does not mean that we are able to bear or to see the fullness of this glory. No matter how much of the glory we experience, we only experience it in part. But one of the goals of prayer is to tap into that glory. To say "thine is the power" is to announce with clarity that God the Father in Heaven inhabits an unapproachable beauty and splendor. For the Christian it is to speak of what the Father shares with the Son Jesus Christ and the Holy Spirit. According to the Jesus, "glory" is one of the bonding elements that holds divinity together. That is why Jesus prayed in John 17:5: "And now, O Father, glorify thou me with thine own self with the glory which I had with thee before the world was."

There are several things which we may mean in prayer when speak of the glory that belongs to God. By this phrase we may speak of the magnificence, excellence, preeminence and even grace of God. (Matt 4:8) This is the majesty that belongs to God, that Kingly majesty of God's person as the supreme ruler of the universe. (Matt 6:13) When we say "thine is . . . the glory" we speak of God's majesty in the sense of the absolute perfection of the God's nature which we cannot attain without

Divine grace. (Rom. 1:23) This Majesty of the Father He gives to the Messiah so that He might have absolutely perfect inward personal excellence. Christ reflects the true likeness of the hidden God and has given it to us that radiance as heritage. (2 Cor. 3:18; 4:4)

The Spirit of God carries with it everything about this glory. It is this glory made Moses so fully alive and radiant that they people could not bear to look at him for its brightness. Our inheritance in paradise is being made fully alive and saturated with the glory of God.

But now in this era as we press in through prayer to the Kabod, glory of God is then extended to cover and clothe us so that signs and wonders occur in our midst. The glory is the garment of the wedding feast which covers our nakedness and shame. The goal of the Messianic epoch is for the glory to become our daily experience and that our inner reality radiates the Life of God. It can be said that part of the fragmentation of the churches and division of believers from believers the absence of the glory. If we press into the glory, we will not work so hard to cover up our nakedness. To us who are believers Christ is the inner reality of the *Kabod*. It is written "Christ in you the hope of (*Kabod*) glory." He is that indwelling presence of the glory that becomes the impetus for our progressive transformation. Without glory there is no real revelation. When we acknowledge the glory as belonging to God we can then move from there to ask for its manifestation upon the earth. Moses knew this, so he asked to be enveloped in the blaze of light and splendor which is the essential expression of Yahweh's holy majesty. We know of course that God refused insisting that Moses would die if such glory was to be manifested to him. (Ex. 33:18 ff) However, God did let Moses see part of the glory through a mask. *In fin*, this is an acknowledgment of the glory as being God's is an indirect way of asking for it to be manifested in our lives. God will impart this beauty, brightness, majesty and wealth which belong to Him to us who are called by His name. The glory is clearly a physical manifestation of God's presence. It can be seen to some extent. But here is the catch, it belongs to God, it is an indication of the presence of God but it is not God. Therefore, it must not be worshipped as God. Fire, cloud,

253

sounds of thunder, lightning miracles signs and wonders can be indicators of the presence but they are not GOD. We will see more and more of this physical manifestations of the glory as we draw near to the return of the ark to Israel. But we must remember in all prayers, "Thine is the Kingdom, the power and the glory, forever." **FOREVER**

"Forever," simply means to all worlds, eternity, all ages. This puts all things which are in God beyond measurable time. As I pray this prayer, I tap into eternity. In my prayer I am connecting worlds and transforming time. I open gateways to other heavenly places, new vistas of life, life, joy, power, experiences. So I pray, "our Father who art in Heaven" and I lift my heart to another dimension. This I do through Him who came from Heaven and taught me to pray—even JESUS THE CHRIST

CHAPTER SEVENTEEN:
GOLDEN CORD

AMEN

In every prayer, "**Amen**" is spoken by all who participate as an affirmation of the God of glory. Power and majesty of the Lord God as the omega point of the entire request is invoked. Not only is it the affirmation of the truth and certainty of the request, it is an affirmation of the nature of the one to whom the prayer is made. Amen is an acronym—I learned from my Rabbi—that stands for Adonai Melech Elohim Naaman.

A= ADNY is an affirmation of the universal Lordship of the God Israel. Of course the name Adonai is usually a substitute for the YHVH which is the name of God. This name Adonai is the name of Divine revelation, power, provision, protection, preservation and peace. When we say it, we invoke the Lordship of YHVH over the four elements: over everything in air, water, wind and earth. By using this word God's people in one swoop put to silence the elemental demons of the ungodly. The God of Israel stands above all who bend the power of fire for ill, who structure the power of water for destruction, who pull on the air to annihilate men and who subvert the gifts of the earth for ill health of man. Yes, even those who supposedly use these elements for good who prescribe honor or their virtues to anything other than the Supreme Being.

M=Melech, in the Hebrew stands for Kingship—this rulership of God over every circumstance is also affirmed when we say "Amen." He is the King of kings. In speaking the word "amen" we proclaim God's authority and dominion over all.

E=Elohim in the Hebrew stands for God. Since it is in the plural, it points to the plural majesty of the Lord. He is the God of all that is God. He rules over all that may be called gods in all worlds. In this one phrase, we silence all false claims to divinity. We subject all principalities and power to Him and make way for the flight of our prayer heavenward.

N=Naaman stands for truth. Truth has to do with the fact of the reality of YHVH over all idols. They are not real-truth but God is truth absolutely. Our God is the embodiment of what is ultimately real. Furthermore, in terms of communication, He will never lie, make any false promise or even deceive those who trust in Him. His strength will not fail. Thus it is written, "they shall not be put to shame that put their trust in Him." When I say "Amen," I affirm all that God is and thus on the basis of His nature I believe that He will answer the prayers uttered. In it also the praying person forgoes all argument with God.

In the Book of Revelation, Jesus refers to Himself as the Amen. In so doing He makes Himself the end and veracity of all true prayer. He is the Lord who is king and God in truth. Ultimately, we get our prayers answered in the eternal realm because we have been connected to the Moshiach by faith. In the Christian context, when we say "Amen," we indeed invoke the whole life and experience of our Lord Jesus Christ.

BIBLIOGRAPHY

Bibles
King James Version of the Bible
New American Standard Version of the Bible

Armstrong, A. H. editor. Classical *Mediterranean Spirituality: Egypt, Greek and Rome* New York: Crossroad, 1986.

Augustine, Aurelius "Confessions" in The Nicene and Post-Nicene Fathers first Series. Schaff, Phillip Editor vol. 1 Grand Rapid: Erdmann, 1979

Boehme, Jacob. *Concerning the Three Principles of the Divine Essence* 2 vols. John Sparrow trans.

Bounds E.M. *On Prayer.* Whitaker House, 1997.

Brown, Colin. The *New International Dictionary of New Testament Theology.* (Grand Rapid: Zondervan, 1976.)

Duewel, Wesley L. Ablaze for God. Grand Rapids: Francis Asbury Press, 1989.

Harkness, Georgia. Disciplines of the Christian Life. Richmond: John Knox Press.1952.

Jones, Rufus "What Does Prayer mean?" in Harry Emerson Fosdick, editor Rufus Jones Speaks to Our Time. New York: Macmillan, 1951.

Fosdick, Harry Emerson, On Being a Real Person. New York: Harper1943.

Hertz, J. H. ed. *Pentateuch and Haftorah: Hebrew Text English Translation and Commentary.* London: Soncino Press, 5761-2001.

Keil, C. F. and Delittzch, F. Commentary on the Old Testament, vol. 1. C, F. Keil "Pentateuch." Peabody: Hendrickson, rpr. 1996.

Lightfoot, John. *A Commentary on the New Testament from the Talmud and Hebraica* 4 vols. Peabody: Hendrickson reprinted from Oxford University Press1859, Grand Rapids: Baker book house, 1979.

Ogbonnaya, A. O. *ChurchNext: The Seven Rewards of the Overcoming Church.* Lansing: Kohanim Press, 2005.

Origen "On Prayer" in The Library of Christian Classics: Alexandrian Christianity. Henry Chadwick editor. Philadelphia: Westminster Press, 1956.

Parker, J. I. Knowing God. Downers Grove: Inter Varsity Press, 1973.

Plotinus "The Six Enneads" trans. Stephen MacKenna and B. S. Page in Great Books of the Western World vol. 17. Chicago: William Benton, 1952.

Scholem, Gershom. Major Trends in Jewish Mysticism. New York: Schoken, 1974.

The Babylonian Talmud. vol. 5 "Tract Hagiya" Michael L. Rodkinson translator (Boston: The Talmud Society, 1918)

Wigglesworth, Smith. On Spirit Filled. Living. New Keningston: Whitaker House, 1999.

Witherington III, Ben. *Jesus the Seer: The Progress of prophesy* Peabody: Hendrickson, 1999

END NOTES

[1] Harry Emerson Fosdick, ed. Rufus Jones Speaks to Our Time. New York: Macmillan Company, 1951, p157.

[2] Howard Thurman, *The Luminous Darkness*. 1965 I borrowed this term from his book. This was among the first books I read when I arrived in Canada to go to school. His Quaker spirituality impacted my life and fitted into what had been going on in my life.

[3] Rufus Jones speaks to our Time, p160ff.

[4] Jacques Ellul. *L'impossible prière*. Paris: Centurion, 1977, p82.

[5] Interlinear Transliterated Bible. Copyright (c) 1994 by Bible soft. 2 Chronicles 7:13-14.

[6] K., & Duncan, E. (1994). The experience of emotions in everyday life. *Cognition and Emotion*, 8, 369-381.

[7] Philo of Alexandria QG 3:42 (taken from Bible Works 7).

[8] My view point on the will is strongly influenced by Schopenhauer's treatise on the will though I do not subscribe to some of his tenets on the human will. Also in this chapter, I use the uppercase Will to refer to the Will of God and the lowercase "will" to refer to the will of man.

[9] "Confessions" *Nicene and Post Nicene Fathers of The Christian Church*, Vol. 1 Grand Rapids: Erdman reprint 1979) p21.

[10] Confessions, p21.
[11] Confessions p4, 12.

[12] St. Augustine. City of God

[13] Charles Spurgeon, Sermon No 3: "the sin of Unbelief.")

[14] Book viii, 19:24.

[15] I have chosen to deal mainly with temptation in this section because the word appears clearly in the Lord's Prayer. But I have done enough study to see that there is a fine distinction which can be made among the four T's. 1. Temptation finds its basis in the human desire and is meant to make man meet his needs by avoiding divine process. 2 Tests are mental processes having to do with the application of the knowledge we have gleaned in our

experiences with the Lord. It is meant to curl out the pearls of wisdom and nuggets of knowledge that we have received in our walk. 3. Trials are directed to our physical endurance. Sometimes they directed to the body's capacity to endure hardship. Paul speaks of this trial in his narrative of experiences for the gospel. 4. We have tribulation when nature, God, and other external circumstances conspire to thwart our very best movement and intentions, causing us suffering for which there is logical explanation. It is not the result personal desires leading to failure which has folded back upon itself to hurt us, nor is it the test our acquired knowledge and presumed wisdom in the things of God or even the mere trial of physical strength which test our endurance. In fact it seems pointless, designed to strip us of all genuine desire for good, knowledge strength and perspective. It is case where the innocent suffer as though they were guilty. This is what led the Greeks to speak of fate and the Hindus to speak of karma. This is what Job went through. Tribulation has led many Believers to argue that Christians will not go through it. For its intensity can open one for temptation and desire so tearing that one is ready to curse God. It reaches beyond human capacity to bear.

[16] E. Stanley Jones, *Songs of Ascent*, p 208.

[17] Ibid.